MW00451726

CAREER EXAMINATION SERIES

THIS IS YOUR **PASSBOOK**® FOR ...

COURT ASSISTANT

NLC®

NATIONAL LEARNING CORPORATION®
passbooks.com

PASSBOOK® SERIES

THE *PASSBOOK® SERIES* has been created to prepare applicants and candidates for the ultimate academic battlefield – the examination room.

At some time in our lives, each and every one of us may be required to take an examination – for validation, matriculation, admission, qualification, registration, certification, or licensure.

Based on the assumption that every applicant or candidate has met the basic formal educational standards, has taken the required number of courses, and read the necessary texts, the *PASSBOOK® SERIES* furnishes the one special preparation which may assure passing with confidence, instead of failing with insecurity. Examination questions – together with answers – are furnished as the basic vehicle for study so that the mysteries of the examination and its compounding difficulties may be eliminated or diminished by a sure method.

This book is meant to help you pass your examination provided that you qualify and are serious in your objective.

The entire field is reviewed through the huge store of content information which is succinctly presented through a provocative and challenging approach – the question-and-answer method.

A climate of success is established by furnishing the correct answers at the end of each test.

You soon learn to recognize types of questions, forms of questions, and patterns of questioning. You may even begin to anticipate expected outcomes.

You perceive that many questions are repeated or adapted so that you can gain acute insights, which may enable you to score many sure points.

You learn how to confront new questions, or types of questions, and to attack them confidently and work out the correct answers.

You note objectives and emphases, and recognize pitfalls and dangers, so that you may make positive educational adjustments.

Moreover, you are kept fully informed in relation to new concepts, methods, practices, and directions in the field.

You discover that you arre actually taking the examination all the time: you are preparing for the examination by "taking" an examination, not by reading extraneous and/or supererogatory textbooks.

In short, this PASSBOOK®, used directedly, should be an important factor in helping you to pass your test.

COURT ASSISTANT

DUTIES
Court Assistants serve as part clerks in Supreme Courts; all County and District Courts; those City Courts with three or more full-time judges; and the City Civil Court. As part clerks, they work under the supervision of higher level court clerical personnel, Chief Clerks, Commissioner of Jurors, or County Clerks and perform court clerical tasks directly related to court proceedings. Court Assistants may also work outside of the courtroom in these same courts, in other city courts, or in the Court of Claims, where they provide procedural information, supervise units staffed by Principal Office Assistants and other subordinate personnel engaged in court support activities such as intake of papers or docketing. They may be designated to act in the absence of the Chief Clerk or Commissioner of Jurors, and may perform duties related to arbitration and the disposition of actions by means of arbitration, and perform other related duties.

SCOPE OF THE EXAMINATION
The multiple-choice written test will cover knowledges, skills, and/or abilities in such areas as:

1. **Clerical checking** - These questions assess candidates' ability to determine whether different sets of names, numbers, letters and/or codes are similar. Material will be presented in three columns, and candidates will be asked to compare the information in the three sets and identify where the sets differ. Candidates must use the directions to determine the correct answer.

2. **Understanding and interpreting written material** - These questions assess candidates' ability to understand brief written passages. Candidates will be provided with short written passages from which words or phrases have been removed. They are required to select from four alternatives the word or phrase that most appropriately completes the sentence when inserted for the missing word or phrase.

3. **Applying facts and information to given situations** -These questions assess candidates' ability to take information which they have read and apply it to a specific situation defined by a given set of facts. Each question contains a brief paragraph which describes a regulation, policy, procedure or law similar to what a Court Assistant may encounter on the job. The selection is followed by a description of a specific situation. Then a question is asked which requires candidates to apply the regulation, policy, procedure or law described in the paragraph to the specific situation. All of the information needed to answer the question will be contained in the paragraph and in the description of the situation.

4. **Court record keeping** - These questions assess candidates' ability to read, combine, and manipulate written information organized from several sources. Candidates will be presented with different types of tables, which contain names, numbers, codes and other information, and must combine and reorganize the information to answer specific questions.

5. **Preparing written material-**
   Format A: These questions assess candidates' ability to present information clearly and accurately, and to organize written information logically and comprehensibly. Candidates will be presented with several sentences and must effectively organize them in a coherent and logical order.
   Format. B: These questions assess candidates' ability to apply rules of English grammar, usage, punctuation, and sentence structure. Candidates will be presented with a series of sentences and must select the sentence that best conforms to standard English grammar, usage, punctuation, and sentence structure.

6. **Legal terminology** - These questions assess candidates' knowledge of basic legal terminology that Court Assistants encounter in their daily work.

HOW TO TAKE A TEST

I. YOU MUST PASS AN EXAMINATION

A. *WHAT EVERY CANDIDATE SHOULD KNOW*

Examination applicants often ask us for help in preparing for the written test. What can I study in advance? What kinds of questions will be asked? How will the test be given? How will the papers be graded?

As an applicant for a civil service examination, you may be wondering about some of these things. Our purpose here is to suggest effective methods of advance study and to describe civil service examinations.

Your chances for success on this examination can be increased if you know how to prepare. Those "pre-examination jitters" can be reduced if you know what to expect. You can even experience an adventure in good citizenship if you know why civil service exams are given.

B. *WHY ARE CIVIL SERVICE EXAMINATIONS GIVEN?*

Civil service examinations are important to you in two ways. As a citizen, you want public jobs filled by employees who know how to do their work. As a job seeker, you want a fair chance to compete for that job on an equal footing with other candidates. The best-known means of accomplishing this two-fold goal is the competitive examination.

Exams are widely publicized throughout the nation. They may be administered for jobs in federal, state, city, municipal, town or village governments or agencies.

Any citizen may apply, with some limitations, such as the age or residence of applicants. Your experience and education may be reviewed to see whether you meet the requirements for the particular examination. When these requirements exist, they are reasonable and applied consistently to all applicants. Thus, a competitive examination may cause you some uneasiness now, but it is your privilege and safeguard.

C. *HOW ARE CIVIL SERVICE EXAMS DEVELOPED?*

Examinations are carefully written by trained technicians who are specialists in the field known as "psychological measurement," in consultation with recognized authorities in the field of work that the test will cover. These experts recommend the subject matter areas or skills to be tested; only those knowledges or skills important to your success on the job are included. The most reliable books and source materials available are used as references. Together, the experts and technicians judge the difficulty level of the questions.

Test technicians know how to phrase questions so that the problem is clearly stated. Their ethics do not permit "trick" or "catch" questions. Questions may have been tried out on sample groups, or subjected to statistical analysis, to determine their usefulness.

Written tests are often used in combination with performance tests, ratings of training and experience, and oral interviews. All of these measures combine to form the best-known means of finding the right person for the right job.

II. HOW TO PASS THE WRITTEN TEST

A. NATURE OF THE EXAMINATION

To prepare intelligently for civil service examinations, you should know how they differ from school examinations you have taken. In school you were assigned certain definite pages to read or subjects to cover. The examination questions were quite detailed and usually emphasized memory. Civil service exams, on the other hand, try to discover your present ability to perform the duties of a position, plus your potentiality to learn these duties. In other words, a civil service exam attempts to predict how successful you will be. Questions cover such a broad area that they cannot be as minute and detailed as school exam questions.

In the public service similar kinds of work, or positions, are grouped together in one "class." This process is known as *position-classification*. All the positions in a class are paid according to the salary range for that class. One class title covers all of these positions, and they are all tested by the same examination.

B. FOUR BASIC STEPS

1) Study the announcement

How, then, can you know what subjects to study? Our best answer is: "Learn as much as possible about the class of positions for which you've applied." The exam will test the knowledge, skills and abilities needed to do the work.

Your most valuable source of information about the position you want is the official exam announcement. This announcement lists the training and experience qualifications. Check these standards and apply only if you come reasonably close to meeting them.

The brief description of the position in the examination announcement offers some clues to the subjects which will be tested. Think about the job itself. Review the duties in your mind. Can you perform them, or are there some in which you are rusty? Fill in the blank spots in your preparation.

Many jurisdictions preview the written test in the exam announcement by including a section called "Knowledge and Abilities Required," "Scope of the Examination," or some similar heading. Here you will find out specifically what fields will be tested.

2) Review your own background

Once you learn in general what the position is all about, and what you need to know to do the work, ask yourself which subjects you already know fairly well and which need improvement. You may wonder whether to concentrate on improving your strong areas or on building some background in your fields of weakness. When the announcement has specified "some knowledge" or "considerable knowledge," or has used adjectives like "beginning principles of…" or "advanced … methods," you can get a clue as to the number and difficulty of questions to be asked in any given field. More questions, and hence broader coverage, would be included for those subjects which are more important in the work. Now weigh your strengths and weaknesses against the job requirements and prepare accordingly.

3) Determine the level of the position

Another way to tell how intensively you should prepare is to understand the level of the job for which you are applying. Is it the entering level? In other words, is this the position in which beginners in a field of work are hired? Or is it an intermediate or advanced level? Sometimes this is indicated by such words as "Junior" or "Senior" in the class title. Other jurisdictions use Roman numerals to designate the level – Clerk I, Clerk II, for example. The word "Supervisor" sometimes appears in the title. If the level is not indicated by the title, check the description of duties. Will you be working under very close supervision, or will you have responsibility for independent decisions in this work?

4) Choose appropriate study materials

Now that you know the subjects to be examined and the relative amount of each subject to be covered, you can choose suitable study materials. For beginning level jobs, or even advanced ones, if you have a pronounced weakness in some aspect of your training, read a modern, standard textbook in that field. Be sure it is up to date and has general coverage. Such books are normally available at your library, and the librarian will be glad to help you locate one. For entry-level positions, questions of appropriate difficulty are chosen – neither highly advanced questions, nor those too simple. Such questions require careful thought but not advanced training.

If the position for which you are applying is technical or advanced, you will read more advanced, specialized material. If you are already familiar with the basic principles of your field, elementary textbooks would waste your time. Concentrate on advanced textbooks and technical periodicals. Think through the concepts and review difficult problems in your field.

These are all general sources. You can get more ideas on your own initiative, following these leads. For example, training manuals and publications of the government agency which employs workers in your field can be useful, particularly for technical and professional positions. A letter or visit to the government department involved may result in more specific study suggestions, and certainly will provide you with a more definite idea of the exact nature of the position you are seeking.

III. KINDS OF TESTS

Tests are used for purposes other than measuring knowledge and ability to perform specified duties. For some positions, it is equally important to test ability to make adjustments to new situations or to profit from training. In others, basic mental abilities not dependent on information are essential. Questions which test these things may not appear as pertinent to the duties of the position as those which test for knowledge and information. Yet they are often highly important parts of a fair examination. For very general questions, it is almost impossible to help you direct your study efforts. What we can do is to point out some of the more common of these general abilities needed in public service positions and describe some typical questions.

1) General information

Broad, general information has been found useful for predicting job success in some kinds of work. This is tested in a variety of ways, from vocabulary lists to questions about current events. Basic background in some field of work, such as sociology or economics, may be sampled in a group of questions. Often these are principles which have become familiar to most persons through exposure rather than through formal training. It is difficult to advise you how to study for these questions; being alert to the world around you is our best suggestion.

2) Verbal ability

An example of an ability needed in many positions is verbal or language ability. Verbal ability is, in brief, the ability to use and understand words. Vocabulary and grammar tests are typical measures of this ability. Reading comprehension or paragraph interpretation questions are common in many kinds of civil service tests. You are given a paragraph of written material and asked to find its central meaning.

3) Numerical ability

Number skills can be tested by the familiar arithmetic problem, by checking paired lists of numbers to see which are alike and which are different, or by interpreting charts and graphs. In the latter test, a graph may be printed in the test booklet which you are asked to use as the basis for answering questions.

4) Observation

A popular test for law-enforcement positions is the observation test. A picture is shown to you for several minutes, then taken away. Questions about the picture test your ability to observe both details and larger elements.

5) Following directions

In many positions in the public service, the employee must be able to carry out written instructions dependably and accurately. You may be given a chart with several columns, each column listing a variety of information. The questions require you to carry out directions involving the information given in the chart.

6) Skills and aptitudes

Performance tests effectively measure some manual skills and aptitudes. When the skill is one in which you are trained, such as typing or shorthand, you can practice. These tests are often very much like those given in business school or high school courses. For many of the other skills and aptitudes, however, no short-time preparation can be made. Skills and abilities natural to you or that you have developed throughout your lifetime are being tested.

Many of the general questions just described provide all the data needed to answer the questions and ask you to use your reasoning ability to find the answers. Your best preparation for these tests, as well as for tests of facts and ideas, is to be at your physical and mental best. You, no doubt, have your own methods of getting into an exam-taking mood and keeping "in shape." The next section lists some ideas on this subject.

IV. KINDS OF QUESTIONS

Only rarely is the "essay" question, which you answer in narrative form, used in civil service tests. Civil service tests are usually of the short-answer type. Full instructions for answering these questions will be given to you at the examination. But in case this is your first experience with short-answer questions and separate answer sheets, here is what you need to know:

1) Multiple-choice Questions

Most popular of the short-answer questions is the "multiple choice" or "best answer" question. It can be used, for example, to test for factual knowledge, ability to solve problems or judgment in meeting situations found at work.

A multiple-choice question is normally one of three types—

- It can begin with an incomplete statement followed by several possible endings. You are to find the one ending which *best* completes the statement, although some of the others may not be entirely wrong.
- It can also be a complete statement in the form of a question which is answered by choosing one of the statements listed.
- It can be in the form of a problem – again you select the best answer.

Here is an example of a multiple-choice question with a discussion which should give you some clues as to the method for choosing the right answer:

When an employee has a complaint about his assignment, the action which will *best* help him overcome his difficulty is to
- A. discuss his difficulty with his coworkers
- B. take the problem to the head of the organization
- C. take the problem to the person who gave him the assignment
- D. say nothing to anyone about his complaint

In answering this question, you should study each of the choices to find which is best. Consider choice "A" – Certainly an employee may discuss his complaint with fellow employees, but no change or improvement can result, and the complaint remains unresolved. Choice "B" is a poor choice since the head of the organization probably does not know what assignment you have been given, and taking your problem to him is known as "going over the head" of the supervisor. The supervisor, or person who made the assignment, is the person who can clarify it or correct any injustice. Choice "C" is, therefore, correct. To say nothing, as in choice "D," is unwise. Supervisors have and interest in knowing the problems employees are facing, and the employee is seeking a solution to his problem.

2) True/False Questions

The "true/false" or "right/wrong" form of question is sometimes used. Here a complete statement is given. Your job is to decide whether the statement is right or wrong.

SAMPLE: A roaming cell-phone call to a nearby city costs less than a non-roaming call to a distant city.

This statement is wrong, or false, since roaming calls are more expensive.

This is not a complete list of all possible question forms, although most of the others are variations of these common types. You will always get complete directions for answering questions. Be sure you understand *how* to mark your answers – ask questions until you do.

V. RECORDING YOUR ANSWERS

Computer terminals are used more and more today for many different kinds of exams.

For an examination with very few applicants, you may be told to record your answers in the test booklet itself. Separate answer sheets are much more common. If this separate answer sheet is to be scored by machine – and this is often the case – it is highly important that you mark your answers correctly in order to get credit.

An electronic scoring machine is often used in civil service offices because of the speed with which papers can be scored. Machine-scored answer sheets must be marked with a pencil, which will be given to you. This pencil has a high graphite content which responds to the electronic scoring machine. As a matter of fact, stray dots may register as answers, so do not let your pencil rest on the answer sheet while you are pondering the correct answer. Also, if your pencil lead breaks or is otherwise defective, ask for another.

Since the answer sheet will be dropped in a slot in the scoring machine, be careful not to bend the corners or get the paper crumpled.

The answer sheet normally has five vertical columns of numbers, with 30 numbers to a column. These numbers correspond to the question numbers in your test booklet. After each number, going across the page are four or five pairs of dotted lines. These short dotted lines have small letters or numbers above them. The first two pairs may also have a "T" or "F" above the letters. This indicates that the first two pairs only are to be used if the questions are of the true-false type. If the questions are multiple choice, disregard the "T" and "F" and pay attention only to the small letters or numbers.

Answer your questions in the manner of the sample that follows:

32. The largest city in the United States is
    A. Washington, D.C.
    B. New York City
    C. Chicago
    D. Detroit
    E. San Francisco

1) Choose the answer you think is best. (New York City is the largest, so "B" is correct.)
2) Find the row of dotted lines numbered the same as the question you are answering. (Find row number 32)
3) Find the pair of dotted lines corresponding to the answer. (Find the pair of lines under the mark "B.")
4) Make a solid black mark between the dotted lines.

VI. BEFORE THE TEST

Common sense will help you find procedures to follow to get ready for an examination. Too many of us, however, overlook these sensible measures. Indeed, nervousness and fatigue have been found to be the most serious reasons why applicants fail to do their best on civil service tests. Here is a list of reminders:

- Begin your preparation early – Don't wait until the last minute to go scurrying around for books and materials or to find out what the position is all about.
- Prepare continuously – An hour a night for a week is better than an all-night cram session. This has been definitely established. What is more, a night a week for a month will return better dividends than crowding your study into a shorter period of time.
- Locate the place of the exam – You have been sent a notice telling you when and where to report for the examination. If the location is in a different town or otherwise unfamiliar to you, it would be well to inquire the best route and learn something about the building.
- Relax the night before the test – Allow your mind to rest. Do not study at all that night. Plan some mild recreation or diversion; then go to bed early and get a good night's sleep.
- Get up early enough to make a leisurely trip to the place for the test – This way unforeseen events, traffic snarls, unfamiliar buildings, etc. will not upset you.
- Dress comfortably – A written test is not a fashion show. You will be known by number and not by name, so wear something comfortable.
- Leave excess paraphernalia at home – Shopping bags and odd bundles will get in your way. You need bring only the items mentioned in the official notice you received; usually everything you need is provided. Do not bring reference books to the exam. They will only confuse those last minutes and be taken away from you when in the test room.
- Arrive somewhat ahead of time – If because of transportation schedules you must get there very early, bring a newspaper or magazine to take your mind off yourself while waiting.
- Locate the examination room – When you have found the proper room, you will be directed to the seat or part of the room where you will sit. Sometimes you are given a sheet of instructions to read while you are waiting. Do not fill out any forms until you are told to do so; just read them and be prepared.
- Relax and prepare to listen to the instructions
- If you have any physical problem that may keep you from doing your best, be sure to tell the test administrator. If you are sick or in poor health, you really cannot do your best on the exam. You can come back and take the test some other time.

VII. AT THE TEST

The day of the test is here and you have the test booklet in your hand. The temptation to get going is very strong. Caution! There is more to success than knowing the right answers. You must know how to identify your papers and understand variations in the type of short-answer question used in this particular examination. Follow these suggestions for maximum results from your efforts:

1) Cooperate with the monitor

The test administrator has a duty to create a situation in which you can be as much at ease as possible. He will give instructions, tell you when to begin, check to see that you are marking your answer sheet correctly, and so on. He is not there to guard you, although he will see that your competitors do not take unfair advantage. He wants to help you do your best.

2) Listen to all instructions

Don't jump the gun! Wait until you understand all directions. In most civil service tests you get more time than you need to answer the questions. So don't be in a hurry. Read each word of instructions until you clearly understand the meaning. Study the examples, listen to all announcements and follow directions. Ask questions if you do not understand what to do.

3) Identify your papers

Civil service exams are usually identified by number only. You will be assigned a number; you must not put your name on your test papers. Be sure to copy your number correctly. Since more than one exam may be given, copy your exact examination title.

4) Plan your time

Unless you are told that a test is a "speed" or "rate of work" test, speed itself is usually not important. Time enough to answer all the questions will be provided, but this does not mean that you have all day. An overall time limit has been set. Divide the total time (in minutes) by the number of questions to determine the approximate time you have for each question.

5) Do not linger over difficult questions

If you come across a difficult question, mark it with a paper clip (useful to have along) and come back to it when you have been through the booklet. One caution if you do this – be sure to skip a number on your answer sheet as well. Check often to be sure that you have not lost your place and that you are marking in the row numbered the same as the question you are answering.

6) Read the questions

Be sure you know what the question asks! Many capable people are unsuccessful because they failed to *read* the questions correctly.

7) Answer all questions

Unless you have been instructed that a penalty will be deducted for incorrect answers, it is better to guess than to omit a question.

8) Speed tests

It is often better NOT to guess on speed tests. It has been found that on timed tests people are tempted to spend the last few seconds before time is called in marking answers at random – without even reading them – in the hope of picking up a few extra points. To discourage this practice, the instructions may warn you that your score will be "corrected" for guessing. That is, a penalty will be applied. The incorrect answers will be deducted from the correct ones, or some other penalty formula will be used.

9) Review your answers

     If you finish before time is called, go back to the questions you guessed or omitted to give them further thought. Review other answers if you have time.

10) Return your test materials

     If you are ready to leave before others have finished or time is called, take ALL your materials to the monitor and leave quietly. Never take any test material with you. The monitor can discover whose papers are not complete, and taking a test booklet may be grounds for disqualification.

VIII. EXAMINATION TECHNIQUES

1) Read the general instructions carefully. These are usually printed on the first page of the exam booklet. As a rule, these instructions refer to the timing of the examination; the fact that you should not start work until the signal and must stop work at a signal, etc. If there are any *special* instructions, such as a choice of questions to be answered, make sure that you note this instruction carefully.

2) When you are ready to start work on the examination, that is as soon as the signal has been given, read the instructions to each question booklet, underline any key words or phrases, such as *least, best, outline, describe* and the like. In this way you will tend to answer as requested rather than discover on reviewing your paper that you *listed without describing*, that you selected the *worst* choice rather than the *best* choice, etc.

3) If the examination is of the objective or multiple-choice type – that is, each question will also give a series of possible answers: A, B, C or D, and you are called upon to select the best answer and write the letter next to that answer on your answer paper – it is advisable to start answering each question in turn. There may be anywhere from 50 to 100 such questions in the three or four hours allotted and you can see how much time would be taken if you read through all the questions before beginning to answer any. Furthermore, if you come across a question or group of questions which you know would be difficult to answer, it would undoubtedly affect your handling of all the other questions.

4) If the examination is of the essay type and contains but a few questions, it is a moot point as to whether you should read all the questions before starting to answer any one. Of course, if you are given a choice – say five out of seven and the like – then it is essential to read all the questions so you can eliminate the two that are most difficult. If, however, you are asked to answer all the questions, there may be danger in trying to answer the easiest one first because you may find that you will spend too much time on it. The best technique is to answer the first question, then proceed to the second, etc.

5) Time your answers. Before the exam begins, write down the time it started, then add the time allowed for the examination and write down the time it must be completed, then divide the time available somewhat as follows:

- If 3-1/2 hours are allowed, that would be 210 minutes. If you have 80 objective-type questions, that would be an average of 2-1/2 minutes per question. Allow yourself no more than 2 minutes per question, or a total of 160 minutes, which will permit about 50 minutes to review.
- If for the time allotment of 210 minutes there are 7 essay questions to answer, that would average about 30 minutes a question. Give yourself only 25 minutes per question so that you have about 35 minutes to review.

6) The most important instruction is to *read each question* and make sure you know what is wanted. The second most important instruction is to *time yourself properly* so that you answer every question. The third most important instruction is to *answer every question.* Guess if you have to but include something for each question. Remember that you will receive no credit for a blank and will probably receive some credit if you write something in answer to an essay question. If you guess a letter – say "B" for a multiple-choice question – you may have guessed right. If you leave a blank as an answer to a multiple-choice question, the examiners may respect your feelings but it will not add a point to your score. Some exams may penalize you for wrong answers, so in such cases *only,* you may not want to guess unless you have some basis for your answer.

7) Suggestions
   a. Objective-type questions
      1. Examine the question booklet for proper sequence of pages and questions
      2. Read all instructions carefully
      3. Skip any question which seems too difficult; return to it after all other questions have been answered
      4. Apportion your time properly; do not spend too much time on any single question or group of questions
      5. Note and underline key words – *all, most, fewest, least, best, worst, same, opposite,* etc.
      6. Pay particular attention to negatives
      7. Note unusual option, e.g., unduly long, short, complex, different or similar in content to the body of the question
      8. Observe the use of "hedging" words – *probably, may, most likely,* etc.
      9. Make sure that your answer is put next to the same number as the question
      10. Do not second-guess unless you have good reason to believe the second answer is definitely more correct
      11. Cross out original answer if you decide another answer is more accurate; do not erase until you are ready to hand your paper in
      12. Answer all questions; guess unless instructed otherwise
      13. Leave time for review

   b. Essay questions
      1. Read each question carefully
      2. Determine exactly what is wanted. Underline key words or phrases.
      3. Decide on outline or paragraph answer

4. Include many different points and elements unless asked to develop any one or two points or elements
5. Show impartiality by giving pros and cons unless directed to select one side only
6. Make and write down any assumptions you find necessary to answer the questions
7. Watch your English, grammar, punctuation and choice of words
8. Time your answers; don't crowd material

8) Answering the essay question

Most essay questions can be answered by framing the specific response around several key words or ideas. Here are a few such key words or ideas:

M's: manpower, materials, methods, money, management
P's: purpose, program, policy, plan, procedure, practice, problems, pitfalls, personnel, public relations

a. Six basic steps in handling problems:
    1. Preliminary plan and background development
    2. Collect information, data and facts
    3. Analyze and interpret information, data and facts
    4. Analyze and develop solutions as well as make recommendations
    5. Prepare report and sell recommendations
    6. Install recommendations and follow up effectiveness

b. Pitfalls to avoid
    1. *Taking things for granted* – A statement of the situation does not necessarily imply that each of the elements is necessarily true; for example, a complaint may be invalid and biased so that all that can be taken for granted is that a complaint has been registered
    2. *Considering only one side of a situation* – Wherever possible, indicate several alternatives and then point out the reasons you selected the best one
    3. *Failing to indicate follow up* – Whenever your answer indicates action on your part, make certain that you will take proper follow-up action to see how successful your recommendations, procedures or actions turn out to be
    4. *Taking too long in answering any single question* – Remember to time your answers properly

IX. AFTER THE TEST

Scoring procedures differ in detail among civil service jurisdictions although the general principles are the same. Whether the papers are hand-scored or graded by machine we have described, they are nearly always graded by number. That is, the person who marks the paper knows only the number – never the name – of the applicant. Not until all the papers have been graded will they be matched with names. If other tests, such as training and experience or oral interview ratings have been given, scores will be combined. Different parts of the examination usually have different weights. For example, the written test might count 60 percent of the final grade, and a rating of training and experience 40 percent. In many jurisdictions, veterans will have a certain number of points added to their grades.

After the final grade has been determined, the names are placed in grade order and an eligible list is established. There are various methods for resolving ties between those who get the same final grade – probably the most common is to place first the name of the person whose application was received first. Job offers are made from the eligible list in the order the names appear on it. You will be notified of your grade and your rank as soon as all these computations have been made. This will be done as rapidly as possible.

People who are found to meet the requirements in the announcement are called "eligibles." Their names are put on a list of eligible candidates. An eligible's chances of getting a job depend on how high he stands on this list and how fast agencies are filling jobs from the list.

When a job is to be filled from a list of eligibles, the agency asks for the names of people on the list of eligibles for that job. When the civil service commission receives this request, it sends to the agency the names of the three people highest on this list. Or, if the job to be filled has specialized requirements, the office sends the agency the names of the top three persons who meet these requirements from the general list.

The appointing officer makes a choice from among the three people whose names were sent to him. If the selected person accepts the appointment, the names of the others are put back on the list to be considered for future openings.

That is the rule in hiring from all kinds of eligible lists, whether they are for typist, carpenter, chemist, or something else. For every vacancy, the appointing officer has his choice of any one of the top three eligibles on the list. This explains why the person whose name is on top of the list sometimes does not get an appointment when some of the persons lower on the list do. If the appointing officer chooses the second or third eligible, the No. 1 eligible does not get a job at once, but stays on the list until he is appointed or the list is terminated.

X. HOW TO PASS THE INTERVIEW TEST

The examination for which you applied requires an oral interview test. You have already taken the written test and you are now being called for the interview test – the final part of the formal examination.

You may think that it is not possible to prepare for an interview test and that there are no procedures to follow during an interview. Our purpose is to point out some things you can do in advance that will help you and some good rules to follow and pitfalls to avoid while you are being interviewed.

What is an interview supposed to test?
The written examination is designed to test the technical knowledge and competence of the candidate; the oral is designed to evaluate intangible qualities, not readily measured otherwise, and to establish a list showing the relative fitness of each candidate – as measured against his competitors – for the position sought. Scoring is not on the basis of "right" and "wrong," but on a sliding scale of values ranging from "not passable" to "outstanding." As a matter of fact, it is possible to achieve a relatively low score without a single "incorrect" answer because of evident weakness in the qualities being measured.

Occasionally, an examination may consist entirely of an oral test – either an individual or a group oral. In such cases, information is sought concerning the technical knowledges and abilities of the candidate, since there has been no written examination for this purpose. More commonly, however, an oral test is used to supplement a written examination.

Who conducts interviews?

The composition of oral boards varies among different jurisdictions. In nearly all, a representative of the personnel department serves as chairman. One of the members of the board may be a representative of the department in which the candidate would work. In some cases, "outside experts" are used, and, frequently, a businessman or some other representative of the general public is asked to serve. Labor and management or other special groups may be represented. The aim is to secure the services of experts in the appropriate field.

However the board is composed, it is a good idea (and not at all improper or unethical) to ascertain in advance of the interview who the members are and what groups they represent. When you are introduced to them, you will have some idea of their backgrounds and interests, and at least you will not stutter and stammer over their names.

What should be done before the interview?

While knowledge about the board members is useful and takes some of the surprise element out of the interview, there is other preparation which is more substantive. It *is* possible to prepare for an oral interview – in several ways:

1) Keep a copy of your application and review it carefully before the interview

This may be the only document before the oral board, and the starting point of the interview. Know what education and experience you have listed there, and the sequence and dates of all of it. Sometimes the board will ask you to review the highlights of your experience for them; you should not have to hem and haw doing it.

2) Study the class specification and the examination announcement

Usually, the oral board has one or both of these to guide them. The qualities, characteristics or knowledges required by the position sought are stated in these documents. They offer valuable clues as to the nature of the oral interview. For example, if the job involves supervisory responsibilities, the announcement will usually indicate that knowledge of modern supervisory methods and the qualifications of the candidate as a supervisor will be tested. If so, you can expect such questions, frequently in the form of a hypothetical situation which you are expected to solve. NEVER go into an oral without knowledge of the duties and responsibilities of the job you seek.

3) Think through each qualification required

Try to visualize the kind of questions you would ask if you were a board member. How well could you answer them? Try especially to appraise your own knowledge and background in each area, *measured against the job sought*, and identify any areas in which you are weak. Be critical and realistic – do not flatter yourself.

4) Do some general reading in areas in which you feel you may be weak

For example, if the job involves supervision and your past experience has NOT, some general reading in supervisory methods and practices, particularly in the field of human relations, might be useful. Do NOT study agency procedures or detailed manuals. The oral board will be testing your understanding and capacity, not your memory.

5) Get a good night's sleep and watch your general health and mental attitude

You will want a clear head at the interview. Take care of a cold or any other minor ailment, and of course, no hangovers.

What should be done on the day of the interview?

Now comes the day of the interview itself. Give yourself plenty of time to get there. Plan to arrive somewhat ahead of the scheduled time, particularly if your appointment is in the fore part of the day. If a previous candidate fails to appear, the board might be ready for you a bit early. By early afternoon an oral board is almost invariably behind schedule if there are many candidates, and you may have to wait. Take along a book or magazine to read, or your application to review, but leave any extraneous material in the waiting room when you go in for your interview. In any event, relax and compose yourself.

The matter of dress is important. The board is forming impressions about you – from your experience, your manners, your attitude, and your appearance. Give your personal appearance careful attention. Dress your best, but not your flashiest. Choose conservative, appropriate clothing, and be sure it is immaculate. This is a business interview, and your appearance should indicate that you regard it as such. Besides, being well groomed and properly dressed will help boost your confidence.

Sooner or later, someone will call your name and escort you into the interview room. *This is it.* From here on you are on your own. It is too late for any more preparation. But remember, you asked for this opportunity to prove your fitness, and you are here because your request was granted.

What happens when you go in?

The usual sequence of events will be as follows: The clerk (who is often the board stenographer) will introduce you to the chairman of the oral board, who will introduce you to the other members of the board. Acknowledge the introductions before you sit down. Do not be surprised if you find a microphone facing you or a stenotypist sitting by. Oral interviews are usually recorded in the event of an appeal or other review.

Usually the chairman of the board will open the interview by reviewing the highlights of your education and work experience from your application – primarily for the benefit of the other members of the board, as well as to get the material into the record. Do not interrupt or comment unless there is an error or significant misinterpretation; if that is the case, do not hesitate. But do not quibble about insignificant matters. Also, he will usually ask you some question about your education, experience or your present job – partly to get you to start talking and to establish the interviewing "rapport." He may start the actual questioning, or turn it over to one of the other members. Frequently, each member undertakes the questioning on a particular area, one in which he is perhaps most competent, so you can expect each member to participate in the examination. Because time is limited, you may also expect some rather abrupt switches in the direction the questioning takes, so do not be upset by it. Normally, a board member will not pursue a single line of questioning unless he discovers a particular strength or weakness.

After each member has participated, the chairman will usually ask whether any member has any further questions, then will ask you if you have anything you wish to add. Unless you are expecting this question, it may floor you. Worse, it may start you off on an extended, extemporaneous speech. The board is not usually seeking more information. The question is principally to offer you a last opportunity to present further qualifications or to indicate that you have nothing to add. So, if you feel that a significant qualification or characteristic has been overlooked, it is proper to point it out in a sentence or so. Do not compliment the board on the thoroughness of their examination – they have been sketchy, and you know it. If you wish, merely say, "No thank you, I have nothing further to add." This is a point where you can "talk yourself out" of a good impression or fail to present an important bit of information. Remember, *you close the interview yourself.*

The chairman will then say, "That is all, Mr. _____, thank you." Do not be startled; the interview is over, and quicker than you think. Thank him, gather your belongings and take your leave. Save your sigh of relief for the other side of the door.

How to put your best foot forward

Throughout this entire process, you may feel that the board individually and collectively is trying to pierce your defenses, seek out your hidden weaknesses and embarrass and confuse you. Actually, this is not true. They are obliged to make an appraisal of your qualifications for the job you are seeking, and they want to see you in your best light. Remember, they must interview all candidates and a non-cooperative candidate may become a failure in spite of their best efforts to bring out his qualifications. Here are 15 suggestions that will help you:

1) Be natural – Keep your attitude confident, not cocky

If you are not confident that you can do the job, do not expect the board to be. Do not apologize for your weaknesses, try to bring out your strong points. The board is interested in a positive, not negative, presentation. Cockiness will antagonize any board member and make him wonder if you are covering up a weakness by a false show of strength.

2) Get comfortable, but don't lounge or sprawl

Sit erectly but not stiffly. A careless posture may lead the board to conclude that you are careless in other things, or at least that you are not impressed by the importance of the occasion. Either conclusion is natural, even if incorrect. Do not fuss with your clothing, a pencil or an ashtray. Your hands may occasionally be useful to emphasize a point; do not let them become a point of distraction.

3) Do not wisecrack or make small talk

This is a serious situation, and your attitude should show that you consider it as such. Further, the time of the board is limited – they do not want to waste it, and neither should you.

4) Do not exaggerate your experience or abilities

In the first place, from information in the application or other interviews and sources, the board may know more about you than you think. Secondly, you probably will not get away with it. An experienced board is rather adept at spotting such a situation, so do not take the chance.

5) If you know a board member, do not make a point of it, yet do not hide it

Certainly you are not fooling him, and probably not the other members of the board. Do not try to take advantage of your acquaintanceship – it will probably do you little good.

6) Do not dominate the interview

Let the board do that. They will give you the clues – do not assume that you have to do all the talking. Realize that the board has a number of questions to ask you, and do not try to take up all the interview time by showing off your extensive knowledge of the answer to the first one.

7) Be attentive

You only have 20 minutes or so, and you should keep your attention at its sharpest throughout. When a member is addressing a problem or question to you, give him your undivided attention. Address your reply principally to him, but do not exclude the other board members.

8) Do not interrupt

A board member may be stating a problem for you to analyze. He will ask you a question when the time comes. Let him state the problem, and wait for the question.

9) Make sure you understand the question

Do not try to answer until you are sure what the question is. If it is not clear, restate it in your own words or ask the board member to clarify it for you. However, do not haggle about minor elements.

10) Reply promptly but not hastily

A common entry on oral board rating sheets is "candidate responded readily," or "candidate hesitated in replies." Respond as promptly and quickly as you can, but do not jump to a hasty, ill-considered answer.

11) Do not be peremptory in your answers

A brief answer is proper – but do not fire your answer back. That is a losing game from your point of view. The board member can probably ask questions much faster than you can answer them.

12) Do not try to create the answer you think the board member wants

He is interested in what kind of mind you have and how it works – not in playing games. Furthermore, he can usually spot this practice and will actually grade you down on it.

13) Do not switch sides in your reply merely to agree with a board member

Frequently, a member will take a contrary position merely to draw you out and to see if you are willing and able to defend your point of view. Do not start a debate, yet do not surrender a good position. If a position is worth taking, it is worth defending.

14) Do not be afraid to admit an error in judgment if you are shown to be wrong

The board knows that you are forced to reply without any opportunity for careful consideration. Your answer may be demonstrably wrong. If so, admit it and get on with the interview.

15) Do not dwell at length on your present job

The opening question may relate to your present assignment. Answer the question but do not go into an extended discussion. You are being examined for a *new* job, not your present one. As a matter of fact, try to phrase ALL your answers in terms of the job for which you are being examined.

Basis of Rating

Probably you will forget most of these "do's" and "don'ts" when you walk into the oral interview room. Even remembering them all will not ensure you a passing grade. Perhaps you did not have the qualifications in the first place. But remembering them will help you to put your best foot forward, without treading on the toes of the board members.

Rumor and popular opinion to the contrary notwithstanding, an oral board wants you to make the best appearance possible. They know you are under pressure – but they also want to see how you respond to it as a guide to what your reaction would be under the pressures of the job you seek. They will be influenced by the degree of poise you display, the personal traits you show and the manner in which you respond.

ABOUT THIS BOOK

This book contains tests divided into Examination Sections. Go through each test, answering every question in the margin. At the end of each test look at the answer key and check your answers. On the ones you got wrong, look at the right answer choice and learn. Do not fill in the answers first. Do not memorize the questions and answers, but understand the answer and principles involved. On your test, the questions will likely be different from the samples. Questions are changed and new ones added. If you understand these past questions you should have success with any changes that arise. Tests may consist of several types of questions. We have additional books on each subject should more study be advisable or necessary for you. Finally, the more you study, the better prepared you will be. This book is intended to be the last thing you study before you walk into the examination room. Prior study of relevant texts is also recommended. NLC publishes some of these in our Fundamental Series. Knowledge and good sense are important factors in passing your exam. Good luck also helps. So now study this Passbook, absorb the material contained within and take that knowledge into the examination. Then do your best to pass that exam.

———

EXAMINATION SECTION

EXAMINATION SECTION

TEST 1

DIRECTIONS: Each question or incomplete statement is followed by several suggested answers or completions. Select the one that BEST answers the question or completes the statement. *PRINT THE LETTER OF THE CORRECT ANSWER IN THE SPACE AT THE RIGHT.*

1. While waiting for jury selection, one of the prospective jurors asks you how long a typical trial lasts.
   Which of the following is the MOST appropriate response?
   A. Trials can be lengthy.
   B. The length of trials varies widely, but every aspect of it is important.
   C. Civil trials typically last three to five days, while criminal trials are generally five to ten days.
   D. Decline to respond for fear of appearing biased.

   1._____

2. One of the jurors appears faint and starts to wobble while seated in the jury box.
   How should you handle the situation?
   A. Let one of the other jurors come to the ailing juror's aid first.
   B. Alert the court officer of what you see and ask that the trial be held indefinitely.
   C. Politely interject the trial proceedings and ask the juror if he or she is feeling well.
   D. Alert the court officer who may or may not escort the juror out of the courtroom.

   2._____

3. During trial, you believe that you see the defendant winking at one of the jurors. No one else seems to notice their interaction, including the judge.
   Which of the following actions would you take?
   A. Alert the judge in chambers
   B. Tell the court officer during a break in trial
   C. Interrupt the trial to make all parties aware of the behavior
   D. Confirm with the juror in question that the defendant is winking at her to determine if the feeling is mutual

   3._____

4. During a recess in the trial, the defendant's expert witness is seen chatting with one of the alternate jurors outside the courthouse. While it is unclear what they are talking about, it seems to be a friendly exchange of information.
   What should you do before the court is called back to order?
   A. Tell the juror she must disclose her conversation with the expert witness in open court
   B. Tell the expert witness he must disclose the conversation with the juror in open court
   C. Inform the plaintiff's attorney about the conversation
   D. Inform the judge about the conversation

   4._____

Questions 5-8.

DIRECTIONS: Questions 5 through 8 are to be answered on the basis of the following fact pattern.

After a TRO is issued to the plaintiff, the ex-wife of the defendant, both parties are free to go. The defendant appeared in court and rigorously opposed his ex-wife's request. His ex-wife already has sole custody of their three children and he seems incredibly distraught by the judge's grant of her request.

5. In a follow-up hearing, where the plaintiff is requesting to extend a TRO, the defendant does not show up. Instead, the defendant's brother appears at the hearing on his behalf. Is the defendant's brother permitted to voice his concerns about extending the TRO?
   The defendant's brother
   A. is not a party to the action and must wait outside of the courtroom during proceedings.
   B. is welcome to testify on his brother's behalf
   C. can testify on his brother's behalf as long as he remains calm while doing so
   D. can testify on his brother's behalf so long as the plaintiff's sister can testify on her behalf

5.____

6. A TRO is a _____ restraining order, while a QDRO is a qualified _____ order.
   A. temporary; domicile relations
   B. territorial; domicile relations
   C. temporary; domestic revision
   D. temporary; domestic relations

6.____

7. How many alternate jurors are typically sworn in for trial?
   A. Up to 12   B. Up to 14   C. Up to 10   D. Up to 6

7.____

Questions 8-10.

DIRECTIONS: Questions 8 through 10 are to be answered on the basis of the following fact pattern.

While those waiting for the court to open file into the hallway, an argument breaks out between two women and one man. When you intervene between the parties, you discover the two women are arguing over custody of a child – who is standing nearby – and the man is one of their attorneys. Barbara is the biological mother of the child. Tina raised the child from birth. Tina and her attorney, Bill, came with the child to court today.

8. Which party should stay with the child?
   A. The biological mother, Barbara, of the child should stay with the child while they await for court to begin.
   B. Tina and Bill should stay with the child since she raised the child from birth.

8.____

C. The parties should separate and the child should come with you to a sequestered part of the courthouse.
D. Tina and Bill should stay with the child as petitioners of the court, Barbara should wait in a separate area away from all three and refrain from contact.

9. Which of the following are Barbara and her attorney MOST likely to request in court?   9._____
    A. An order of protection   B. Order to expunge
    C. Order to impeach   D. Deposition

10. Should you tell the judge about the behavior of the parties during the hearing?   10._____
    A. You can inform the judge if asked, but not during the hearing itself.
    B. You can inform the judge if asked, but should wait until a hearing is not in session.
    C. Before the hearing is set to begin, you should inform the judge of your encounter with the parties and let the judge decide how to best confront the situation between all involved.
    D. No.

Questions 11-14.

DIRECTIONS: Questions 11 through 14 are to be answered on the basis of the following fact pattern.

At district court, a trial of a group of alleged rapists has drawn a huge crowd of spectators at each day of the hearings. Two of the defendants are locals of Nassau County, while the other is a local of Richmond County. The trial date has been set and moved multiple times.

11. Which of the following will the defendants MOST likely be charged with?   11._____
    A. An information   B. A felony
    C. A misdemeanor   D. An indictment

12. In reading the charge, which of the following is LEAST likely to appear?   12._____
    A. The name of the attorneys of record
    B. The names of the victims
    C. The number of counts of each crime
    D. The name of the judge hearing the case

13. There are likely to be multiples of which during this trial?   13._____
    A. Multiple court officers   B. Multiple attorneys
    C. Multiple charges   D. All of the above

14. The venue of the trial is MOST likely to be   14._____
    A. Nassau County   B. Richmond County
    C. Determined by the jury   D. Determined by the judge

Questions 15-17.

DIRECTIONS: Questions 15 through 17 are to be answered on the basis of the following fact pattern.

In the Supreme Court Foreclosure Part, a variety of parties are awaiting for hearings to begin. Homeowners, attorneys, creditors, and trustees anxiously talk amongst themselves. Based on your knowledge of foreclosure procedures, answer the following questions.

15. As you approach the foreclosure part, a woman rushes toward you. She is incredibly upset and begins to cry as soon as she begins speaking. She tells you that she cannot wait any longer for her hearing to begin because her mother just had an accident and she must rush to the hospital.
If she misses her court date, what should she be MOST concerned with as it relates to her foreclosure case?
   A. Having to reschedule her court date to defend herself
   B. Defaulting and, therefore, her creditor(s) prevailing against her
   C. Answering a motion to show cause from the bank
   D. Answering a complaint from the bank

15.____

16. One of the most frequent questions you are asked is whether a bank can accelerate the mortgage loan against a homeowner/borrower after the homeowner has made a few late payments.
Acceleration is
   A. requiring a borrower to immediately pay off the balance of the loan
   B. the amount of money owed on the mortgage
   C. the document showing the ownership of a mortgage or deed of trust
   D. the basic repayment plan the homeowner/borrower initially agreed to when purchasing the home

16.____

17. Homeowners in foreclosure sometimes file simultaneously for bankruptcy. The automatic stay is a function unique to bankruptcy.
An automatic stay is defined as
   A. a large lump sum payment due as the last payment on a loan
   B. an injunction automatically issued by the bankruptcy court when someone files for bankruptcy
   C. an optional injunction that requires creditors to call the debtor and seek a settlement
   D. another term meaning "to stay a motion" or to hold a request from the court temporarily

17.____

18. Dave approaches the clerk's desk and asks how, generally, judges make their decisions on legal matters. The MOST correct answer would be based on
   A. case law, or the body of all court decisions which govern or provide precedent on the same legal issue before the judge
   B. case law, personal opinion and oral arguments by attorneys
   C. case law, oral arguments by attorneys, and the defendant's rap sheet
   D. "stare decisis" or that which has already been decided

18.____

19. Which hearing below will MOST likely be heard in the Commercial Division of the Suffolk County Supreme courthouse?
    A. Divorce petition between Bill and Amy
    B. A custody dispute between Jim and John
    C. A business dispute between ABC Corp. and XYZ, Inc.
    D. A petition for expungement of a stockbroker's record

19.____

20. Richard may face criminal charges for allegedly embezzling thousands of dollars from his company's business account.
    If a grand jury decides there is enough evidence to move forward with criminal charges against Richard, they
    A. return an information
    B. return an indictment
    C. issue a warrant
    D. issue a seizure

20.____

21. At trial, the prosecutor asks many pointed questions at Richard. The prosecutor believes Richard is lying on the stand.
    When an attorney attempts to reduce the credibility of the other side's witness, they are said to be trying to _____ the witness on the stand.
    A. objectify   B. anger   C. impeach   D. frustrate

21.____

22. During a lengthy trial, four jurors conspire with one another to enter votes of "not guilty" and hatch a plan to sway other jurors in their favor in an attempt to close out deliberations early.
    What is the likely outcome of the trial?
    A. Hung jury
    B. Mistrial
    C. Acquittal
    D. Defensive charge

22.____

23. The judge's charge to the jury is also known as
    A. closing statements
    B. quid pro quo
    C. jury instructions
    D. sua sponte

23.____

24. Who is the only party responsible for delivering the sentence to the convicted?
    A. Bailiff
    B. Jury
    C. Judge
    D. Jury foreperson

24.____

25. A motion for directed verdict is made
    A. without the jury present
    B. with only the jury foreperson present
    C. with the entire jury present
    D. with only the alternate jurors present

25.____

KEY (CORRECT ANSWERS)

1.	C		11.	B
2.	D		12.	B
3.	A		13.	D
4.	D		14.	D
5.	A		15.	B
6.	D		16.	A
7.	D		17.	B
8.	D		18.	A
9.	A		19.	C
10.	C		20.	B

21.	C
22.	B
23.	C
24.	C
25.	A

TEST 2

DIRECTIONS: Each question or incomplete statement is followed by several suggested answers or completions. Select the one that BEST answers the question or completes the statement. *PRINT THE LETTER OF THE CORRECT ANSWER IN THE SPACE AT THE RIGHT.*

1. Juror #12 is a close friend of your brother's, Tom. Tom starts to strike up a conversation with you outside of the courtroom.
   How should you respond?
   A. Politely decline to engage, unless he or she is asking for directions
   B. Politely decline to engage, unless he or she would like to talk about the case
   C. Politely decline to engage, unless he or she knows you personally
   D. Engage the conversation remaining mindful of the appearance of bias and immediately ceasing the conversation if the trial at hand comes up

   1.____

2. A charge of attempted murder is LEAST likely to accompany a charge of
   A. murder   B. burglary   C. robbery   D. assault

   2.____

Questions 3-4.

DIRECTIONS: Questions 3 and 4 are to be answered on the basis of the following fact pattern.

Mary approaches you inside the Albany County Supreme Court and says that she has been served with a lawsuit. She is confused about the entire lawsuit process and is confused as to what area of the courthouse she should be in. She believes, but is not entirely sure, that her sister may be suing her over money she lent her then subsequently lost gambling in the casino.

3. Which of the following is the MOST appropriate response you can provide Mary with regard to her being served?
   She should have a copy of the _____ with her and refer to it, which will tell her where she would report within the courthouse.
   A. answer   B. complaint   C. summons   D. information

   3.____

4. Mary produces the document and asks you if there is anything she can do to respond to the lawsuit.
   What is the MOST appropriate answer?
   She should
   A. file an answer, and perhaps seek legal counsel
   B. seek legal counsel
   C. check in at the Preliminary Conference desk
   D. file an injunction, and perhaps seek legal counsel

   4.____

5. Who decides whether the jurors are allowed to take notes during the trial?
   A. The judge
   B. The plaintiff's attorney, since they are bringing the case to court
   C. Jurors are always allowed to take notes during trials
   D. Jurors are never allowed to take notes during trials.

   5.____

6. During a trial, one of the jurors writes a question for one of the witnesses on a piece of paper and hands it to the court officer.
   What is the CORRECT procedure?
   The court officer
   A. may, but is not required to, pass the written question to the judge
   B. must pass the written question to the judge, who may or may not ask the witness the question posed
   C. must decline receipt of the written message
   D. passes the written question to the court assistant who may or may not read the question aloud

   6._____

7. If questions arise during the jury deliberation process, what is the role of the court officer?
   A. To deliver the written question from the jury foreperson to the judge
   B. To repeat the question orally as told to the court officer by the jury foreperson to the judge
   C. To read the written question in open court with all parties present other than the defendant
   D. To record the written question in the docket

   7._____

8. A juror has informed you that she accidentally read information about the case she is serving on while she was at the supermarket last night.
   How should you respond to her?
   A. Berate her for not being more diligent in seeking out information about the case
   B. Inform the court officer that the juror should be replaced
   C. Remove the juror from the jury box and replace him or her with an alternate juror yourself
   D. Inform the judge immediately

   8._____

9. Which court proceeding takes place CLOSEST in time to an arrest?
   A. Arraignment   B. Sentencing
   C. Trial   D. Jury selection

   9._____

10. Which of the following is LEAST likely to occur at the conclusion of a trial?
    A. Sentencing   B. Appeal
    C. Reversal   D. Plea bargaining

    10._____

11. You overhear two jurors talking about the case in the hallway during recess. From their conversation, it appears that they are related to one another.
    You should
    A. do nothing as it's none of your business
    B. make sure no one else hears them
    C. simply tell them not to discuss the case between themselves
    D. tell the judge

    11._____

12. How many jurors typically serve on a trial?   12._____
    A. 12   B. 18   C. 16   D. 6

13. During jury selection, the judge has already excused 25 prospective jurors   13._____
for cause. How many more jurors can be excused for cause before reaching
the excusal limit?
    A. 5
    B. 10
    C. The judge has reached the limit
    D. There is no excusal limit "for cause"

14. Which of the following is the jury usually prohibited from doing during a trial on which   14._____
they are serving?
    A. Visiting the scene of the alleged crime
    B. Read or listen to news about the trial from outside sources
    C. Research case law that applies to the trial
    D. All of the above

15. In New York City, jury trials are conducted at which of the following courts?   15._____
    A. Supreme Court   B. New York City Civil Court
    C. New York City Criminal Court   D. All of the above

16. A trial involving an alleged assault and battery is MOST likely to occur at   16._____
which New York City court?
    A. Town and Village Court   B. New York City Civil Court
    C. New York City Criminal Court   D. County Court

17. In vacating a default, which must the petitioner file FIRST?   17._____
    A. Notice of motion   B. Emergency affidavit
    C. Legal back   D. Injunction

18. Order the steps of a typical trial from first to last.   18._____
    I. Opening statements   II. Jury selection
    III. Deliberations   IV. Oath and preliminary instructions
    The CORRECT answer is:
    A. I, II, III, IV   B. IV, III, II, I   C. I, II, IV, III   D. II, IV, I, III

19. On appeal, three justices hear a case that was already decided in the lower   19._____
courts. The issue before them is a complicated issue involving a determination
of legal guardian.
An opinion from the entire panel of justices is known as a(n)
    A. per curiam decision   B. affirmative decision
    C. stare decisis   D. en banc order

20. One of the judges agrees with the decision of the court, but disagrees with   20._____
the reasoning of the conclusion. This judge decides to write his own opinion.
This is deemed a
    A. dissenting opinion   B. remedial decision
    C. concurring opinion   D. recurrent opinion

21. Suppose that one of the judges disagrees entirely with the ruling.   21.____
How will the judgment be altered because of the disagreement?
The judgment
   A. is unaffected because the majority voted in agreement with the trial court
   B. is unaffected because this judge did not author a dissenting opinion
   C. is unaffected because oral arguments were not made before the panel
   D. will be overturned

22. The appellate court still requires _____, even if it is established by the trial   22.____
court, known as original _____.
   A. domicile; venue   B. venue; jurisdiction
   C. jurisdiction; jurisdiction   D. jurisdiction; domicile

23. The legal theory upon which a case is based is called a   23.____
   A. basis   B. decisis
   C. cause of action   D. precedent

24. Sarah and her friend, Ashley, burglarized a number of homes in Kings   24.____
County over the summer. They were only apprehended after one of their other
friends overheard them talking about their crimes. At the time, both Sarah and
Ashley were 18 and legally minors.
A minor is legally defined as:
   A. In New York, a minor is anyone under the age of 18
   B. Anyone under 18
   C. A legally emancipated individual
   D. An infant or individual under the age of legal competence

25. The BEST place to refer back to the testimony of one witness is   25.____
   A. the docket
   B. the judge's notes which can be obtained freely from chambers
   C. the stenographer's transcript
   D. clerk notes which, in some instances, are available online

---

KEY (CORRECT ANSWERS)

1.	D		11.	D
2.	A		12.	A
3.	B		13.	D
4.	B		14.	D
5.	A		15.	D
6.	B		16.	C
7.	A		17.	A
8.	D		18.	D
9.	A		19.	A
10.	D		20.	C

21.	A
22.	C
23.	C
24.	D
25.	C

TEST 3

DIRECTIONS: Each question or incomplete statement is followed by several suggested answers or completions. Select the one that BEST answers the question or completes the statement. *PRINT THE LETTER OF THE CORRECT ANSWER IN THE SPACE AT THE RIGHT.*

1. The pre-trial hearing is MOST likely to take place after _____, but before _____.   1.____
   A. arraignment; jury selection
   B. deliberations; closing statements
   C. assignment; adjudication
   D. plea bargain; opening statement

2. During a court recess, you see one of the jurors walking into the judge's   2.____
   chambers. You immediately
   A. halt the juror and demand he or she return to the deliberation room
   B. allow the juror to proceed, but ask the judge about the incident later
   C. allow the juror to proceed and assume they know one another personally
   D. allow the juror to proceed, but inform the court officer of the incident

3. When reading an indictment in court, each charge represents a(n)   3.____
   A. allegation of a crime
   B. proven criminal act
   C. evidentiary plea
   D. legal certainty

4. After a defendant has been acquitted, he or she will likely be   4.____
   A. free to leave the courthouse
   B. remanded to federal prison
   C. detained until further notice
   D. formally sentenced

5. Jeremiah, a defense attorney, has approached you in the hallways of the   5.____
   New York Civil Court. He is concerned that his client, Dave, may become
   violent during court proceedings.
   How do you handle Jeremiah's request to closely supervise Dave while court is
   in session?
   A. Inform the judge of Jeremiah's request and allow proceedings to continue
      as normal
   B. Ask that a court officer be present during court proceedings
   C. Request the judge to sequester the jury while Dave is present
   D. Ignore Jeremiah's request for now, until you see how Dave behaves
      yourself

6. Jury sequestration is   6.____
   A. extremely common given the complex nature of most criminal trials
   B. becoming increasingly common
   C. more common in civil cases than in criminal trials
   D. rare

7. At arraignment, the defendant is MOST likely to   7.____
   A. state his case
   B. convince the judge of his or her innocence
   C. enter a plea
   D. gather information on his or her case from the State's attorney

8. A warrant can be issued for an individual's arrest or for   8.____
   A. search of premises outlined in the warrant itself
   B. testimony
   C. deposition of the arrested individual
   D. evidence found at the scene

9. The responsibility to record notes for the judge and listen to issues of law   9.____
   that may need to be researched later are reserved for the
   A. court officer   B. stenographer
   C. judge's clerk   D. jury

10. Information about the charges against the defendant, as well as the   10.____
    parties involved in the case, can MOST likely be found in the
    A. judge's notes   B. docket
    C. information   D. discovery report

11. The opening statements in a trial are delivered by the   11.____
    A. defendant   B. plaintiff   C. attorneys   D. judge

12. When the judge sustains the objection of an attorney who is asking a   12.____
    question of the witness on the stand, the witness must
    A. answer the question as asked
    B. wait for counsel to re-phrase the question in a proper form or ask another
       question before answering
    C. refuse to answer the question
    D. the witness may step down

13. An expert is permitted to   13.____
    A. review the plaintiff's evidence, draw a reasonable conclusion and give
       testimony to that effect
    B. review the defendant's evidence, draw a reasonable conclusion and
       submit his or her opinion in writing to the judge
    C. give his or her opinion based on the facts in evidence and provide the
       reasoning for that opinion
    D. provide an opinion in open court

14. Prosecutor and defense counsel have both made closing arguments in the trial of   14.____
    Samuel Smith Jones. Mr. Jones is being tried for capital murder for the alleged
    murder of his mother and sister.
    Which party is entitled to a rebuttal in closing arguments?
    A. The prosecutor
    B. The defense
    C. The defense, but only after the plaintiff has given their closing argument
    D. The defense, but only if the plaintiff waives their right to make a closing
       argument

15. When a jury cannot agree on a verdict, a(n) _____ occurs and the result is   15.____
    a _____.
    A. mistrial; acquittal   B. mistrial; hung jury
    C. hung jury; mistrial   D. acquittal; mistrial

16. Nominal damages are   16.____
    A. damages awarded in name only, indicating no substantial harm was done
    B. damages to recompense the injured for the infliction of emotional distress
    C. damages to recompense the initiator of the lawsuit
    D. a reimbursement of filing fees, awarded to the person who can prove they
       are injured

17. The type of recovery being sought by the plaintiff is known as the   17.____
    A. order   B. punishment
    C. remedy   D. issue

18. Robert approaches the clerk's desk in a panic. He says that he filed a   18.____
    lawsuit last week against his cousin, Mike, but neglected to add his cousin's
    friend, Rory, to the suit.
    Robert must _____ the compliant.
    A. amend   B. refile   C. re-serve   D. redact

19. In a foreclosure action, which of the following will the borrower MOST likely 19.____
    be asked about in terms of securing a second or third mortgage?
    A. Business terms   B. Collateral
    C. Damages   D. Remedy

20. Maya has asked you about Article 7A proceedings.   20.____
    Article 7A hearings allow
    A. tenants being foreclosed upon to file a class action against the landlord
    B. at least 1/3 of tenants to ask the court to appoint an administrator to run
       the building in select circumstances
    C. tenants to forego paying the rent when living conditions in the building
       become inhabitable
    D. tenants to book their landlord from collecting rent when living conditions in
       the building become inhabitable

21. The Housing Court, sometimes referred to as Landlord and Tenant Court,   21.____
    is held at the
    A. Town and Village Court   B. New York City Civil Court
    C. New York City Criminal Court   D. County Court

22. Without an attorney, how much money can one sue for in Town or Village   22.____
    Courts, outside of New York City?
    A. Up to $3,000   B. Up to $5,000
    C. Up to $2,500   D. Up to $2,000

14

23. Judith wants to sue her neighbor, Samantha, in small claims court after Samantha borrowed Judith's lawnmower and refused to return it. Judith has begun a petition in small claims court for recovery of the lawnmower. How will the case proceed?
    A. The case will not go forward, because only money damages can be sought in small claims court.
    B. The case will not go forward, because small claims court cannot compel Samantha to return the lawnmower.
    C. The case will not go forward, because the lawnmower exceeds the small claims court limit.
    D. Judith will likely prevail.

23.____

24. Daniel wants to file for probate of his father's estate. The filing fee is based on
    A. Daniel's assets
    B. Daniel's age
    C. The size of the estate
    D. The age at which Daniel's father passed

24.____

25. Family court will hear each of the following cases EXCEPT
    A. custody and visitation   B. adoption
    C. juvenile delinquency   D. estate

25.____

KEY (CORRECT ANSWERS)

1.	A		11.	C
2.	A		12.	B
3.	A		13.	C
4.	A		14.	A
5.	B		15.	C
6.	D		16.	A
7.	C		17.	C
8.	A		18.	A
9.	C		19.	B
10.	B		20.	B

21.	B
22.	A
23.	A
24.	C
25.	D

15

TEST 4

1. Jason is currently a student at SUNY Buffalo. He is worried that his recent conviction will affect his financial aid package with the college.
   How will Jason's conviction of drug possession affect his financial aid?
   It will
   A. remain unaffected
   B. remain unaffected as long as Jason is represented by counsel
   C. automatically be cancelled for a period of time
   D. be cancelled indefinitely

   1.____

2. Who is responsible for drafting the Pre-Sentence report that judges use in sentencing convicted defendants?
   A. Defendant's attorney
   B. Probation officer
   C. Court assistant
   D. Judge's law clerk

   2.____

3. Restitution cannot be made for
   A. breach of contract
   B. assault and battery
   C. lost wages
   D. future losses

   3.____

4. In a bench trial, the _____ serves as the ultimate fact finder.
   A. jury   B. judge   C. bailiff   D. law clerk

   4.____

5. The role of the bankruptcy trustee is to represent the
   A. interest of the bankruptcy estate and the creditors of the debtor
   B. debtor against all creditors
   C. largest creditor of the debtor
   D. smallest creditor of the debtor

   5.____

6. The bankruptcy estate typically includes _____ at the time of the filing.
   A. all property of the debtor, including interests in property
   B. the home where the debtor resides
   C. the home and personal vehicle of the debtor
   D. all personal property, but not real property, of the debtor

   6.____

7. When a party to a lawsuit cannot afford the cost of the lawsuit, the Court
   A. may permit that party to proceed without being required to pay for court costs
   B. disallows payment for foreclosure proceeds
   C. does not require that party to pay for filing fees
   D. requires that party to settle the matter in ADR

   7.____

8. An answer is a formal response to which document?　　　　　　　　　　8.____
    A. indictment   B. discovery   C. complaint   D. summons

9. Ishmael sued his former employer, Igor, for loss of wages. Igor lost the case   9.____
and now wishes to appeal the ruling.
When Igor appeals the case, he becomes an
    A. appellee   B. appellant   C. respondent   D. defendant

10. Damiano has been sentenced to six years for armed robbery and ten years   10.____
for grand larceny. He is sentenced to serve his prison terms concurrently.
What is the MAXIMUM amount of time he will spend behind bars?
    A. Six years   B. Sixteen years
    C. Ten years   D. Four years

11. What does the exclusionary rule exclude in a criminal trial?   11.____
    A. Testimony that is deemed hearsay by a judge in a court of competent
       jurisdiction
    B. Evidence obtained in violation of a defendant's constitutional or statutory
       rights
    C. Depositions that are unsworn or not notarized
    D. Affidavits that are unsworn or not notarized

12. David is being arraigned and needs to enter a plea for the crime he allegedly   12.____
committed while he was with his friend, Robert. Robert pleads guilty during his
arraignment yesterday, but David has been advised by his attorney to plead no
contest, also known as
    A. nolo contendere   B. pro se   C. quid pro quo   D. qui tam

13. Adoptions can be heard in which two courts?   13.____
    A. Family court and surrogate court
    B. Foreclosure court and family court
    C. Family court and commercial court
    D. Family court and court of claims

14. Which party may NOT file a paternity petition?   14.____
    A. The child's mother
    B. The man who believes he may be the father of the child
    C. The child or the child's guardian
    D. The child's teacher or other close associate

15. Amy was married to Bob at the time her child was born. John believes he is   15.____
the father of Amy's baby.
Who is presumed to be the father of Amy's child?
    A. Bob
    B. John
    C. Neither can be presumed; a DNA test must be administered in this
       circumstance
    D. Neither can be presumed; each has to petition the court separately

16. Parties that represent themselves during court hearings are referred to as
_____ litigants.
    A. qui tam   B. pro se   C. en banc   D. quid quo pro

16.____

17. Normally, guardianship petitions must be filed in _____ court.
    A. family   B. surrogates   C. probate   D. civil

17.____

18. At what age can a child's own preference be taken under consideration in
guardianship or custody hearings?
    A. 12   B. 14   C. 17   D. 16

18.____

19. Civil litigation claims against the State of New York or other State-related
agencies are heard exclusively in the
    A. Civil Court   B. Criminal Court
    C. Court of Claims   D. Surrogate Court

19.____

20. Preliminary conferences are automatically scheduled by the Court within
_____ days after a Request for Judicial Intervention (RJI).
    A. 30   B. 45   C. 50   D. 55

20.____

21. There are two junior attorneys that have been sent to cover the preliminary
conference of their case *Abe v. Gabe* in part 22 of the court. Both attorneys
approach the clerk's desk to ask what the "return date" on a motion refers to.
The return date is the date the
    A. motion will be conferenced and/or orally argued at the discretion of the
       court
    B. attorneys must return for more information
    C. attorneys must return with the clients
    D. attorneys must return to complete discovery

21.____

22. Decisions made on motions and pro se litigants must be
    A. mailed or a copy provided of the decision
    B. made available for photocopy or fax
    C. made available for scan, but not photocopied or faxed
    D. uploaded to the court website so it can be easily accessed online

22.____

23. A stipulation of settlement represents a formal agreement between the
    A. judge and the parties resolving the case
    B. litigants and their attorneys resolving the dispute
    C. clerk and the litigants representing a near end to the dispute at issue
    D. judge and the clerk representing a notation of the resolution

23.____

24. A motion to vacate a default in foreclosure part represents an attempt by the
homeowner or borrower to
    A. reverse the court's finding of default
    B. reverse the court's finding of dereliction
    C. obtain a new hearing
    D. reschedule a hearing due to a missed court date

24.____

25. The Personal Appearance Part in the Civil Court is where which types of   25.____
    cases are heard?
    Cases where
    A. one or both parties are self-represented
    B. the plaintiff is self-represented
    C. the defendant is self-represented
    D. clerk is the fact finder

KEY (CORRECT ANSWERS)

1.	C		11.	B
2.	B		12.	A
3.	D		13.	A
4.	B		14.	D
5.	A		15.	A
6.	A		16.	B
7.	A		17.	A
8.	C		18.	B
9.	B		19.	C
10.	C		20.	B

21.	A
22.	A
23.	B
24.	A
25.	A

EXAMINATION SECTION

TEST 1

DIRECTIONS: Each question or incomplete statement is followed by several suggested answers or completions. Select the one that BEST answers the question or completes the statement. *PRINT THE LETTER OF THE CORRECT ANSWER IN THE SPACE AT THE RIGHT.*

Questions 1-5.

DIRECTIONS: Questions 1 through 5 are to be answered on the basis of the following fact pattern.

Bill initiated a lawsuit against his landlord, Amy, last year. Bill claims Amy did not upkeep common areas in the four-apartment building where Bill resides. These common areas include the hallway, entryway, and parking lot of the building. Bill is not represented by an attorney, but Amy is represented by Maureen. The parties have failed to settle the matter outside of court. Bill, Amy, and Maureen are ready to move forward with court proceedings.

1. The magistrate judge sets the pre-trial conference between the parties for March 30 at 9:30 A.M. The parties required to attend the pretrial conference are
    A. Maureen, Bill, and the judge
    B. the judge only
    C. Bill and Amy
    D. Bill, Amy, and Maureen

1.____

2. During the pre-trial conference, the judge wants the parties to stipulate to as many issues as possible before trial. The judge instructs the parties to focus on undisputed facts. An example of a stipulation would be:
    A. Both parties agree the parking lot is not a common area
    B. Maureen files a motion to vacate
    C. Bill wants to expedite the case and start trial the following Monday
    D. Amy files a counterclaim against Bill for failure to pay rent on time

2.____

3. A pre-trial conference is attended by the required parties if the case does not settle before trial. However, a pre-trial conference cannot be set until
    A. the jury is selected
    B. the attorneys have entered appearances
    C. initial pleadings, including the complaint and answer, have been filed
    D. the court clerk is selected

3.____

4. Which deadline is MOST likely to be set by the judge during the pre-trial conference?
    The deadline
    A. to decide which juror will serve as foreperson
    B. to decide which courthouse the trial will take place
    C. for all discovery to be completed
    D. for the judge to select a law clerk to transcribe court proceedings

4.____

5. Bill will be appearing as a
   5._____
   A. defendant
   B. pro se litigant
   C. respondent
   D. en banc party

Questions 6-9.

DIRECTIONS: Questions 6 through 9 are to be answered on the basis of the following fact pattern.

Adam, Barbara, Cameron, and David appear for jury duty on June 15. Adam and Barbara have each served on a trial before; Adam served on a criminal trial while Barbara served on a civil trial. The trial Adam served on lasted three months, and he would prefer not to serve on a trial ever again. Cameron and David have never served on a trial before and are unsure of what to expect.

6. While prospective jurors wait to be called by the clerk, Adam and Cameron
   6._____
   spark up a conversation. Adam tells Cameron that if he were selected to be a
   juror Cameron may be isolated from his family and friends for weeks.
   What is Adam referring to?
   A. Ex-parte communications, which prohibit jurors from speaking with
      anyone else during the trial
   B. Voir dire, which may require one to be questioned in judge's chambers
      about past dealings
   C. Jury sequestration or juror isolation from the public to prevent contact with
      outside influences
   D. Individual depositions of jurors prior to the start of a trial

7. Barbara overhears the conversation between Adam and Cameron and
   7._____
   interjects. She explains that not all juries operate the same way. She explains
   that in the middle of the trial in which she served, the defendant filed a motion
   requesting a bench trial.
   A bench trial is a trial without a
   A. plaintiff's attorney
   B. jury
   C. defendant's attorney
   D. bailiff

8. The court's clerk finally begins jury selection. He or she calls how many jurors
   8._____
   from the jury selection list?
   A. 9
   B. 6
   C. 10
   D. 12

9. Cameron and David are selected and take a seat in the jury box. The judge
   9._____
   provides an overview of the case and tells the prospective jurors that the case
   involves armed robbery. As a teenager, David was mugged at gunpoint while
   walking home from school. He raises his hand and tells the judge he may be
   biased in the trial because of his personal experience.
   The defendant's attorney will ask that David be excused
   A. with good reason
   B. for cause
   C. without prejudice
   D. with prejudice

10. Which of the following does NOT occur during the judge's charge to the jury?   10.____
    A. A discussion of the standard of proof jurors should apply to the case
    B. A reminder that opening and closing arguments are considered evidence
    C. A note that jurors should base their conclusions on the evidence presented at trial
    D. A reminder that jurors are required to adhere to the relevant laws in rendering a verdict

11. Which of the following does the court reporter NOT record   11.____
    A. testimony of the witnesses
    B. objections made by the attorneys
    C. the judge's respective rulings of objections
    D. ex-parte communications

Questions 12-16.

DIRECTIONS: Questions 12 through 16 are to be answered on the basis of the following fact pattern.

Michael is accused of felony theft of an automobile. The vehicle was taken from an 18-unit apartment building parking lot sometime during the night of August 15. The vehicle was driven for approximately five miles before the driver crashed it into a parked car. The driver fled the scene. The owner of the vehicle, Jeffrey, was asleep in his apartment during the time the vehicle was stolen. Michael and Jeffrey are represented by counsel.

12. Given the charge of felony theft of an automobile, Michael now faces how long   12.____
    a term of incarceration?
    A. One year or more   B. One year or less
    C. Six months   D. Five years or more

13. During Jeffrey's testimony, one of the jurors, Samantha, realizes she was in   13.____
    the building where the car was stolen on the night of the theft. She was
    sleeping over her sister's apartment for the night and remembers seeing a
    bright blue Porsche – Jeffrey's car – in the parking lot before bed. She
    immediately informs the bailiff who tells the judge.
    How will the judge MOST likely move forward in the case?
    A. Declare a mistrial
    B. Acquit Michael of all charges
    C. Excuse the juror and replace here with an alternate juror and continue the trial
    D. Demand the attorneys in the case submit post-hearing briefs on the issue

14. In open court, the judge asks Samantha details about why she was in the   14.____
    apartment at the time Michael allegedly stole Jeffrey's car and what, if
    anything, she remembers about that night. Samantha says she did not see or
    hear anything suspicious, but does remember Michael being in the apartment
    building in one of the common areas. Michael's attorney files a motion for a
    mistrial after Samantha's testimony to the court. Why?

A. Samantha's testimony has substantially prejudiced the other jurors who heard Michael was in the building on the night of the theft.
B. There is not enough substantive evidence to continue the trial against Michael.
C. Samantha should have been removed as a juror at the beginning of the trial.
D. The case must be filed in the court closest to where the car was found, not where it was allegedly taken.

15. If the judge declares a mistrial, what effect would that determination have on the jury verdict?
    A. No effect; the jury must still render a decision on the merits
    B. The jury need only to determine damages.
    C. The jury does not need to render a verdict.
    D. Only six jurors need to serve after the judge declares a mistrial.

15.____

16. After all evidence has been presented, it is clear Michael did not commit the crime. Michael was in another state at the time of the theft and could not have committed felony theft of Jeffrey's automobile. Before the case is submitted to a jury, Michael's attorney submits a motion that argues no reasonable jury could find for Jeffrey. Michael's attorney asks the judge to instruct the jury to find Michael not guilty.
    Michael's attorney is requesting a(n) _____, because Michael clearly did not commit the crime.
    A. reduced charge   B. substitute charge
    C. acquittal   D. directed verdict

16.____

17. During the direct examination of one of the plaintiff's witnesses, the defendant's attorney objects. Defendant's attorney believes opposing counsel asked a leading question. The judge sustains defendant's objection.
    How must plaintiff's counsel proceed?
    A. The witness may answer the question as asked.
    B. Plaintiff's counsel must re-phrase the question in a proper form or ask another question.
    C. Plaintiff's counsel must stop his or her line of questioning completely.
    D. The witness may step down.

17.____

18. An expert is permitted to
    A. review the plaintiff's evidence, draw a reasonable conclusion, and give testimony to that effect
    B. review the defendant's evidence, draw a reasonable conclusion, and submit his or her opinion in writing to the judge
    C. give his or her opinion based on the facts in evidence and provide the reasoning for that opinion
    D. provide an opinion in open court

18.____

19. Which party, as a matter of right, is entitled to a rebuttal in closing arguments?   19._____
    A. The plaintiff
    B. The defense
    C. The defense, but only after the plaintiff has given their closing argument
    D. The defense, but only if the plaintiff waives their right to make a closing argument

20. When a jury cannot agree on a verdict, a(n) _____ occurs and the result   20._____
    is a(n) _____.
    A. mistrial; acquittal   B. mistrial; hung jury
    C. hung jury; mistrial   D. acquittal; mistrial

21. Generally speaking, the role of the foreperson, also known as the presiding   21._____
    juror, is to
    A. announce the verdict
    B. preside over discussion of the jurors
    C. preside over the votes of the jurors
    D. all of the above

22. A request to poll the jury serves what purpose?   22._____
    Jury polling
    A. ensures the verdict to be recorded is accurate
    B. allows jurors to resolve any conflicts of interests prior to the start of trial
    C. helps the jury selection process move faster
    D. allows the judge to ensure each juror will be impartial and unbiased while hearing evidence

23. In which of the following scenarios would a bailiff MOST likely intervene?   23._____
    A. The plaintiff and defense attorneys are chatting with one another outside the courtroom.
    B. The judge and his or her law clerk are overheard talking about the case in judge's chambers.
    C. One of the jurors is talking with the defense attorney inside the courtroom before others have entered the room.
    D. The plaintiff and the defendant's attorney are heard talking in the hallway.

24. Which of the following would be submitted only after a verdict is rendered?   24._____
    A. Motion to dismiss   B. Motion in limine
    C. Motion to exclude   D. Motion in arrest of judgment

25. In many jurisdictions, a motion for a new trial must be filed before a party   25._____
    can file a(n)
    A. exculpatory plea   B. motion for mistrial
    C. acquittal by default   D. appeal

KEY (CORRECT ANSWERS)

1.	A		11.	D
2.	A		12.	A
3.	C		13.	C
4.	C		14.	A
5.	B		15.	C
6.	C		16.	D
7.	B		17.	B
8.	D		18.	C
9.	B		19.	A
10.	B		20.	C

21.	D
22.	A
23.	C
24.	D
25.	D

TEST 2

DIRECTIONS: Each question or incomplete statement is followed by several suggested answers or completions. Select the one that BEST answers the question or completes the statement. *PRINT THE LETTER OF THE CORRECT ANSWER IN THE SPACE AT THE RIGHT.*

Questions 1-5.

DIRECTIONS: Questions 1 through 5 are to be answered on the basis of the following fact pattern.

James and Sean started an accounting practice five years ago. Business quickly soured and James and Sean decided to each start their own competing business practices. While James' business flourished, Sean's practice has floundered. Sean believes James spoke poorly about him to their mutual friends, ruining his professional reputation, and went behind his back to steal clients. Sean now wants to sue James civilly.

1. How would Sean begin a civil suit against James?   1.____
   A. Sean needs to file an interpleader to compel James to court.
   B. Sean must file a motion to compel proceedings.
   C. Sean must file a complaint against Sean in the proper court.
   D. Sean can outline the facts of his case to the clerk who will transcribe the issues.

2. Sean must also file a summons with the clerk.   2.____
   What is the role of the summons in initiating a lawsuit?
   A. It puts the other party on notice that a lawsuit has been filed against them.
   B. It compels discovery in a court of proper jurisdiction.
   C. It requires the other party to answer by initiating a cross-motion.
   D. It gives the other party extended time to file a counterclaim.

3. Sean's attorney and James' attorney begin the process of exchanging   3.____
   information about the witnesses each side plans to call and the evidence that
   will be presented at trial.
   This process is called
   A. interrogation   B. discovery   C. compulsion   D. demurrer

4. One of James' and Sean's former clients is moving to London. James' and   4.____
   Sean's attorneys agree to take her deposition now and use it at trial in the
   event she will not be able to appear.
   At trial, her testimony will be _____ and part of the record.
   A. read into evidence   B. ex parte
   C. sequestered   D. assumed credible

5. After being notified that a lawsuit has been filed against him, James has an   5.____
   opportunity to answer the _____ that has been filed against him.
   A. pleadings   B. motion to compel
   C. interpleader   D. complaint

27

6. Venue refers to the district or county within a state where the   6.____
    A. lawsuit began   B. lawsuit must be heard
    C. plaintiff resides   D. plaintiff is domiciled

7. After both parties have agreed on a jury, the jurors are _____ by the   7.____
    court clerk before they are impaneled.
    A. instructed to take notes   B. sworn in
    C. fingerprinted   D. arranged

8. Can the prosecution compel a defendant in a criminal trial to take the stand   8.____
    and testify?
    A. Yes; he or she must explain what happened in open court
    B. Yes; he or she must take the stand and testify they are using their Fifth
       Amendment right against self-incrimination.
    C. Yes; he or she must take the stand but they can refuse to answer any
       question they choose.
    D. No.

9. Criminal charges are brought against a person in all of the following ways,   9.____
    EXCEPT
    A. citation   B. information   C. indictment   D. subpoena

Questions 10-15.

DIRECTIONS: Questions 10 through 15 are to be answered on the basis of the following fact
              pattern.

    Jason's brother, Andrew, has been arrested. Jason appears at the courthouse as soon as
he hears this news. He does not know why Andrew has been arrested, but suspects it may be
related to his tumultuous relationship with his ex-girlfriend, who has filed a temporary restraining
order against Andrew.

10. If Andrew was not arrested on a warrant, when will he be able to file a plea of   10.____
    guilty, not guilty, or no contest?
    A. At arraignment   B. At trial
    C. At a preliminary conference   D. At indictment

11. If Andrew is released from custody without a payment of money on the   11.____
    promise that he will appear for all hearings and for trial, the judge has released
    Andrew
    A. on his own recognizance   B. with time served
    C. after a concurrent term   D. on exculpatory evidence

12. In the alternative, if the judge sets bail for Andrew's release, he or she does 　　　12._____
so with the intent of
    A. punishing Andrew
    B. ensuring Andrew will appear for trial and all pre-trial hearings for which he
       must be present
    C. setting a fine dependent on the type of crime alleged
    D. releasing Andrew into the custody of his responsible brother, Jason

13. Which of the following should NOT be a factor a judge may use in deciding 　　　13._____
the amount of Andrew's bail?
    A. The risk of Andrew's fleeing
    B. The type of crime Andrew is alleged to have committed
    C. Andrew's age, race, and sex
    D. The safety of the community

14. During Andrew's initial appearance, the judge explains to Andrew that he has 　　　14._____
a right to a trial by jury.
If Andrew does not want a trial by jury, what type of trial will he receive?
    A. An expedited trial　　　　　B. A bench trial
    C. A summation　　　　　　　　D. An information

15. Andrew pleads no contest to the charges in his initial appearance. 　　　15._____
Andrew is effectively
    A. not admitting guilt or disputing the charge alleged
    B. admitting guilt
    C. denying the charge but admitting he will pay any fines incurred
    D. deferring his plea until a later date

Questions 16-19.

DIRECTIONS:　Questions 16 through 19 are to be answered on the basis of the following fact
　　　　　　　pattern.

　　　Jameson and Avery are neighbors. Jameson moved and purchased a home in the lot
next to Avery's lot three months ago. Avery is suing Jameson for building a fence on Avery's
property. Jameson attests the fence is actually being built on his own property and there is no
boundary dispute. Jameson and Avery are both represented by counsel. A number of motions
are filed by each party and discovery has been a lengthy process thus far.

16. Both parties serve each other requests to answer questions in writing under 　　　16._____
oath. Avery's attorney demands Jameson answer questions about the
purchase of his home and dealings with the contractors building the fence.
Jameson demands Avery answer questions about the property line dividing
their property.
This type of discovery is called
    A. interrogatories　　　　　B. demands
    C. summons　　　　　　　　D. written decision

17. Avery's attorney would like to depose the property surveyor, Abe.   17.____
Can Jameson and/or Jameson's attorney attend Abe's deposition?
    A. No, because Abe will be Avery's witness
    B. No, because Avery can share the information with Jameson's counsel at a later date
    C. No, because Abe's testimony may not be inadmissible in court so Jameson's presence would be futile
    D. Yes

18. Which of the following will NOT occur at the pre-trial conference between the   18.____
parties?
    A. A deadline for discovery will be set.
    B. A trial date will be set.
    C. The judge will encourage stipulations between the parties.
    D. The judge will ask for oral arguments.

19. During discovery, both parties ascertain that Jameson built the fence on his   19.____
side of the property line. Jameson's attorney asks the court to dismiss the
case because there is no longer a legally sound basis to proceed.
This request to the court is a motion to
    A. relinquish   B. dismiss   C. vacate   D. suppress

20. Which type of evidence suggests a fact by implication or inference?   20.____
    A. Exculpatory   B. Demandable
    C. Circumstantial   D. Ascertainable

21. Sam sued David civilly last September. Sam prevailed in the original suit.   21.____
David has appealed. David is now the _____ and Sam is the _____.
    A. petitionery; respondent   B. appellant; appellee
    C. appellant; petitioner   D. respondent; appellee

22. If an appellate court remands a case back to the lower trial court, which   22.____
of the following instructions may be imposed on the trial court.
    A. A new trial be held
    B. The trial court's judgment be modified or corrected
    C. The trial court reconsider the facts and/or the evidence presented
    D. All of the above

23. Which of the following motions may only be filed after all of the evidence has   23.____
been presented?
    A. Motion in limine   B. Motion for directed verdict
    C. Motion for summary judgment   D. Motion for admission

24. When is it permissible for parties to settle a suit?   24.____
    A. Before the trial begins   B. During the trial
    c. While the jury is deliberating   D. All of the above

25. Summations are typically a part of _____ and discuss the evidence and the
inferences that can be drawn from that evidence.
    A. closing arguments
    B. indictments
    C. hearings on the merits
    D. ex-parte communications

25._____

KEY (CORRECT ANSWERS)

1.	C		11.	A
2.	A		12.	B
3.	B		13.	C
4.	A		14.	B
5.	D		15.	A
6.	B		16.	A
7.	B		17.	D
8.	D		18.	D
9.	D		19.	B
10.	A		20.	C

21.	B
22.	D
23.	B
24.	D
25.	A

TEST 3

DIRECTIONS: Each question or incomplete statement is followed by several suggested answers or completions. Select the one that BEST answers the question or completes the statement. *PRINT THE LETTER OF THE CORRECT ANSWER IN THE SPACE AT THE RIGHT.*

Questions 1-4.

DIRECTIONS: Questions 1 through 4 are to be answered on the basis of the following fact pattern.

Steven is on trial for embezzlement. The case is complex; there are eight witnesses for the prosecution and twelve witnesses for the defense, including character witnesses. Steven has filed a cross-claim against his former employer, and plaintiff, ABC Corp., Inc. for defamation of character. Steven maintains that he never stole a dime from ABC Corp., Inc. and wants ABC Corp., Inc. to issue him a public apology when the trial is over.

1. The BEST place to refer back to the testimony of one witness is   1.____
   A. the docket   B. the judge's notes
   C. the stenographer's transcript   D. clerk notes

2. Steven's attorney presents evidence that his client was not working on the   2.____
   days the theft from ABC Corp. allegedly occurred.
   What kind of evidence is Steven's counsel presenting to the court?
   A. Alibi   B. Exculpatory
   C. Exclusionary   D. Exemplary

3. Alexandra, a friend of Steven, testifies for the prosecution in Steven's case.   3.____
   Alexandra testifies that Steven told her that he embezzled money from ABC
   Corp. Steven's attorney objects to Alexandra's testimony because it is
   A. exculpatory   B. hearsay   C. untrue   D. impeachment

4. At the close of Steven's trial, oral arguments are made by _____ to the   4.____
   court, summarizing their position on the evidence that has been presented and
   their theories on the case in its entirety.
   A. jurors   B. plaintiffs   C. attorneys   D. defense

Questions 5-8.

DIRECTIONS: Questions 5 through 8 are to be answered on the basis of the following fact pattern.

April 16 is turning out to be a very busy day at the courthouse. In the morning, three cases were withdrawn by the plaintiff without a hearing, six cases were dismissed without prejudice by the judge, and two cases were settled out of court.

5. How many were decided by the judge on April 16?   5.____
   A. 0   B. 2   C. 6   D. 3

6. How many cases were heard before the judge?   6.____
   A. 3   B. 6   C. 2   D. 8

7. How many cases would the court reporter need to be present for?   7.____
   A. 6   B. 3   C. 2   D. 8

8. How many of the cases were awarded damages?   8.____
   A. 2   B. 6   C. 3   D. 0

Questions 9-12.

DIRECTIONS: Questions 9 through 12 are to be answered on the basis of the following fact
              pattern.

   Miranda has initiated a lawsuit against her former friend, Anne, for breach of contract.
Miranda referred Anne's interior design services to Miranda's boss. Anne went to Miranda's
boss' house for an initial consultation and, even though Anne agreed to design three rooms in
the house, she never followed through with the contract. Miranda is incredibly embarrassed by
the entire situation. Anne, however, maintains that she has a reasonable excuse for not
finishing the work.

9. In addition to money damages, Miranda would also like the court to compel   9.____
   Anne to execute the contract or, in other words, actually design the rooms.
   This remedy is deemed
   A. compulsion under order   B. specific performance
   C. remedy at law   D. joint and several liability

10. Miranda alleges that she suffered pain and suffering from Anne's inability to   10.____
    execute the contract.
    What type of damages are pain and suffering categorized as?
    A. Punitive   B. Special   C. Specific   D. Compensatory

11. Miranda lives in New York. Anne lives in New Jersey. Miranda's boss   11.____
    lives in Connecticut. When Miranda files suit in New York, the judge initially
    indicates that she does not have
    A. authority   B. jurisdiction   C. venue   D. domicile

12. The contract that is alleged to have been breached exists between Anne and   12.____
    Miranda's boss, not Miranda. Therefore, there is no legal cause of action for
    the case to proceed. Miranda's boss is free to file the claim against Anne at a
    later date if she so chooses.
    The court will
    A. dismiss the action without prejudice
    B. deny the action without prejudice
    C. sustain the action
    D. abdicate as necessary

13. Nominal damages are   13._____
   A. damages awarded in name only, indicating no substantial harm was done
   B. damages to recompense the injured for the infliction of emotional distress
   C. damages to recompense the initiator of the lawsuit
   D. a reimbursement of filing fees, awarded to the person who can prove they are injured

14. The type of recovery being sought by the plaintiff is known as the   14._____
   A. order   B. punishment   C. remedy   D. issue

15. Robert approaches the clerk's desk in a panic. He says that he filed a   15._____
   lawsuit against his cousin, Mike, but neglected to add his cousin's friend, Roy, to the suit.
   What action is Robert attempting to take?
   A. Amending the complaint
   B. Adding an addendum to the summons
   C. Re-issuing a summons
   D. Redacting the answer

Questions 16-20.

DIRECTIONS: Questions 16 through 20 are to be answered on the basis of the following fact pattern.

Daniel and Patrick sue one another civilly. Daniel sues Patrick for intentional infliction of emotional distress and Patrick countersues Daniel for assault. Both causes of action stem from a physical altercation which took place at a youth hockey game where Daniel's and Patrick's sons played against one another. At trial, the judge found that Daniel started the fight and attacked Patrick and found, by extension, that Patrick was not a contributor in the altercation.

Daniel appealed the decision to an appellate court. Daniel's attorney argued that the trial court erred, as a matter of law, in finding that Daniel was the sole initiator of the altercation and ignored evidence to the contrary. Appellate courts generally render decisions by a panel. The panel in Daniel's appeal was comprised of three justices. The appellate court agreed with the trial court's finding of fault.

16. The ultimate disposition of this case was the appellate court   16._____
   A. affirmed the lower court's decision
   B. remanded the lower court's decision
   C. reversed the lower court's decision
   D. acquitted Daniel of all charges

17. An opinion from the entire panel of justices is known as a   17._____
   A. per curiam decision   B. affirmative decision
   C. stare decisis   D. en banc order

18. One of the judges agrees with the decision of the court, but disagrees with
    the reasoning of the conclusion. This judge decides to write his own opinion.
    This is deemed a
    A. dissenting opinion
    B. remedial decision
    C. concurring opinion
    D. recurrent opinion

18.____

19. Suppose that one of the judges disagrees entirely with the ruling.
    How will the judgment be altered because of the disagreement?
    The judgment
    A. is unaffected because the majority voted in agreement with the trial court
    B. is unaffected because this judge did not author a dissenting opinion
    C. is unaffected because oral arguments were not made before the panel
    D. will be overturned

19.____

20. The appellate court still requires _____, even if it is established by the trial
    court, known as original _____.
    A. domicile; venue
    B. venue; jurisdiction
    C. jurisdiction; jurisdiction
    D. jurisdiction; domicile

20.____

21. The legal theory upon which a case is based is called a
    A. basis
    B. decisis
    C. cause of action
    D. precedent

21.____

Questions 22-25.

DIRECTIONS: Questions 22 through 25 are to be answered on the basis of the following fact
              pattern.

Last July, Sarah stole Alexis's car and took it for a joyride along Main Street. After a long
joyride, Sarah decided to pick up Ashley at Ashley's apartment. Although Ashley asked when
Sarah bought a new car, Sarah lied and told Ashley that it was her aunt's car that she borrowed
with permission. Sarah and Ashley went on another joyride, this time driving up to 90 miles per
hour on the highways around town. After three hours, Ashley asked to go home and Sarah
obliged. After Sarah dropped Ashley back off at her apartment, Sarah sped through a busy
intersection and crashed the car. The car was totaled.
    Alexis has filed a lawsuit against both Sarah and Ashley.

22. Alexis is determined to sue both Sarah and Ashley for conversion, or the
    wrongful act of dominion or control over another person's property. However,
    after meeting with her attorney, Alexis decided she may not be able to prove
    each _____ of the alleged crime against Ashley.
    A. stage   B. element   C. circumstance D. remedy

22.____

23. After Alexis initiated her lawsuit against Sarah and Ashley, Ashley requested
    the court remove her from the lawsuit altogether. She attested that she could
    not have participated in a crime if she did not know the car was stolen. Her
    request to the court will come in the form of a(n)
    A. notice   B. motion   C. termination   D. demand

23.____

24. Ashley's attorney asks the judge to instruct the jury that it can consider mitigating factors in rendering a verdict against Ashley.
An example of a mitigating factor in this scenario would MOST likely be

    A. Ashley does not known Alexis
    B. Sarah is no longer friends with Alexis
    C. Ashley asked Sarah about the origins of the car and Sarah's reply was untruthful
    D. Ashley and Sarah were working in cahoots to steal Alexis's car

24.____

25. During the time of the crime Sarah was a minor. A minor is legally defined as

    A. someone who cannot think for themselves
    B. anyone under 21
    C. a legally emancipated individual
    D. an infant or individual under the age of legal competence

25.____

KEY (CORRECT ANSWERS)

1.	C		11.	B
2.	B		12.	A
3.	B		13.	A
4.	C		14.	C
5.	C		15.	A
6.	B		16.	A
7.	A		17.	A
8.	D		18.	C
9.	B		19.	A
10.	D		20.	C

21.	C
22.	B
23.	B
24.	C
25.	D

TEST 4

DIRECTIONS: Each question or incomplete statement is followed by several suggested answers or completions. Select the one that BEST answers the question or completes the statement. *PRINT THE LETTER OF THE CORRECT ANSWER IN THE SPACE AT THE RIGHT.*

Questions 1-4.

DIRECTIONS: Questions 1 through 4 are to be answered on the basis of the following fact pattern.

A complex civil litigation suit is set to begin between ABC Insurance Corp. and DEF Indemnity Corp. Adam represents ABC Insurance and Jane represents DEF Indemnity Corp. Multiple extensions have been granted to either side to conduct more extensive discovery. At the last conference scheduled before trial, the presiding judge is notably frustrated at the requested delays from both Adam and Jane. The presiding judge would like both parties to stipulate to as many points as possible.

1. Adam and Jane appear in the permanent record as _____ unless either are withdrawn or are otherwise removed from the case.
   A. attorneys in time
   B. attorneys of record
   C. attorneys of the case
   D. permanent attorneys

   1._____

2. The judge asks whether the parties have attempted to settle this matter in another forum, such as binding _____.
   A. decision-making
   B. arbitration
   C. neutral court
   D. judgment arena

   2._____

3. While the judge would like the parties to settle, he quickly realizes that it is not a possibility between these two parties. Adam and Jane continue to argue about various issues including expert witnesses. Adam argues that Jane's expert witness, who will testify about financial crimes, is a quack. In response, Jane offers that her witness be _____, or testify under oath at a date prior to trial.
   A. sworn in   B. indemnified   C. deposed   D. saddled

   3._____

4. Which of the following is the LEAST appropriate behavior of the judge during a pre-trial conference?
   A. Providing advice on Adam or Jane's legal strategy for trial
   B. Asking the parties to stipulate to the facts
   C. Remaining indifferent about the witnesses each party plans to call at trial
   D. Setting a date for trial more than three months away

   4._____

5. A lawsuit with a single cause of action being breach of contract will be classified as what type of suit?
   A. Criminal   B. Divisional   C. Situational   D. Civil

   5._____

6. Sheila's mother passed away last week. She comes to the courthouse and asks about the probate process. You inform her that probate may not be necessary if she is the person named in the will as the individual who will administer her mother's estate. This individual is otherwise known as the
    A. administrator   B. guarantor   C. creditor   D. executor

6.____

7. Brandy would like her juvenile record expunged. What is she seeking to do? She is requesting
    A. her record, or a portion of her record, be removed
    B. her record be sealed
    C. her record be unsealed
    D. to make her record unavailable to creditors

7.____

8. Having never met Jamie, a pro se litigant, Judge Smith strikes up a friendly conversation about the recent political climate in the elevator with him on the way to the courtroom. In the courtroom that afternoon, Jamie enters his appearance and says, "You and I are clearly already on the same page, Judge" in open court. Jamie's adversary, Courtney, requests that the judge recuses himself from the case. Why?
    A. Jamie and Judge Smith's political affiliations are unsavory.
    B. Judge Smith is clearly biased as evidenced by Jamie's comment.
    C. Judge Smith and Jamie have partaken in en banc communications.
    D. Judicial discrimination is appropriate if a conflict of interest would affect a judge's ruling.

8.____

9. Emily appears at court with a crumbled notice in her hands. She has a complaint in her hands and indicates that she never answered or responded to the complaint, hoping it would go away or resolve itself.
    Emily is currently
    A. in default   B. owes restitution
    C. in declaratory judgment   D. subsidiary

9.____

10. A conditional release from incarceration is known as
    A. an expungement   B. a restitution
    C. parole   D. reduced sentence

10.____

11. Tom paid a contractor to cut down a large pine tree in front of his house. The tree had grown so tall that it has started to interfere with the power lines running parallel to the street. As the contractor cut down the tree, a large gust of wind blew and the tree crashed down on top of his neighbor, Dane's, roof. Dane is suing Tom for failure to exercise the degree of care that a reasonable person would have exercised in the same circumstance.
    Dane is suing Tom for
    A. lack of judgment   B. breach of contract
    C. negligence   D. conversion

11.____

12. Lawyers are generally prohibited from asking _____ questions of their own witnesses because they are suggestive, or prompt, the witness to answer in a certain way.
    A. leading   B. direct   C. cross   D. sustainable

12._____

13. One process that is generally private, and not heard in open court, is(are)
    A. testimony of expert witnesses   B. swearing in of jurors
    C. objections   D. plea bargaining

13._____

14. The burden of proof in a civil case is _____ stringent than that in a criminal case.
    A. less   B. more   C. equally   D. substantially

14._____

15. May jurors consider arguments made during an attorney's opening or closing arguments as evidence or fact?
    A. Yes, but only if compelling
    B. Yes, but only under the circumstances explained by the judge
    C. Yes, unconditionally
    D. No

15._____

16. In reviewing the court transcript, which of the following is the attorney LEAST likely to find?
    A. The judge's opinions on the case   B. Testimony of the petitioner
    C. Attorneys of record   D. Names of the expert witnesses

16._____

17. A mandatory injunction has the effect of
    A. requiring a party to do a particular act
    B. providing the option of a party to do a particular act
    C. requiring a party to report their actions
    D. providing the party an option to report their actions

17._____

18. James approaches the clerk's desk and asks how, generally, judges make their decisions on legal matters.
The MOST correct answer would be: Based on
    A. case law, or the body of all court decisions which govern or provide precedent on the same legal issue before the judge
    B. case law, personal opinion, and oral arguments by attorneys
    C. case law, oral arguments by attorneys, and the defendant's rap sheet
    D. "stare decisis" or that which has already been decided

18._____

19. Which of the following individuals is LEAST likely to serve on a jury?
    A. Susan, who has been called numerous times but never served on a jury
    B. Bill, a supporter of labor unions and freelance political columnist
    C. Gary, who served on a murder trial 10 years ago
    D. Amy, a 16-year-old genius who just finished her junior year of college

19._____

20. If a grand jury decides there is enough evidence to move forward with criminal charges against a group or individual, they return a(n)
    A. information   B. indictment   C. warrant   D. seizure

20._____

21. When an attorney attempts to reduce the credibility of the other side's
    witness, they are said to be trying to _____ the witness.
    A. objectify   B. anger   C. impeach   D. frustrate

    21.____

22. During a lengthy murder trial, it is discovered that two of the jurors have been
    romantically involved. They have conspired with one another to enter votes of
    "not guilty" and attempt to sway other jurors in their favor in an attempt to close
    out deliberations early.
    What is the likely outcome of the trial?
    A. Hung jury   B. Mistrial
    C. Acquittal   D. Defensive charge

    22.____

23. The judge's charge to the jury is also known as
    A. voir dire   B. en banc
    C. jury instructions   D. sua sponte

    23.____

24. Who is MOST likely to deliver the sentence to the convicted?
    A. Bailiff   B. Jury
    C. Judge   D. Jury foreperson

    24.____

25. A motion for directed verdict is made
    A. without the jury present
    B. with only the jury foreperson present
    C. with the entire jury present
    D. with only the alternate jurors present

    25.____

KEY (CORRECT ANSWERS)

1.	B		11.	C
2.	B		12.	A
3.	C		13.	D
4.	A		14.	A
5.	D		15.	D
6.	D		16.	A
7.	A		17.	A
8.	D		18.	A
9.	A		19.	D
10.	C		20.	B

21.	C
22.	B
23.	C
24.	C
25.	A

_____

41

EXAMINATION SECTION

TEST 1

DIRECTIONS: Each question or incomplete statement is followed by several suggested answers or completions. Select the one that BEST answers the question or completes the statement. *PRINT THE LETTER OF THE CORRECT ANSWER IN THE SPACE AT THE RIGHT.*

Questions 1-5.

DIRECTIONS: Questions 1 through 5 are to be answered on the basis of the following fact pattern.

When Family Court opens on Monday morning, Desiree rushes to the clerk's desk in a panic. Her ex-boyfriend, Alex, has made threats against her and her children and she would like to file a restraining order as soon as possible. She has never been in court before and does not have any idea of what to expect or what she may need, but she is in fear of her and her children's lives.

1. While Desiree fears for her safety, she cannot obtain a final order of protection against Alex. Why?
   A. A judge has not yet been assigned to the case.
   B. A judge has not been assigned, so there has been no finding of a family offense being committed and Alex has not agreed to the order.
   C. Desiree's children should be present for the request to the court unless they are under age 18.
   D. Alex has not agreed to the order.

1.____

2. A temporary restraining order only lasts until
   A. the close of the case
   B. the beginning of an appeal
   C. the next time the petitioner is in court
   D. it is extended indefinitely

2.____

3. Desiree asks how long a final order of protection lasts. The MOST appropriate response is
   A. two or ten years
   C. one year
   B. two or five years
   D. six months

3.____

4. Which party is responsible for drafting the petition to the judge for a temporary restraining order?
   A. The judge
   C. The clerk
   B. The party seeking the order
   D. A spectator

4.____

5. After Desiree starts her case, Alex is served with a summons. Three weeks later, Desiree returns to the courthouse to say that she has changed her mind and no longer fears for her safety.
   Desiree must
   A. withdraw her petition for a restraining order
   B. start an anger management program
   C. withdraw her petition with prejudice as she will not be able to file again
   D. recuse herself

5.____

6. Jamie has hired legal counsel to represent him in the purchase of commercial buildings across New York State. With his attorney's help, he has secured the purchase of nine different office buildings totaling $2 million. Last week, Jamie discovered that his attorney forged his signature on the sale of four of those properties and collected the proceedings. Assume the threshold for filing a suit in Albany County is $50,000, Nassau County is $200,000, and New York County is $500,000.
   Where can Jamie sue his attorney for malpractice?
   A. New York County   B. Albany County
   C. Nassau County   D. All of the above

6.____

7. Which of the following matters is LEAST likely to be heard in the Albany County – Commercial Division?
   A. Commercial class actions
   B. Transactions governed by the Uniform Commercial Code
   C. Divorce
   D. Shareholder derivate action

7.____

8. Which of the following matters is LEAST likely to be heard in Suffolk County District Court?
   A. Small claims matter of $1,000,000   B. Arraignment in a felony case
   C. Petty larceny (theft of $200)   D. Shoplifting

8.____

9. Which of the following is LEAST likely to be heard in the Landlord and Tenant Court?
   A. Non-payment proceedings   B. Hold-over proceedings
   C. Evictions   D. Adoptions

9.____

10. Dave approaches the clerk's desk and insists that he has a tenant in his building who refuses to pay rent and will not vacate the premises.
    Dave seeks assistance on initiating _____ proceedings.
    A. Annulment   B. Hold-over   C. Numeration   D. Abandonment

10.____

11. John and Jill need to file for bankruptcy and would like to do so together.
    John and Jill would file which type of petition?
    A. Separate   B. Tenants   C. Survivor   D. Joint

11.____

44

12. Rich would like to know what advice he can give his brother who was
arrested last night for driving under the influence of alcohol. Rich's brother is
scheduled to be arraigned this morning. While you may not be authorized to
give legal advice, it is prudent to know that a plea of nolo contendere has the
same effect as a plea of _____, but is not an admission of guilt.
   A. acquittal   B. remorse   C. not guilty   D. guilty

12._____

13. Emily arrives in court for her bankruptcy hearing. Emily is not working,
does not have any savings. She does not own any property, jewelry,
collectibles, or other precious items of value.
Emily's bankruptcy petition will MOST likely be classified as a _____ case.
   A. nolo contendere   B. no asset
   C. no prohibition   D. Chapter 13

13._____

14. Assume the same facts as above. Emily is a full-time student and took out
a student loan before filing bankruptcy.
The trustee has informed Emily her student loan is a _____ debt.
   A. dischargeable   B. non-dischargeable
   C. immediate   D. short term

14._____

15. A party in interest in bankruptcy is defined as a party who
   A. has standing to be heard in a matter to be decided in the bankruptcy case
   B. standing to disrupt the court
   C. intends to file a brief
   D. intends to petition for early release

15._____

16. A petty offense is one that is punishable by _____ or less in prison.
   A. six months   B. one year   C. three years   D. four years

16._____

17. Town and village courts have jurisdiction over
   A. vehicle and traffic matters   B. small claims
   C. civil matters   D. all of the above

17._____

18. The highest civil court in New York is the
   A. Supreme Court   B. City Court
   C. Civil Court   D. Court of Appeals

18._____

19. The highest criminal court in New York is the
   A. New York City Criminal Court   B. Court of Appeals
   C. County Courts   D. Village Courts

19._____

Questions 20-23.

DIRECTIONS: Questions 20 through 23 are to be answered on the basis of the following fact pattern.

Amy is a Guardians ad Litem ("GAL") for the New York Housing Court. She volunteered for the Court because she wanted to help people resolve their housing disputes. The judge has appointed Amy as Gerald's GAL in his case. Gerald is involved in a minor dispute with his landlord.

20.   Amy believes that Gerald's housing issues stem from his poor money management. Can Amy manage Gerald's checkbook and other personal finances as they relate to his housing case?
    A. Yes, because his finances relate to his housing case
    B. Yes, because he clearly cannot manage his money on his own
    C. Yes, but only if Gerald asks her to
    D. No

20.____

21.   Amy is NOT allowed to do which of the following things?
    A. Meet with Gerald
    B. Meet with Gerald's landlord
    C. Allow Gerald's landlord into Gerald's apartment
    D. Ensure the landlord completes repairs as promised

21.____

22.   A GAL works in which party's best interest?
    A. Gerald's landlord   B. Gerald
    C. The appointed party   D. The judge

22.____

23.   Amy has fallen ill and cannot meet her obligations as a GAL. Which party can remove Amy as Gerald's GAL?
    A. Gerald   B. Gerald's landlord
    C. The judge   D. The clerk

23.____

24.   Pro per is another term for _____ or a self-represented person.
    A. pro tem   B. pro se   C. qui tam   D. quid pro

24.____

25.   Sanctions are defined as a
    A. penalty or other type of enforcement used to bring about compliance with the law
    B. penalty specific to international trade law
    C. federal penalty reserved for those who lie under oath
    D. misdemeanor crime punishable by more than four years in prison

25.____

KEY (CORRECT ANSWERS)

1.	A		11.	D
2.	C		12.	D
3.	B		13.	B
4.	C		14.	B
5.	A		15.	A
6.	D		16.	A
7.	C		17.	D
8.	A		18.	D
9.	D		19.	B
10.	B		20.	D

21.	C
22.	C
23.	C
24.	B
25.	A

TEST 2

Questions 1-5.

DIRECTIONS: Questions 1 through 5 are to be answered on the basis of the following fact pattern.

Edwin has been served with a lawsuit from his former accountant, Bob. Bob claims Edwin never paid him for his accounting services after he filed Edwin's personal income tax and business income tax returns. Edwin has come to the clerk's desk confused and angry.

1. Edwin wants to know what the basis of Bob's legal claim is against him. Where can Edwin find more information about the case?
   A. The internet
   B. The complaint
   C. The subpoena
   D. The arraignment

   1.____

2. Edwin claims that he was audited by the IRS shortly after Bob filed his personal income taxes. Edwin wants to sue Bob in connection with his being audited. In order to do so, Edwin would need to
   A. re-sue
   B. re-file
   C. countersue
   D. cross-claim

   2.____

3. Bob filed taxes for Edwin and Edwin's wife. While Edwin's wife is not listed on the Complaint in Edwin's suit against Bob, Edwin's wife would also like to appear as a party to the case. Is this possible?
   A. No, because Edwin's wife may be unavailable for trial
   B. No, because Edwin's wife is not initiating the suit
   C. No, because Edwin can only sue Bob himself
   D. Yes

   3.____

4. Which of the following courts is MOST appropriate for Edwin's suit against Bob?
   A. Housing Court
   B. Surrogates Court
   C. Civil Court
   D. Criminal Court

   4.____

5. Which of the following is MOST likely to be the legal basis of Bob's suit against Edwin?
   A. Breach of contract
   B. Negligence
   C. Assault
   D. Defamation

   5.____

6.   The Housing Court is made of parts. The resolution part presides over all   6.____
pre-trial matters in a case and attempts to settle the case. Jeremy appears at
Housing Court for his trial that begins this morning.
Is Jeremy's case appropriate for the pre-trial part of the Housing Court?
    A. Yes, as pre-trial matters preclude this
    B. Yes, as a check in before the trial can start
    C. No, the trial part is separate and distinct from the pre-trial part of Housing
        Court
    D. No, the trial part only hears cases on Mondays

Questions 7-8.

DIRECTIONS: Questions 7 and 8 are to be answered on the basis of the following text.

    Jenny received a notice from the marshal that she is being evicted from her apartment.
She wants to ignore the notice, but comes to the courthouse at the urging of her boyfriend.

7.   Her boyfriend warns her that if she does not take care of the notice, she and   7.____
her _____ may be _____ from the apartment.
    A. property; removed   B. removed; property
    C. property; removal   D. assets; removed

8.   At the courthouse, the clerk instructs Jenny to complete an affidavit in   8.____
support of a(n)
    A. order for removal   B. petition
    C. order to show cause   D. justification

9.   Because Jenny never answered the original petition for eviction from her   9.____
landlord, her landlord obtained a _____ judgment against her. Jenny now
needs to complete an affidavit in support of an order to show cause to _____ a
judgment based on failure to answer.
    A. vacate; default   B. vacate; demand
    C. default; vacate   D. default; validate

10.   A clerk in the Resolution Part of Housing Court can do all of the following   10.____
EXCEPT
    A. answer questions about the court calendar
    B. answer questions about the judge's rules
    C. assist the judge as necessary
    D. provide detailed legal analysis and/or advice

11.   A judge may direct parties in a dispute to mediation, which is a form of   11.____
    A. neutrality
    B. alternative dispute resolution
    C. alternative judgment
    D. non-binding analysis of the legal dispute

12. Joel and Rachel would like to place their daughter into foster care.
    Do Joel and Rachel need an attorney to represent them in court?
    A. Yes, as foster care placements are complicated
    B. Yes, unless they do not have money to hire a lawyer
    C. No, legal representation is not required but they do have a right to have the court appoint an attorney if they cannot afford one
    D. No, unless they change their minds after the placement has taken place

    12.____

13. The New York Court of Claims is the only court where one can seek damages against
    A. the State of New York or other state-related agencies
    B. New York City
    C. municipalities in Richmond County
    D. New York State colleges

    13.____

14. While City Courts such as Binghamton City Court handle criminal and civil matters, the amount in dispute can only be up to
    A. $20,000,000   B. $15,000   C. $1,000,000   D. $5,000,000

    14.____

15. Beatrice is having issues understanding her mother's will. Her mother is living, but Beatrice wants to ensure she understands all of the terms of the will while her mother is still alive.
    Beatrice is not the named executor, which is defined as
    A. someone named in the will appointed to wind up the affairs of the deceased person
    B. the person who inherits all of the deceased person's property
    C. the attorney of the estate
    D. the judge who presides over the estate

    15.____

16. A person who is named in the will to inherit money or other property is the
    A. executrix   B. devisee   C. custodian   D. beneficiary

    16.____

17. Matters of will and probate are heard in which court?
    A. Civil Court   B. Family Court
    C. Surrogates Court   D. Criminal Court

    17.____

18. A revocable trust is a trust that can be
    A. rescinded by the grantor after creation
    B. overruled by a judge
    C. nullified by the beneficiaries
    D. canceled outright without warning to the trust remainders

    18.____

19. James approaches the clerk's desk seeking assistance regarding a child support matter. James lost his job a few months ago and can no longer pay his child support.
    What is the LEAST appropriate advice you can give James?
    A. He is prudent for coming to the court to seek assistance as there are serious penalties for non-payment of child support.
    B. A support order can be modified.

    19.____

C. Without income, he cannot possibly pay child support, so he should wait until he is found in contempt of court.
D. Penalties for non-payment include interception of tax refunds, suspension of personal and business licenses, and seizure of bank accounts.

20. As a clerk for the New York Court of Appeals, you are asked to determine whether a case from one of the trial courts has been upheld or reversed. If the case has been upheld, it is recorded in the docket as
    A. remanded   b. retained   C. affirmed   D. affiant

    20.____

21. If a case has been reversed or sent back to the trial court from the New York Court of Appeals, the word _____ will be recorded in the docket.
    A. retained   B. reversed   C. remanded   D. replevin

    21.____

22. Sue does not agree with the finding of the Family Court. She asks if an order can be appealed.
    The MOST appropriate response is:
    A. No, as all orders are final
    B. No, as Family Court does not pose any legal issues requiring appeal
    C. No, given that Sue is not represented by an attorney
    D. Yes, she may appeal from an order

    22.____

23. Joe, John, and Beth are involved in a paternity suit. Joe believes he is the father of Beth's baby, Sarah, but John maintains that he is the father.
    What document would be MOST helpful for the court in resolving this matter?
    A. John and Beth's marriage license
    B. Joe and Beth's marriage license
    C. Sarah's birth certificate
    D. Beth's medical records

    23.____

24. Abel is concerned that his cousin, Ted, is not able to afford legal representation in his trial for armed robbery. Ted must be considered _____ or otherwise unable to afford to hire a lawyer before defense counsel is appointed by the court.
    A. responsible   B. indigent   C. not guilty   D. petty

    24.____

25. Which of the following is heard and determined outside of the courtroom?
    A. Hearing   B. Plea bargain
    C. Testimony   D. Evidence

    25.____

KEY (CORRECT ANSWERS)

1.	B		11.	B
2.	C		12.	C
3.	D		13.	A
4.	C		14.	B
5.	A		15.	A
6.	C		16.	D
7.	A		17.	C
8.	C		18.	A
9.	C		19.	C
10.	D		20.	C

21.	C
22.	D
23.	C
24.	B
25.	B

EXAMINATION SECTION
TEST 1

DIRECTIONS: Each question or incomplete statement is followed by several suggested answers or completions. Select the one that BEST answers the question or completes the statement. *PRINT THE LETTER OF THE CORRECT ANSWER IN THE SPACE AT THE RIGHT.*

1. An affidavit and a summons are similar in that an affidavit and a summons   1.____
   A. both require an answer
   B. both may be filed with a court of proper jurisdiction
   C. outline the particulars of the case
   D. are both served on each party in a lawsuit

2. A judgment of the court refers to a(n)   2.____
   A. final order and decision on a matter before the Court that is binding on both parties
   B. reservation by the judge to defer a decision to a later date
   C. award by the judge granting monetary payment to the plaintiff
   D. request by the defendant to dismiss the case against the plaintiff

3. A pretrial conference typically requires the presence of the   3.____
   A. attorneys representing the parties and the case and the judge
   B. judge only
   C. named parties in the lawsuit and the judge
   D. named parties in the lawsuit, attorneys, and the judge

4. Gary, a local business owner, has discovered one of his customers is suing him for monetary and punitive damages in court. Gary would like to represent himself at trial.   4.____
   Gary is a(n) _____ litigant.
   A. Qui Tam   B. In Limine   C. Pro Se   D. Pro Tem

5. A subpoena duces tecum requires its recipient to   5.____
   A. appear and produce documents   B. appear and provide testimony
   C. appear with a witness   D. appear

6. A capital offense is characterized by its punishment. A capital offense is punishable by   6.____
   A. large money payment, payable in a lump sum
   B. lien on real property
   C. death
   D. an automatic sentence of 20 years

7. Bankruptcy law is governed by _____ law, rather than _____ law. Therefore, bankruptcy hearings are heard in _____ courts.
   A. State, Federal, District
   B. District, State, Federal
   C. Federal, District, State
   D. Federal, State, District
                 7.____

8. Michelle is the subject of a wage garnishment. She is a full-time student at Brooklyn College and also works full time as an administrative assistant for an accountant in Queens. After receiving notice of the wage garnishment, she decides to quit her job and take a part-time job as a receptionist at a dental office.
Are Michelle's dental office wages subject to garnishment?
   A. No, because she is only working part time.
   B. No, because the garnishment was issued while she was working at her last job.
   C. Yes, because she obtained new employment.
   D. Yes.
                 8.____

9. A trial which was scheduled to begin in Queens in October is now being moved to Albany. The trial is still scheduled to begin in October.
The change of the trial location is an example of a change in
   A. venue
   B. locale
   C. environment
   D. jurisdiction
                 9.____

10. Plaintiff's attorney has withdrawn as counsel and is being replaced by another attorney who comes highly recommended by a family friend of the plaintiff.
Where is the change of attorney MOST appropriately recorded?
   A. Disclosure statement
   B. Docket
   C. Letter to the Judge
   D. Deposition
                 10.____

11. A bench trial is a trial without a(n)
   A. plaintiff's attorney
   B. jury
   C. defendant's attorney
   D. bailiff
                 11.____

12. Mark's son, Jeff, has been arrested and is being held on $50,000 bail. Mark is visibly upset and angrily demands to know why bail is required in order for Jeff to be released from prison.
The MOST correct answer is:
   A. Bail is absolutely required of all prisoners awaiting trial.
   B. Bail is required to release Jeff because he committed a felony.
   C. Bail is not always required, but can be established to ensure a person's appearance at court when required.
   D. Bail is only required when a probation officer has not yet been assigned.
                 12.____

13. In classifying her debts in bankruptcy, Alicia attests that she owes $10,000 in personal credit card debt, $5,000 business loan to a credit union, and $200,000 mortgage.
Which debts will be classified as consumer debt?
A. Credit card debt, business loan, and mortgage
B. The business loan only
C. Credit card debt and business loans
D. Credit card debt and mortgage

13.____

14. A warrant has been issued by Judge Walker for John Smith. There are typically two types of warrants that can be issued.
They are
A. search and arrest
B. seize and arrest
C. detain and arrest
D. summons and arrest

14.____

15. The role of the court stenographer is to
A. assist the bailiff in maintaining order in the courtroom
B. serve as an additional support to the court clerk
C. transcribe the dialogue of court proceedings in short form to create the trial transcript
D. record the final judgment and transcribe the judge's rationale for sentencing

15.____

16. Precedent refers to:
A. The same plaintiff and same defendant from another lawsuit are named in the present suit
B. A defendant is on trial again after being found innocent in an earlier trial
C. An earlier case or decision of a court that is considered authority in the present case because of an identical or similar question of law
D. A series of lawsuits involving the same plaintiff in each case

16.____

17. An automatic stay has what effect on a debtor in a bankruptcy petition?
A. Allows the debtor to appoint a trustee for his/her petition
B. Stops lawsuits, foreclosures, garnishments, and most collection activities against the debtor the moment a bankruptcy petition is filed
C. Provides the debtor with additional time to arrange their assets before filing the petition
D. Allows the debtor to attend court hearings on the status of their bankruptcy petition

17.____

18. A joint petition in bankruptcy refers to a bankruptcy
A. petition filed by a husband and wife together
B. petition filed by business partners
C. petition filed by family members
D. petitioned by the largest creditor of the debtor

18.____

19. A misdemeanor is punishable by _____ or _____, whereas a felony is
    punishable by _____ or _____.
    A. two years, less; two years, more   B. six months, less; six months, more
    C. one year, less; one year, more   D. one year, more; one year, less

20. Gail has filed for Chapter 7 bankruptcy. She has read online that some of
    her property will be considered non-exempt assets.
    Non-exempt assets is property that
    A. can be sold to satisfy claims of the creditors
    B. is exempt from being included in the bankruptcy estate
    C. does not need to be reported to the trustee
    D. can be considered "charge offs" for tax purposes

21. A motion represents a _____ to the court, requiring a decision by the judge.
    A. request   B. demand   C. action   D. plea

22. A jury verdict that a criminal defendant is not guilty, or a finding by a judge
    that there is insufficient evidence to support a conviction is known as a(n)
    A. information   B. acquiescence
    C. acquittal   D. compromise in settlement

23. An affidavit is accurately defined as a(n)
    A. statement made in the presence of a court of competent jurisdiction
    B. written statement that is notarized then sent to a court of competent
       jurisdiction
    C. oral statement transcribed by his or her attorney
    D. written or printed statement made under oath

24. Under what circumstances does an alternate juror help decide a case?
    A. Only when called on to replace a regular juror
    B. When a regular juror has trouble making a decision in the case
    C. When the bailiff asks the alternate jurors' opinion on the case
    D. Only during bench trials

25. A case that is dismissed with prejudice prevents which of the following:
    The filing of
    A. an identical suit in a later filing
    B. a suit by the same plaintiff in a later filing
    C. a suit by the same defendant in a later filing
    D. the same suit in the same courthouse in a later filing

KEY (CORRECT ANSWERS)

1.	B		11.	B
2.	A		12.	C
3.	A		13.	D
4.	C		14.	A
5.	A		15.	C
6.	C		16.	C
7.	D		17.	B
8.	D		18.	A
9.	A		19.	C
10.	B		20.	A

21.	A
22.	C
23.	D
24.	A
25.	A

———————

TEST 2

DIRECTIONS: Each question or incomplete statement is followed by several suggested answers or completions. Select the one that BEST answers the question or completes the statement. *PRINT THE LETTER OF THE CORRECT ANSWER IN THE SPACE AT THE RIGHT.*

1. There are various forms of discovery that can be requested by either party in a lawsuit.
   _____ is the form of discovery that consists of written questions that are answered in writing and under oath.
   A. Depositions
   B. Examinations before trial
   C. Interrogatories
   D. Affidavits

   1.____

2. At what point in a trial are jury instructions delivered by the judge?
   A. Before the trial begins
   B. After opening arguments
   C. After the defense rests
   D. Before the jury is to begin deliberations

   2.____

3. In a bench trial, the _____ serves as the fact finder.
   A. jury
   B. judge
   C. bailiff
   D. law clerk

   3.____

4. The role of the bankruptcy trustee is to represent the
   A. interests of the bankruptcy estate and the creditors of the debtor
   B. debtor against all creditors
   C. largest creditor of the debtor
   D. small creditor of the debtor

   4.____

5. The bankruptcy estate typically includes _____ at the time of filing.
   A. all property of the debtor, including interests in real property
   B. the home where the debtor resides
   C. the home and personal vehicle of the debtor
   D. all personal property, but not real property, of the debtor

   5.____

6. An amicus curiae brief is filed by a person or entity with a(n) _____ in, but that is not a _____ in the case.
   A. outcome; party
   B. interest; party
   C. party; outcome
   D. party; interest

   6.____

7. An answer is a formal response to which document?
   A. Deposition
   B. Discovery
   C. Complaint
   D. Advice

   7.____

8. Donovan sued his former employer, Ink Securities, LLC and his former boss, Steve, for unpaid wages. Ink Securities lost the case and now wishes to appeal the ruling.
   When Steve and Ink Securities, LLC appeal the case, what do they become?
   A. Appellees
   B. Appellants
   C. Plaintiffs
   D. Defendants

   8.____

9. In an indictment or information, each count represents a(n)   9.____
   - A. proven crime
   - B. request by the court
   - C. decision on the merits
   - D. allegation

10. Allison is sentenced to six years for armed robbery and ten years for   10.____
    grand larceny. She is sentenced to serve her prison terms concurrently.
    What is the MAXIMUM amount of time Allison will spend behind bars?
    - A. Six years
    - B. Sixteen years
    - C. Ten years
    - D. Four years

11. An appellate review de novo is one that provides no _____ to the ruling of   11.____
    the trial judge.
    - A. deference
    - B. credibility
    - C. assignability
    - D. advancement

12. Mary Ellen's house is worth $700,000, her car is worth $10,000, and she has   12.____
    cash and other financial assets worth $50,000. Creditors in Mary Ellen's
    bankruptcy have secured an interest in Mary Ellen's personal and real property
    amounting to $650,000.
    How much equity remains in Mary Ellen's property?
    - A. $90,000
    - B. $50,000
    - C. $10,000
    - D. $110,000

13. Ex parte communications are generally strictly forbidden because the   13.____
    - A. other party is not privy to the information that is shared, creating the
      appearance of bias in a case
    - B. associated cost to appeal a case with ex parte communications is an
      undue burden to the plaintiff
    - C. defendant usually prevails when ex parte communications occur
    - D. jury is not privy to the information that is shared, creating the appearance
      of bias in a case

14. What does the exclusionary rule exclude in a criminal trial?   14.____
    - A. Testimony that is deemed hearsay by a judge in a court of competent
      jurisdiction
    - B. Evidence obtained in violation of a defendant's constitutional or statutory
      rights
    - C. Depositions that are unsworn or not notarized
    - D. Affidavits that are unsworn or not notarized

15. Grand juries convene to determine whether there is _____ to believe an   15.____
    individual committed an offense.
    - A. burden of proof
    - B. reasonable belief
    - C. probable cause
    - D. an absolute determination

16. A liquidated claim is a claim that can be satisfied by   16.____
    - A. a fixed amount of money
    - B. real property
    - C. personal property
    - D. a percentage of property that will be sold

17. A motion to lift the automatic stay is a request to take action in a bankruptcy case that would otherwise violate the automatic stay.
This motion is filed by the
 A. debtor's attorney   B. bankruptcy trustee
 C. creditor(s)   D. trustee's attorney

17.____

18. David is being arraigned and needs to enter a plea for the crime he allegedly committed while he was with his friend, Robert. Robert pleaded guilty during his arraignment yesterday, but David has been advised by his attorney to plead no contest, also known as
 A. nolo contendere   B. pro se
 C. quid pro quo   D. qui tam

18.____

19. Under federal law, a petty offense is any misdemeanor which is punishable by a period of _____ or less, a fine of not more than $5,000, or both.
 A. one year   B. six months   C. two years   D. 1 month

19.____

20. If a case is remanded by a Court of Appeals, what effect does this have on the case at bar?
 A. The attorneys on the case are replaced for both the plaintiff and defendant.
 B. The appellant becomes the appellee in a new trial.
 C. The case is sent back to the trial, or lower, court.
 D. The trial court has the right to enter a determination to the Court of Appeals which may materially affect the outcome of the case.

20.____

21. Sentencing Guidelines are set by which entity or government entity?
 A. The Bureau of Prisons
 B. Immigration and Customs Enforcement
 C. Department of Justice
 D. U.S. Sentencing Commission

21.____

22. Sequestered juries are prevented from
 A. being biased by outside influences during deliberations
 B. speaking with one another during deliberations
 C. relying on alternate juror votes in rendering a decision in a trial
 D. hearing testimony from witnesses deemed to have hearsay evidence

22.____

23. A statute is a law passed by the
 A. courts   B. judicial branch
 C. legislature   D. executive branch

23.____

24. If an element or issue in a case has not arisen, or no longer applies to the matter at hand because it has ended before trial, the issue is considered
 A. triable   B. factual
 C. indeterminate   D. moot

24.____

25. Susan would like to file a restraining order on her ex-husband, John, and may want to sue him criminally and civilly. She asks for advice on the rules of conducting a lawsuit.
These rules are otherwise known as
  A. procedure   B. terms   C. requirements D. issues

25.____

KEY (CORRECT ANSWERS)

1.	C		11.	A
2.	D		12.	D
3.	B		13.	A
4.	A		14.	B
5.	A		15.	C
6.	B		16.	A
7.	C		17.	C
8.	B		18.	A
9.	D		19.	B
10.	C		20.	C

21.	D
22.	A
23.	C
24.	D
25.	A

TEST 3

DIRECTIONS: Each question or incomplete statement is followed by several suggested answers or completions. Select the one that BEST answers the question or completes the statement. *PRINT THE LETTER OF THE CORRECT ANSWER IN THE SPACE AT THE RIGHT.*

1. The delivery of writs or summons to one party in a lawsuit is also known as
    A. demand for interrogatories
    B. requests for information
    C. service of process
    D. statement on the record

1._____

2. The time in which a lawsuit must be filed or a criminal prosecution must begin is called
    A. tolling period
    B. statute of limitations
    C. timely prosecution
    D. Article III hearing

2._____

3. A subpoena requires its recipient to appear and provide _____, while a subpoena duces tecum requires its recipient to appear and provide _____.
    A. documents; testimony
    B. a witness; testimony
    C. documents; a witness
    D. testimony; documents

3._____

4. _____ is the process of selecting a jury by questioning prospective jurors to ascertain their qualifications and determine if there is a basis for challenge, such as a conflict or other reason for disqualification.
    A. sua sponte
    B. de jure
    C. voir dire
    D. jury statement

4._____

5. In executing a warrant, law enforcement has court authorization to make an arrest, _____, or both.
    A. conduct a search
    B. question a suspect
    C. subpoena a suspect's attorney
    D. require a personal appearance by the suspect

5._____

6. A Chapter 7 case where there are no available assets of the debtor that would satisfy any portion of a creditor's unsecured claims is referred to as a(n)
    A. liquidation case
    B. no asset case
    C. unranked estate
    D. dischargeable debt

6._____

7. Bill and Tim are neighbors. They are currently engaged in a heated dispute over the boundary of the property line that separates their lots. Bill has sued Tim for harassment as he claims Tim parks his delivery truck in the driveway that is on Bill's property. A judge has issued a court order which prevents Tim from parking any vehicle in the driveway in dispute until further research can be completed by the attorneys for either side.
    The court order issued is
    A. injunction
    B. restraining order
    C. issue
    D. home confinement

7._____

8. If a case is dismissed without prejudice, that court has made no decision on   8._____
    the merits and the parties are allowed to
    A. question the final ruling   B. file the case at a later date
    C. find new attorneys/representation   D. ignore the final ruling

9. May a deposition be used later in trial?   9._____
    A. Yes, but only if the witness was represented by an attorney
    B. Yes, as it is an oral statement made before an officer authorized by law to
       administer oaths
    C. No, because it is a written statement that can be retracted at any time
    D. No

10. Madeline asks for advice regarding the discovery process. She is unsure what   10._____
    it entails.
    Discovery is the
    A. procedure that governs the exchange of information, particularly the
       disclosure of evidence, between the parties before trial
    B. procedure that governs the appearance of the testifying witnesses at trial
    C. rules of evidence both parties must adhere to during the trial
    D. exchange of motions and subpoenas before trial

11. The docket is an important component of court proceedings because   11._____
    A. it is a log containing the complete history of each case
    B. it is accessible to the jury who can better understand the procedural
       history of each case.
    C. the judge enters the journal entries guaranteeing the docket's accuracy
    D. each court docket is at least 100 separate entries

12. Information presented in testimony or in documents used to persuade a judge   12._____
    or jury in deciding a case in favor of one side or the other is termed
    A. disclosure   B. deposition   C. evidence   D. indictment

13. Samuel is on trial for armed robbery. Samuel's attorney, Maxine, presents   13._____
    evidence her client was not in the state during the robbery and does not own a
    weapon of any kind.
    What kind of evidence is Maxine presenting to the court?
    A. Alibi   B. Exculpatory
    C. Exclusionary   D. Exemplary

14. Samantha and Steven are separately called as witnesses in the trial of Adam   14._____
    Jones, who is being tried for murder. Steven testifies that he saw Adam
    commit the crime behind a local bar. Samantha testifies that Steven told her
    what Adam did.
    Adam's attorney objects to Samantha's testimony because it is
    A. exculpatory   B. hearsay
    C. untrue   D. impeachment

63

15. After filing bankruptcy, Katherine sells her home to her daughter. Katherine's home is currently worth $300,000. She sells it to her daughter for $5. Katherine's sale of her home is deemed a

    A. insider transaction   B. joint administration
    C. transfer of jurisprudence   D. fraudulent transfer

15.____

16. When a trial is deemed invalid and must start again with a new jury, the trial is called a

    A. acquittal   B. mistrial   C. in limine   D. no asset case

16.____

17. Oral arguments are an opportunity for _____ to summarize their position before the court.

    A. jurors   B. plaintiffs   C. the accused   D. attorneys

17.____

18. During jury selection, the judge grants each side the right to exclude a certain number of prospective jurors without reason.
This grant is also called a _____ challenge.

    A. prospective   B. per curiam   C. peremptory   D. petition

18.____

19. Who prepares the pre-sentence report for the court?

    A. The plaintiff's attorney   B. The jury
    c. The defendant's attorney   D. The court's probation officer

19.____

20. The legal doctrine that allows for the delay or pausing of the statute of limitations is referred to as

    A. extended delay   B. tolling
    C. transferring   D. tort

20.____

21. At trial, William was convicted of harassment and the negligent infliction of emotional distress. His attorney appealed the decision to the Court of Appeals. The Court of Appeals disagreed with the lower court and acquitted William of all charges.
The Court of Appeals _____ the lower court's decision.

    A. remanded   b. reversed   C. returned   D. rescinded

21.____

22. The preparation of schedules requires the disclosure of

    A. assets, liabilities, and other financial information
    B. past convicted crimes
    C. past arrests
    D. past employment

22.____

23. The punishment ordered by a court for a defendant convicted of a crime is logged in the docket as the official

    A. disposition of the case   B. sentence
    C. dismissal of the case   D. order

23.____

24. John's trial is set to begin a month before Judge Smith. In a pre-trial
hearing, it is determined that John is not a resident of the state where the trial
will take place, and the alleged crime was not committed in the state. Judge
Smith quickly realizes the court does not have jurisdiction and dismisses the
case so that it can be filed with a court of proper jurisdiction.
Judge Smith's action, without prompting from either the plaintiff or defendant, is
referred to as
   A. per diem   B. pro tem   C. sua sponte   D. en banc

24.____

25. In criminal cases, prosecutors must prove a defendant's guilt beyond a
reasonable doubt.
In most civil trials, the _____ is by a preponderance of the evidence.
   A. clear and convincing   B. standard of proof
   C. evidence   D. degree and necessity

25.____

KEY (CORRECT ANSWERS)

1.	C		11.	A
2.	B		12.	C
3.	D		13.	B
4.	C		14.	B
5.	A		15.	D
6.	B		16.	B
7.	A		17.	D
8.	B		18.	C
9.	B		19.	D
10.	A		20.	B

21.	B
22.	A
23.	B
24.	C
25.	B

TEST 4

DIRECTIONS: Each question or incomplete statement is followed by several suggested answers or completions. Select the one that BEST answers the question or completes the statement. *PRINT THE LETTER OF THE CORRECT ANSWER IN THE SPACE AT THE RIGHT.*

1. The _____ is the final decision by the fact finder (judge or jury) that determines the guilt or innocence of a criminal defendant, or the outcome of a civil case.
   A. order
   C. verdict
   B. punishment
   D. decision

   1._____

2. Following precedent, or adhering to the decisions in prior cases involving the same issue is known as _____, the Latin term meaning "to stand by things decided."
   A. pro tempura
   C. stare decisis
   B. en banc
   D. quid pro quo

   2._____

3. One of the largest areas of civil law, a _____ is a wrongful or illegal act which causes injury to another.
   A. criminal
   B. tort
   C. defendant
   D. punitive

   3._____

4. Stacy wants to sue Bob, who sold her a used car last year. Stacy alleges that Bob knowingly sold her a stolen car. Stacy paid Bob $5,000 for the car and in exchange Bob provided her with the keys to the car and a coupon for four free oil changes. No other documents were exchanged between Bob and Stacy.
   What document would prove who the legal owner of the car truly is?
   A. A wobbler
   C. Schedule of ownership
   B. Disclosure statement
   D. Title

   4._____

5. Michelle walks into a local courthouse and demands to speak with the clerk. She is upset that her neighbor, Rich, has not picked up the leaves on his property all season. She feels strongly his failure to do so will drive property prices down and, additionally, the leaves keep blowing into her yard.
   The clerk informs Michelle that she is free to contact an attorney, but should know that she will not likely be able to proceed with a lawsuit because
   A. there is no cause of action
   B. the courts cannot force Rich to pick up his leaves or prevent the leaves from blowing onto Michelle's property
   C. the statute of limitations will pass by the time Michelle contacts an attorney
   D. punitive damages are not likely to be awarded, so filing a lawsuit will be frivolous

   5._____

6. Latin for a "guilty mind," this term is synonymous with "intent" and for some crimes, it must be present when the person committed the criminal act in order to be found guilty.

    A. Pro se   B. Mens rea   C. Pro tem   D. En banc

6._____

7. Compensatory damages are different from punitive damages in that: Compensatory damages

    A. are recovered for injury or economic loss, while punitive are awarded over and above compensatory damages for the purpose of punishment and to serve as a deterrent to others

    B. and punitive damages both make the injured party whole, but compensatory damages can be up to 10% more than the actual claim

    C. serve as a deterrent to others, while punitive damages are recovered for injury or economic loss

    D. are incurred from the moment the crime occurs, thereby accruing interest, whereas punitive damages are awarded in a lump sum

7._____

8. Malfeasance is defined as doing something illegal or morally wrong, and is usually associated with a(n)

    A. abuse of authority committed by a public official

    B. torts committed in a public setting

    C. crimes that are punishable by one year or more in prison

    D. a crime committed by a judge, court officer, or registered attorney

8._____

9. A title abstract search on a home would provide the researcher with a

    A. list of people who made bids to buy the property

    B. list of real estate agents who worked on selling the home as well as a list of real estate agents representing potential buyers of the home

    C. history of ownership that establishes the present state of a title

    D. history of individuals who lived in the home at one point in time

9._____

10. A crime that can be classified as either a felony or a misdemeanor is often referred to as a

    A. deciding factor   B. wobbler

    C. precedent   D. information

10._____

11. A formal response to a complaint that pleads for dismissal due to a lack of a legal basis for a lawsuit is called

    A. an answer   B. an affidavit

    C. a motion in limine   D. demurrer

11._____

12. Administrative law concerns _____ agencies, such as the U.S. Department of Housing and Urban Development (HUD) or the U.S. Department of Education.

    A. government   B. municipal

    C. administrative   D. elected

12._____

13. Daniel committed and is currently being sentenced for his involvement in
    an armed robbery. His attorney is seeking alternative sanctions given that
    Daniel was present during the commission of the crime, but did not actively
    participate.
    His attorney asks the court for
    A. alternative sanctions   B. sentencing by statute
    C. diminished capacity   D. demurrer

13.____

14. The attorney who appears in the permanent records or files of a case is known
    as the _____ unless he or she withdraws or is otherwise removed from the
    case.
    A. attorney of the case   B. attorney of record
    C. attorney in time   D. permanent attorney

14.____

15. Mark and Cindy are divorcing. Cindy did not request money for support
    from Mark prior to the final court hearing, therefore her rights to _____ are
    waived.
    A. child support   B. compensatory damages
    C. punitive damages   D. alimony

15.____

16. Attorneys for the plaintiff and the defendant agree that each side needs
    more time to conduct additional discovery before trial.
    The parties jointly request a(n)
    A. recess   B. voir dire
    C. adjournment   D. information

16.____

17. Instead of using a judge, amicable parties may decide to submit to _____
    for a decision.
    A. adjudication   B. arbitration
    C. meritorious decision   D. jury trial

17.____

18. The first court appearance of a person accused of a crime, where he or she
    is advised of his or her rights is called a(n)
    A. plea meeting   B. pretrial conference
    C. jury selection   D. arraignment

18.____

19. Charlie is behind on his child support and alimony payments to his ex-wife,
    Miranda. The court garnishes his wages to satisfy the amount in _____ that is
    overdue and unpaid.
    A. arrears   B. damages   C. satisfaction   D. lien

19.____

20. Joel became aware that he was being sued by his former business partner   20._____
    when he was served with a verified complaint by a process server last May.
    Joel decided to ignore the complaint altogether and believed that, eventually,
    the lawsuit would go away.
    What is Joel's status in the suit?
    A. He owes his former business partner punitive damages, because he
        failed to respond or answer.
    B. He is a defendant that will be forced to go to trial to answer to the
        charges.
    C. He is in default as he failed to answer or respond to the plaintiff's claims.
    D. He is in limbo as he did not answer the complaint but the trial date has
        not yet been set.

21. The permanent home of a person is referred to as their _____; where a   21._____
    person can have many residences, they can only have one of these.
    A. domicile   B. address
    C. place of business   D. permanency

22. Missy has been paroled after serving 60 months of her 120-month prison   22._____
    sentence. Parole is effectively a release
    A. into the custody of a responsible person
    B. from incarceration after serving part of a sentence
    C. from incarceration after serving more than half or a majority of a sentence
    D. into the custody of a probation officer who will continue to monitor the
        individual indefinitely

23. A petitioner is also known as the _____ or the person starting the lawsuit.   23._____
    A. applicant   B. plaintiff   C. respondent   D. defendant

24. After learning more about the circumstances surrounding the alleged   24._____
    armed robbery committed by Justin and three of his friends, the state's
    prosecutor decides to replace the original armed robbery charge against Justin
    for conspiracy to commit a felony.
    The prosecutor asks the court grant her request to enter a
    A. new charge   B. substitute charge
    C. felonious charge   D. determination of guilt

25. At a pretrial hearing to determine the credibility of the state's expert witness,   25._____
    the witness appeared and gave testimony followed by oral arguments by both
    the plaintiff's attorney and the defendant's attorney. Following the conference,
    each party decided they would like to review the record of what was said during
    that hearing prior to the trial. There was a stenographer during the pretrial
    hearing.
    Each party needs to request a(n)
    A. docket   B. witness log   C. transcript   D. disclosure

KEY (CORRECT ANSWERS)

1.	C		11.	D
2.	C		12.	A
3.	B		13.	A
4.	D		14.	B
5.	A		15.	D
6.	B		16.	C
7.	A		17.	B
8.	A		18.	D
9.	C		19.	A
10.	B		20.	C

21.	A
22.	B
23.	B
24.	B
25.	C

EXAMINATION SECTION
TEST 1

DIRECTIONS: Each question or incomplete statement is followed by several suggested answers or completions. Select the one that BEST answers the question or completes the statement. *PRINT THE LETTER OF THE CORRECT ANSWER IN THE SPACE AT THE RIGHT.*

Questions 1-5.

DIRECTIONS: Questions 1 through 5 are to be answered on the basis of the following fact pattern.

Astrid's son, Carlos, attends the local high school. Carlos and another student, Manny, have been bullying another student both on and off school premises. The high school principal has notified the New York Police Department School Safety Unit of the issue. The principal has also been in touch with Astrid and Manny's mother, Mary. Mary believes Carlos is a bad influence to her son, Manny. After obtaining Astrid's phone number, Mary called Astrid and made threats towards her and Carlos. She indicated that if Carlos did not stay away from her son, Manny, she would have them both killed. The next day after school, Carlos is jumped by a group of teenagers and his leg is broken in the brawl. Astrid sues Manny, Mary, and the school district. Mary intends to countersue.

1. Who is the complainant?
   A. Manny   B. Mary   C. Astrid   D. Carlos   1._____

2. Which of the following is NOT a possible cause of action?   2._____
   A. Harassment
   B. Assault
   C. Negligence
   D. Breach of Contract

3. What key information is missing from the complaint?   3._____
   A. The name of the bullied student
   B. The location where Carlos was jumped
   C. The name of the high school principal
   D. The name of the police officer at the NYPD School Safety Unit who was originally notified on the issue

4. Is Mary obligated to countersue because she or her son, Manny, may have been involved in the assault against Carlos?   4._____
   A. Yes; she must answer the suit and countersue as required
   B. Yes; she must countersue to clear her son's name
   C. No; Mary is not obligated to countersue and can simply answer to the claims as alleged
   D. No; Mary is not obligated to countersue but she is obligated to countersue on Manny's behalf

5. Assume that Carlos and Manny are minors.
   What effect, if any, would this fact have on the lawsuit that is filed?
   A. The legal guardians of Carlos and Manny will need to file, and answer, the lawsuit on their behalf.
   B. Carlos and Manny do not need to appear in court.
   C. Minors cannot sue other people.
   D. The lawsuit is unaffected by their age.

5._____

6.

6._____

Mary Williams	Mary S. Williams	Mary S. Williams
1 Court Way	1 Court Way	1 Court Way
Smithtown, NY 10170	Smithtown, NY 10170	Smith Town, NY 10170

Which selection below accurately describes the addresses as listed above?
   A. All three addresses are the same.
   B. The first and the third address are the same.
   C. None of the addresses are the same.
   D. The second and third address are the same.

Questions 7-9.

DIRECTIONS: Questions 7 through 9 are to be answered on the basis of the following table.

Schedule – Judge Presser		
Petitioner	**Respondent**	**Status**
Williams	Smith	Dismissed with prejudice
Jones	Johnson	Continued
Adams	Doe	Dismissed with prejudice
Ash	Link	Adjourned
Lam	Garcia	Settled

7. How many cases were adjourned?
   A. 3   B. 1   C. 4   D. 5

7._____

8. In how many cases were money damages awarded by the judge?
   A. 0   B. 3   C. 4   D. 5

8._____

9. How many cases will be heard again?
   A. 2   B. 1   C. 3   D. 5

9._____

10. A warrant for the arrest of Benjamin Lang. Lang lives in Suffolk County, New York. What is recorded on the warrant?
    Lang's
    A. venue   B. domicile
    C. jurisdiction   D. subject matter jurisdiction

10._____

Questions 11-13.

DIRECTIONS: Questions 11 through 13 are to be answered on the basis of the following table.

455888912	455888812	455888912	455888812
Civil Court	Civil Court	Civil Court	Civil Court
Contract	Contract	Contract	Contract
Pam L. Williams	Pam Williams	Pam Williams	Pam L. Williams

11. Which selection below accurately describes the case captions as listed above?   11.____
    A. All of the captions are the same.
    B. Caption 1 and Caption 3 are the same.
    C. Caption 2 and Caption 4 are the same.
    D. None of the captions are the same.

12. Which digit above is dissimilar in two of the above captions?   12.____
    A. The seventh digit   B. The fifth digit
    C. The sixth digit   D. The eighth digit

13. The notation "contract" in each caption above describes the _____ of the   13.____
    case.
    A. Cause of action   B. Remedy at issue
    C. Order of the court   D. Disposition

14. Melinda was seen stealing money from a car on Atlantic Avenue in Brooklyn.   14.____
    Samuel witnessed the crime from his apartment and called the police. Officer
    Tang recorded the call in the police log. Samuel does not own a car and
    reported the crime anonymously. Later that same evening, Jeremy returned
    his car and found the passenger window had been broken and $500 was stolen
    from the glove compartment. Jeremy called the police to report the crime.
    In the judge's docket, the petitioner of the case against Melinda is MOST likely
    A. Jeremy   B. Samuel
    C. Officer Tang   D. The petitioner is anonymous

15. Judge Oswald hears cases in the Surrogate Court.   15.____
    Which of the following would NOT be in Judge Oswald's court calendar?
    A. Adoption   B. Wills
    C. Estate and Probation   D. Negligence

Questions 16-19.

DIRECTIONS: Questions 16 through 19 are to be answered on the basis of the following fact
             pattern.

    Judge Laredo, Smith and Ora hear no-fault cases in the 10th Judicial District throughout
the week. Judge Laredo hears cases the first Monday of each month. Judge Smith hears
cases with amounts in dispute over $10,000 on Tuesday, Wednesday, and Friday. Judge Ora
hears cases without amounts in dispute below $25,000 on Tuesdays only.

16. Geico and ABC Chiropractic are parties to a no-fault dispute with an amount in dispute of $8,500.
    If Judge Laredo is unavailable, what day can the case be heard?
    A. Wednesday   B. Friday   C. Monday   D. Tuesday

16.____

17. Blue Health Medical and Progressive Insurance are parties to a no-fault dispute which is scheduled to be heard February 18th. Blue Health demands Progressive reimburse the provider $5,000 for the primary surgeon fees and $12,000 in assistant surgeon fees.
    Which judge will hear the matter and on which day?
    A. Judge Smith on Friday   B. Judge Smith on Tuesday
    C. Judge Smith on Wednesday   D. Judge Ora on Tuesday

17.____

18. A no-fault dispute is being heard on Monday, June 10th.
    Which statement below must be TRUE?
    A. The amount in dispute is above $10,000.
    B. The amount in dispute is less than $25,000.
    C. The amount in dispute is less than $10,000.
    D. Judge Laredo is hearing the case.

18.____

19. What information must be obtained in order to properly schedule the court calendar?
    A. The amount in dispute for each case
    B. The parties in each case
    C. Verification the dispute is "no-fault in nature"
    D. All of the above

19.____

20. A victim impact statement is an oral or _____ statement that may be read in court.
    A. recorded   B. transcribed   C. written   D. visualized

20.____

21. The clerk in the Surrogates Court will need to have access to what information in the preparation of adoption hearings?
    A. Personal information of a child's current or prior legal guardian
    B. Emancipation petition documentation
    C. Deed or will
    D. Probate documentation

21.____

Questions 22-25.

DIRECTIONS: Questions 22 through 25 are to be answered on the basis of the following table.

Schedule – Judge Orlando			
Complainant/Plaintiff	Defendant	Case Type	Money Awarded
Williams	Smith	Civil	$5,000
Jones	Johnson	Criminal	No
Adams	Doe	Criminal	$10,000
Ash	Link	Civil	$15,000
Lam	Garcia	Civil	$25,000

22. What is the total amount of money damages from civil disputes?   22._____
    A. $45,000   B. $40,000   C. $5,000   D. 0

23. Which complainant/plaintiff was awarded less than $20,000?   23._____
    A. Williams, Adams, and Ash   B. Jones, Adams, and Ash
    C. Lam, Williams, and Jones   D. Jones, Adams, and Lam

24. How many criminal cases were heard by Judge Orlando?   24._____
    A. 4   B. 5   C. 2   D. 3

25. Which defendants are responsible for paying more than $10,000?   25._____
    A. Doe and Link   B. Link and Garcia
    C. John and Doe   D. Smith and Garcia

KEY (CORRECT ANSWERS)

1.	C		11.	D
2.	D		12.	A
3.	B		13.	A
4.	C		14.	A
5.	A		15.	D
6.	C		16.	D
7.	B		17.	D
8.	A		18.	D
9.	A		19.	D
10.	B		20.	C

21.	A
22.	A
23.	A
24.	C
25.	B

TEST 2

DIRECTIONS: Each question or incomplete statement is followed by several suggested answers or completions. Select the one that BEST answers the question or completes the statement. *PRINT THE LETTER OF THE CORRECT ANSWER IN THE SPACE AT THE RIGHT.*

Questions 1-4.

DIRECTIONS: Questions 1 through 4 are to be answered on the basis of the following text.

After a lengthy trial with multiple ___1___, Jim was acquitted of armed robbery and conspiracy. On the other hand, his alleged partner, Bob, was ___2___ of armed robbery. The conspiracy charge was dropped against Bob since the 12-person ___3___ found he acted alone. Jim's attorney ___4___.

1. Fill in the blank for #1:
   A. witnesses   B. evidence   C. discretionary D. turbulent   1.____

2. Fill in the blank for #2:
   A. guilty   B. convicted   C. indicted   D. surmised   2.____

3. Fill in the blank for #3:
   A. judge   B. spectator   C. jury   D. bailiff   3.____

4. Fill in the blank for #4:
   A. appealed   B. remanded   C. reversed   D. rescinded   4.____

Questions 5-10.

DIRECTIONS: Questions 5 through 10 are to be answered on the basis of the following table.

Court Schedule - Tuesday			
Judge	Total Cases	Cases Dismissed	Cases with Money Awarded
Presser	10	2	X
O'Dell	5	5	
Williams	6	6	
Sasha	8	7	X

5. How many cases were awarded money damages from Judge Presser's calendar?   5.____
   A. 2   B. 8   C. 6   D. 10

6. How many cases were awarded money damages from Judge Sasha's calendar?   6.____
   A. 8   B. 7   C. 1   D. 0

7. How many cases were dismissed on Tuesday?   7.____
   A. 11   B. 20   C. 7   D. 10

8. How many cases were awarded money damages on Tuesday?   8.____
   A. 9   B. 8   C. 1   D. 10

9. Which judge heard the MOST cases on Tuesday?   9.____
   A. Presser   B. O'Dell   C. Williams   D. Sasha

10. Which judge heard the LEAST cases on Tuesday?   10.____
    A. Presser   B. O'Dell   C. Willliams   D. Sasha

Questions 11-15.

DIRECTIONS: Questions 11 through 15 are to be answered on the basis of the following text.

Judge Smith hears adoption cases on Fridays. Judge Clark hears criminal cases every weekday except Tuesday in the New York City Criminal Court. Judge Clark hears felony criminal cases on Tuesday in Supreme Court. Judge Amy hears felony criminal cases on Thursday in Supreme Court.

11. Daniel is being charged with the murder of his cousin, Jerrell.   11.____
    Which judge can hear the case and on what day?
    A. Judge Smith on Friday   B. Judge Clark on Monday
    C. Judge Amy on Tuesday   D. Judge Clark on Tuesday

12. Jamal lives in Staten Island with his sister, Tisha, and Tisha's boyfriend,   12.____
    Hunter. Hunter and Jamal do not get along and one day last January, Hunter
    and Jamal were involved in a physical altercation. Hunter and Jamal both
    allege that the other assault and battered the other.
    Which judge can hear the case and on what day?
    A. Judge Clark on Tuesday   B. Judge Amy on Thursday
    C. Judge Smith on Friday   D. Judge Clark on Monday

13. Assuming the crime of assault and battery are not felonies, in which court   13.____
    will Jamal and Hunter's dispute be heard?
    A. Supreme Court   B. Surrogates Court
    C. New York City Criminal Court   D. Small Claims Court

14. Assume that Tisha and Hunter have a six-year-old daughter.   14.____
    If Hunter is incarcerated for his role in the physical altercation with Jamal,
    which court would have jurisdiction over Hunter's trial?
    A. Surrogates Court   B. New York City Criminal Court
    C. Bronx Housing Court   D. Richmond County Civil Court

15. What day of the week are the MOST cases heard between all three judges?   15.____
    A. Monday   B. Thursday   C. Tuesday   D. Friday

Questions 16-19.

DIRECTIONS: Questions 16 through 19 are to be answered on the basis of the following table.

Caption #1	Caption #2	Caption #3	Caption #4
Case 12-908	Case 12-909	Case 12-910	Case 12-911
Bronx Housing Court	Civil Court	Civil Court	Surrogates Court
Landlord/Tenant	Assault	Breach of Contract	Guardianship
ABC Property Mgmt v. Sam Smith	Jim Jones v. Sam Hunt	Terrell Williams v. Daniel Tang	In re: Jane Doe

16. Which caption above contains an INCORRECT cause of action?   16.____
    A. 1   B. 2   C. 3   D. 4

17. When were the cases in each of the captions above initiated?   17.____
    A. 2015
    B. 2016
    C. 2012
    D. Unable to determine based on the information provided

18. Which case caption above corresponds to a matter that will NOT have   18.____
    monetary damages awarded?
    A. 1   B. 2   C. 3   D. 4

19. Which case caption has a matter involving an institutional, rather than an   19.____
    individual, petitioner?
    A. 1   B. 2   C. 3   D. 4

20. A pro se litigant wants to initiate a lawsuit against his intrusive neighbor.   20.____
    Assuming the pro se litigant prevails, which form should be served against the
    neighbor after the judgment is entered?
    A. Notice of entry   B. Notice of appeal
    C. Remand service   D. Process discovery

21. A(n) _____ is a hearing for the purpose of determining the amount of   21.____
    damages sue on a claim. The clerk can enter the request on the judge's
    calendar after the opposing party has defaulted.
    A. imposition   B. inquest   C. tardy notice   D. reversal

22. After a judgment is entered, it becomes enforceable for a period of time.   22.____
    For real property, a transcript of _____ is filed with the County Clerk which
    makes the judgment enforceable for a period of ten years.
    A. enforcement   B. judgment
    C. engagement   D. affidavit

23. Sensitive information must be _____ before it becomes public record.   23.____
    A. retained   B. reposed   C. redacted   D. recanted

24. Service of process can be filed upon the individual or upon the _____. The affidavit of service will state the party that received the service.
    A. secretary of state   B. guardian
    C. ad litem   D. second most suitable person

24._____

25. A warrant can be issued to a sheriff or a marshal. The warrant clerk is responsible for reviewing the paperwork and ensuring that all is in order, including
    A. the names of the parties   B. address of the premises
    C. the index number   D. all of the above

25._____

KEY (CORRECT ANSWERS)

1.	A		11.	D
2.	B		12.	D
3.	C		13.	C
4.	A		14.	B
5.	B		15.	D
6.	C		16.	B
7.	B		17.	C
8.	A		18.	D
9.	A		19.	A
10.	B		20.	A

21.	B
22.	B
23.	C
24.	A
25.	D

TEST 3

DIRECTIONS: Each question or incomplete statement is followed by several suggested answers or completions. Select the one that BEST answers the question or completes the statement. *PRINT THE LETTER OF THE CORRECT ANSWER IN THE SPACE AT THE RIGHT.*

1. Supreme Court clerks need to be on notice when a(n) _____ is filed as a judge is not assigned until one that parties files this document and pays the filing fee. A case will never go to trial if this document is never filed.
   A. request for maintenance
   B. request for judicial intervention
   C. remediation
   D. arbitration

   1.____

Questions 2-4.

DIRECTIONS: Questions 1 through 5 are to be answered on the basis of the following chart.

Row	Case Type	Court
1	Divorce	Supreme Court
2	Custody/Visitation	Family Court
3	Child Support	Family Court
4	Paternity	Family Court
5	When Someone Dies	Surrogates Court
6	Guardianship	Surrogate's Court
7	Name Change	Supreme Court
8	Housing	New York City Housing Court

2. Assume that you are advising a pro se litigant on the proper forms to file when representing him or herself. Where would John file a small estate affidavit?
   A. Family Court
   B. Supreme Court
   C. Surrogates Court
   D. New York Civil Court

   2.____

3. Where would Tom's sister, Emmanuela, file a name change?
   A. Supreme Court
   B. Family Court
   C. Surrogates Court
   D. New York City Civil Court

   3.____

4. Tara and her husband, Cassidy, share custody of their twin sons, Drake and Austin. Cassidy would like to petition the court for sole custody. Where would Cassidy file his petition?
   A. New York City Housing Court
   B. Supreme Court
   C. Family Court
   D. Surrogates Court

   4.____

5. Richard is representing himself in a lawsuit against his landlord. Richard   5.____
does not have the financial means to hire an attorney and would like to request
a reduction in the court filing fees. Richard must file a request for a _____
which is made by filing a _____ and sworn _____ which explains his finances
to the court.
   A. fee waiver; notice of motion; affirmation
   B. fee waiver, notice of motion, affidavit
   C. affidavit, notice of motion, fee waiver
   D. affidavit, fee waiver, notice of motion

Questions 6-10.

DIRECTIONS: Questions 6 through 10 are to be answered on the basis of the following text.

    Daniel walks into this local supermarket after lunch and falls in one of the store aisles.
Daniel lies on the floor – which is nearly empty – until one of the store managers finds him,
helps him up, and offers to pay for his groceries. Daniel leaves the store bruised, but not
seriously injured. Two days later, Daniel falls at another grocery store. This time, Daniel
threatens to sue the grocery store. The second grocery store has heard about Daniel and is
concerned that he is falsifying his injuries to gain sympathy and money. The second grocery
store sues Daniel to get ahead of Daniel suing them.

6. Who is the plaintiff in the case?   6.____
   A. The first grocery store   B. The second grocery store
   C. The grocery store manager   D. Daniel

7. Which of the following is the MOST likely cause of action in a suit that Daniel   7.____
   initiates against the grocery store?
   A. Breach of contract   B. Discrimination
   C. Negligence   D. Assault

8. After the lawsuit has commenced, which party would respond or file an answer   8.____
   to the complaint?
   A. Daniel   B. The first grocery store
   C. The second grocery store   D. The grocery store manager

9. Which party is eligible to countersue?   9.____
   A. The first grocery store   B. The second grocery store
   C. The grocery store manager   D. Daniel

10. The lawsuit will likely be dismissed. Why?   10.____
   A. Daniel is clearly not exaggerating his injuries.
   B. Daniel has not sued either grocery store.
   C. The store manager did not take a report of Daniel's injuries.
   D. The first grocery store must sue Daniel first.

11. A settlement between parties is not a final and binding legal agreement until   11.____
   the _____ of settlement is signed by both parties.
   A. amendment   B. agreement   C. stipulation   D. simulation

12. Which of the following are appropriate reasons for filing an Order to Show Cause?
    A. Changing the terms of a court order
    B. Requesting the court to dismiss a case
    C. Bringing the case back to court for any reason
    D. All of the above

12.____

13. Which of the following is NOT an appropriate reason for filing an Order to Show Case?
    A. Asking for more time to do something previously agreed upon by court order
    B. Explaining why either party missed a court date
    C. Submitting financial information for a landlord/tenant dispute
    D. Fixing errors in a stipulation

13.____

Questions 14-17.

DIRECTIONS: Questions 14 through 17 are to be answered on the basis of the following text.

Judge Chin hears child neglect and abuse cases in Family Court on Mondays and Tuesdays. Judge Amy hears divorce cases on Mondays, Wednesdays, and Fridays. Judge Snell hears child support and visitation cases every day of the week except Thursday. Termination of parental rights, foster care placement, and other child support cases are scheduled on Thursdays only with any of the three judges.

14. Tim and Sarah would like to adjust their visitation schedule for their eight-year-old daughter, Samantha. They would like the courts to assist them with this issue as they have been unable to come to an agreement on their own. Which judge will hear the case and on what day?
    A. Judge Snell on Thursday
    B. Judge Snell on Monday
    C. Judge Chin on Monday
    D. Judge Chin on Friday

14.____

15. Amanda would like to file for emancipation from her parents. Which judge is MOST likely to hear her case?
    A. Judge Chin
    B. Judge Amy
    C. Judge Snell'
    D. Any of the judges can hear Amanda's case

15.____

16. Jimmy and Eva are legally separating. Which judge will hear their case and on what day?
    A. Judge Chin on Monday
    B. Judge Snell on Monday
    C. Judge Amy on Monday
    D. Judge Chin on Tuesday

16.____

17. The State of New York intends to file a case against Eric for the abuses
    and neglect of his daughter, Clare. Eric, however, is not Clare's legal guardian.
    Clare's legal guardian is her grandmother, Allison. Even though it is not clear
    that Clare has been neglected, the courts have found that Clare should be
    placed into foster care until it can be determined who the ultimate caregiver
    should be.
    Which judge will MOST likely hear this case?
    A. Judge Amy
    B. Judge Chin
    C. Judge Snell
    D. Any of the judges can hear this case

17.____

Questions 18-25.

DIRECTIONS: Questions 18 through 25 are to be answered on the basis of the following
              chart.

Item	Fee
Obtaining an index number	$210
RJI	$95
Note of Issue	$30
Motion or Cross-Motion	$45
Demand for Jury Trial	$65
Voluntary Discontinuance	$35
Notice of Appeal	$65

18. What is the final cost to obtain an index number, demand a jury trial, and
    file a notice of appeal?
    A. $210   B. $35   C. $65   D. $310

18.____

19. What is the final cost to obtain an RJI and note of issue?
    A. $125   B. $95   C. $30   D. $65

19.____

20. Which of the following is MOST likely to be filed with an RJI?
    A. Demand for jury trial   B. Notice of appeal
    C. Voluntary discontinuance   D. Obtaining an index number

20.____

21. Which of the following is the MOST likely outcome of filing a voluntary
    discontinuance?
    The case
    A. is automatically appealed   B. is dismissed
    C. is rescheduled   D. will be remanded

21.____

22. What is the final cost of filing a notice of appeal?
    A. $35   B. $65   C. $95   D. $120

22.____

23. What is the final cost of all items prior to filing a motion or cross-motion?
    A. $210   B. $95   C. $45   D. $335

23.____

24. Jamal would like to petition the court to compel discovery from his adversary   24.____
and former friend, Bob. He would also like to speed up the date of trial by filing
a demand for jury trial and RJI.
What is the final cost to do so?
   A. $160   B. $95   C. $65   D. $205

25. What is the LEAST costly court document filing fee?   25.____
   A. Notice of motion   B. Demand for jury trial
   C. Note of issue   D. RJI

KEY (CORRECT ANSWERS)

1.	B		11.	C
2.	C		12.	D
3.	A		13.	C
4.	C		14.	B
5.	B		15.	D
6.	B		16.	C
7.	C		17.	D
8.	A		18.	D
9.	D		19.	A
10.	B		20.	D

21.	B
22.	B
23.	D
24.	D
25.	C

TEST 4

DIRECTIONS: Each question or incomplete statement is followed by several suggested answers or completions. Select the one that BEST answers the question or completes the statement. *PRINT THE LETTER OF THE CORRECT ANSWER IN THE SPACE AT THE RIGHT.*

1. A lawsuit for money damages amounting to more than $25,000 can be heard in which court?
   - A. Surrogates Court
   - B. Supreme Court
   - C. New York City Civil Court
   - D. New York City Criminal Court

   1.____

2. Which of the following will NOT be on a Notice of Entry?
   - A. Name of plaintiff
   - B. Name of defendant
   - C. Index number
   - D. Social Security number

   2.____

3. Court clerks are prohibited from which of the following?
   - A. Predicting the judgment of the court
   - B. Explaining available options for a case or problem
   - C. Providing past rulings
   - D. Providing citations or copies of the law

   3.____

4. Court clerks are permitted to do all of the following EXCEPT
   - A. provide forms with instructions
   - B. instruct an individual on how to make a complaint
   - C. analyze the law based on the specifics of a case
   - D. describe court records and their availability

   4.____

5. Mary would like to sue her neighbor, Jacob, for money damages. Mary claims Jacob ran his car into Mary's garage door while it was down and caused $5,000 in damages. For claims below $1,000, the filing fee is $15, while the filing fee is $5 more for claims above $1,000.
   How much is Mary's filing fee?
   - A. $15
   - B. $10
   - C. $20
   - D. $25

   5.____

Questions 6-10.

DIRECTIONS: Questions 6 through 10 are to be answered on the basis of the following table.

Schedule – Judge O'Neill		
Wednesday	**Thursday**	**Friday**
Continued	Dismissed with prejudice	Dismissed with prejudice
Continued	Adjourned	Continued
Settled	Dismissed with prejudice	Dismissed without prejudice
Settled	Continued	Settled
Settled	Continued	Settled

6. How many cases were adjourned this week?
   - A. 5
   - B. 6
   - C. 1
   - D. 2

   6.____

7. How many cases settled this week?　　　　　　　　　　　　　　　　7.___
 A. 5　　　　　B. 4　　　　　C. 3　　　　　D. 8

8. How many cases were dismissed this week?　　　　　　　　　　　　8.___
 A. 6　　　　　B. 4　　　　　C. 5　　　　　D. 7

9. How many cases will likely be heard again or, in other words, how many　　9.___
cases can be re-filed or are otherwise continued?
 A. 6　　　　　B. 5　　　　　C. 7　　　　　D. 8

10. Which day was Judge O'Neill the LEAST busy?　　　　　　　　　　10.___
 A. Thursday　　　　　　　　　　B. Friday
 C. Wednesday　　　　　　　　　D. Each day was equally busy

Questions 11-15.

DIRECTIONS: Questions 11 through 15 are to be answered on the basis of the following text.

At Alex's arraignment, he pled ___1___ to the charge of driving under the influence and vehicular manslaughter. At trial, the prosecutor presented evidence from several ___2___ that testified Alex had a drinking problem. While Alex's defense attorneys ___3___ to that testimony and argued it was hearsay, the judge overruled those objections and allowed the testimony to be entered in the record as originally spoken. At the conclusion of the trial, Alex was found ___4___ and sentenced to community service.

11. Fill in the blank for #1:　　　　　　　　　　　　　　　　　　11.___
 A. nolo　　　　B. contendere　　C. not guilty　　D. guilty

12. Fill in the blank for #2:　　　　　　　　　　　　　　　　　　12.___
 A. witnesses　　B. evidence　　C. testimony　　D. bearer

13. Fill in the blank for #3:　　　　　　　　　　　　　　　　　　13.___
 A. disagreed　　B. objected　　C. qualified　　D. disclaimed

14. Fill in the blank for #4:　　　　　　　　　　　　　　　　　　14.___
 A. arraigned　　B. protested　　C. remanded　　D. guilty

15. An acquittal can also be recorded in court documentation as a finding of　　15.___
 A. reversal　　B. recusal　　C. not guilty　　D. remand

16. Evidence must be found _____ before it can be marked and evaluated by　　16.___
the fact finder, either a judge or jury, in civil and criminal cases.
 A. relevant　　B. redacted　　C. qualified　　D. admissible

17. The party who seeks an appeal from a decision of a court is deemed a(n)　　17.___
_____ and is recorded in court documentation as such.
 A. petitioner　　B. respondent　　C. appellant　　D. re-respondent

18. How would a condominium be recorded in a bankruptcy proceeding?   18.____
     A. Real property   B. Personal property
     C. Intangible asset   D. chattel

19. Which of the following is LEAST likely to be recorded as a written statement   19.____
     describing one's legal and factual arguments?
     A. Attorney's brief   B. Motion
     C. Summons   D. Complaint

20. A lawsuit where one or more members of a large group of individuals sues   20.____
     on behalf of the other individuals in the large group is recorded as a _____
     lawsuit.
     A. introductory   B. class action   C. municipality   D. winning

21. Jamal has filed for bankruptcy. After the trustee has reviewed Jamal's   21.____
     assets, the trustee proposes a plan to the court where Jamal promises property
     that he already owns to satisfy the major of his debt.
     The property Jamal owns that will satisfy the debt is recorded as
     A. demerits   B. collateral   C. debris   D. probate

22. Judge Presser has rendered Emilio's sentence for the charges of armed   22.____
     robbery and kidnapping. Emilio will serve 10 years for armed robbery and 12
     years for kidnapping.
     If Emilio's total time in prison is 12 years, his sentence is recorded as
     A. consecutive   B. demonstrative
     C. concurrent   D. rebated

23. Assume the same facts as the previous question, but assume Emilio serves   23.____
     22 years in prison.
     In this instance, his sentence is recorded as
     A. consecutive   B. demonstrative
     C. concurrent   D. rebated

24. A conviction can also be recorded in court records as a judgment of   24.____
     _____ against a defendant.
     A. guilt   B. remorse   C. retaliation   D. acquittal

25. In bankruptcy, Jamal sells his house to his mother for $5 in an effort to   25.____
     hide it from creditors who will require that he sell it to satisfy his debts.
     This sale is recorded as a
     A. fraudulent transfer   B. falsified sale
     C. remarkable trade   D. clawback trade

KEY (CORRECT ANSWERS)

1.	B		11.	C
2.	D		12.	A
3.	A		13.	B
4.	C		14.	D
5.	C		15.	C
6.	C		16.	D
7.	A		17.	C
8.	B		18.	A
9.	A		19.	C
10.	C		20.	B

21.	B
22.	C
23.	A
24.	A
25.	A

EXAMINATION SECTION
TEST 1

DIRECTIONS: Each question or incomplete statement is followed by several suggested answers or completions. Select the one that BEST answers the question or completes the statement. *PRINT THE LETTER OF THE CORRECT ANSWER IN THE SPACE AT THE RIGHT.*

Questions 1-6.

DIRECTIONS: Questions 1 through 6 consist of descriptions of material to which a filing designation must be assigned.

Assume that the matters and cases described in the questions were referred for handling to a government legal office which has its files set up according to these file designations. The file designation consists of a number of characters and punctuation marks as described below.

The first character refers to agencies whose legal work is handled by this office. These agencies are numbered consecutively in the order in which they first submit a matter for attention, and are identified in an alphabetical card index. To date numbers have been assigned to agencies as follows:

Department of Correction	1
Police Department	2
Department of Traffic	3
Department of Consumer Affairs	4
Commission on Human Rights	5
Board of Elections	6
Department of Personnel	7
Board of Estimate	8

The second character is separated from the first character by a dash. The second character is the last digit of the year in which a particular lawsuit or matter is referred to the legal office.

The third character is separated from the second character by a colon and may consist of either of the following:

    I.   A sub-number assigned to each lawsuit to which the agency is a party. Lawsuits are numbered consecutively regardless of year. (Lawsuits are brought by or against agency heads rather than agencies themselves, but references are made to agencies for the purpose of simplification.)

    or II.   A capital letter assigned to each matter other than a lawsuit according to subject, the subject being identified in an alphabetical index. To date, letters have been assigned to subjects as follows:

Citizenship	A	Housing	E
Discrimination	B	Gambling	F
Residence Requirements	C	Freedom of Religion	G
Civil Service Examinations	D		

These referrals are numbered consecutively regardless of year. The first referral by a particular agency on citizenship, for example, would be designated A1, followed by A2, A3, etc.

If no reference is made in a question as to how many letters involving a certain subject or how many lawsuits have been referred by an agency, assume that it is the first.

For each question, choose the file designation which is MOST appropriate for filing the material described in the question.

1. In January 2010, two candidates in a 2009 civil service examination for positions with the Department of Correction filed a suit against the Department of Personnel seeking to set aside an educational requirement for the title.
    The Department of Personnel immediately referred the lawsuit to the legal office for handling.

    A. 1-9:1   B. 1-0:D1   C. 7-9:D1   D. 7-0:1

1.____

2. In 2014, the Police Department made its sixth request for an opinion on whether an employee assignment proposed for 2015 could be considered discriminatory.

    A. 2-5:1-B6   B. 2-4:6   C. 2-4:1-B6   D. 2-4:B6

2.____

3. In 2015, a lawsuit was brought by the Bay Island Action Committee against the Board of Estimate in which the plaintiff sought withdrawal of approval of housing for the elderly in the Bay Island area given by the Board in 2015.

    A. 8-3:1   B. 8-5:1   C. 8-3:B1   D. 8-5:E1

3.____

4. In December 2014, community leaders asked the Police Department to ban outdoor meetings of a religious group on the grounds that the meetings were disrupting the area. Such meetings had been held from time to time during 2014. On January 31, 2015, the Police Department asked the government legal office for an opinion on whether granting this request would violate the worshippers' right to freedom of religion.

    A. 2-4:G-1   B. 2-5:G1   C. 2-5:B-1   D. 2-4:B1

4.____

5. In 2014, a woman filed suit against the Board of Elections. She alleged that she had not been permitted to vote at her usual polling place in the 2013 election and had been told she was not registered there. She claimed that she had always voted there and that her record card had been lost. This was the fourth case of its type for this agency.

    A. 6-4:4   B. 6-3:C4   C. 3-4:6   D. 6-3:4

5.____

6. A lawsuit was brought in 2011 by the Ace Pinball Machine Company against the Commissioner of Consumer Affairs. The lawsuit contested an ordinance which banned the use of pinball machines on the ground that they are gambling devices.
    This was the third lawsuit to which the Department of Consumer Affairs was a party.

    A. 4-1:1   B. 4-3:F1   C. 4-1:3   D. 3F-4:1

6.____

7. You are instructed by your supervisor to type a statement that must be signed by the person making the statement and by three witnesses to the signature. The typed statement will take two pages and will leave no room for signatures if the normal margin is maintained at the bottom of the second page.
In this situation, the PREFERRED method is to type

    A. the signature lines below the normal margin on the second page
    B. nothing further and have the witnesses sign without a typed signature line
    C. the signature lines on a third page
    D. some of the text and the signature lines on a third page

7._____

8. Certain legal documents always begin with a statement of venue - that is, the county and state in which the document is executed. This is usually boxed with a parentheses or colons.
The one of the following documents that ALWAYS bears a statement of venue in a prominent position at its head is a(n)

    A. affidavit
    B. memorandum of law
    C. contract of sale
    D. will

8._____

9. A court stenographer is to take stenographic notes and transcribe the statements of a person under oath. The person has a heavy accent and speaks in ungrammatical and broken English.
When he or she is transcribing the testimony, of the following, the BEST thing for them to do is to

    A. transcribe the testimony exactly as spoken, making no grammatical changes
    B. make only the grammatical changes which would clarify the client's statements
    C. make all grammatical changes so that the testimony is in standard English form
    D. ask the client's permission before making any grammatical changes

9._____

10. When the material typed on a printed form does not fill the space provided, a Z-ruling is frequently drawn to fill up the unused space.
The MAIN purpose of this practice is to

    A. make the document more pleasing to the eye
    B. indicate that the preceding material is correct
    C. insure that the document is not altered
    D. show that the lawyer has read it

10._____

11. After you had typed an original and five copies of a certain document, some changes were made in ink on the original and were initialed by all the parties. The original was signed by all the parties, and the signatures were notarized.
Which of the following should *generally* be typed on the copies BEFORE filing the original and the copies? The inked changes

    A. but not the signatures, initials, or notarial data
    B. the signatures and the initials but not the notarial data
    C. and the notarial data but not the signatures or initials
    D. the signatures, the initials, and the notarial data

11._____

12. The first paragraph of a noncourt agreement *generally* contains all of the following EXCEPT the

    12.____

    A. specific terms of the agreement
    B. date of the agreement
    C. purpose of the agreement
    D. names of the parties involved

13. When typing an answer in a court proceeding, the place where the word ANSWER should be typed on the first page of the document is

    13.____

    A. at the upper left-hand corner
    B. below the index number and to the right of the box containing the names of the parties to the action
    C. above the index number and to the right of the box containing the names of the parties to the action
    D. to the left of the names of the attorneys for the defendant

14. Which one of the following statements BEST describes the legal document called an acknowledgment?
It is

    14.____

    A. an answer to an affidavit
    B. a receipt issued by the court when a document is filed
    C. proof of service of a summons
    D. a declaration that a signature is valid

15. Suppose you typed the original and three copies of a legal document which was dictated by an attorney in your office. He has already signed the original copy, and corrections have been made on all copies.
Regarding the copies, which one of the following procedures is the PROPER one to follow?

    15.____

    A. Leave the signature line blank on the copies
    B. Ask the attorney to sign the copies
    C. Print or type the attorney's name on the signature line on the copies
    D. Sign your name to the copies followed by the attorney's initials

16. Suppose your office is defending a particular person in a court action. This person comes to the office and asks to see some of the lawyer's working papers in his file. The lawyer assigned to the case is out of the office at the time.
You SHOULD

    16.____

    A. permit him to examine his entire file as long as he does not remove any materials from it
    B. make an appointment for the caller to come back later when the lawyer will be there
    C. ask him what working papers he wants to see and show him only those papers
    D. tell him that he needs written permission from the lawyer in order to see any records

17. Suppose that you receive a phone call from an official who is annoyed about a letter from your office which she just received. The lawyer who dictated the letter is not in the office at the moment.
Of the following, the BEST action for you to take is to

    A. explain that the lawyer is out but that you will ask the lawyer to return her call when he returns
    B. take down all of the details of her complaint and tell her that you will get back to her with an explanation
    C. refer to the proper file so that you can give her an explanation of the reasons for the letter over the phone
    D. make an appointment for her to stop by the office to speak with the lawyer

17.____

18. Suppose that you have taken dictation for an interoffice memorandum. You are asked to prepare it for distribution to four lawyers in your department whose names are given to you. You will type an original and make four copies. Which one of the following is COR-RECT with regard to the typing of the lawyers' names?
The names of all of the lawyers should appear

    A. *only* on the original
    B. on the original and each copy should have the name of one lawyer
    C. on each of the copies but not on the original
    D. on the original and on all of the copies

18.____

19. Regarding the correct typing of punctuation, the GENERALLY accepted practice is that there should be

    A. two spaces after a semi-colon
    B. one space before an apostrophe used in the body of a word
    C. no space between parentheses and the matter enclosed
    D. one space before and after a hyphen

19.____

20. Suppose you have just completed typing an original and two copies of a letter requesting information. The original is to be signed by a lawyer in your office. The first copy is for the files, and the second is to be used as a reminder to follow up.
The PROPER time to file the file copy of the letter is

    A. after the letter has been signed and corrections have been made on the copies
    B. before you take the letter to the lawyer for his signature
    C. after a follow-up letter has been sent
    D. after a response to the letter has been received

20.____

21. A secretary in a legal office has just typed a letter. She has typed the copy distribution notation on the copies to indicate *blind copy distribution*. This *blind copy* notation shows that

    A. copies of the letter are being sent to persons that the addressee does not know
    B. copies of the letter are being sent to other persons without the addressee's knowledge
    C. a copy of the letter will be enlarged for a legally blind person
    D. a copy of the letter is being given as an extra copy to the addressee

21.____

22. Suppose that one of the attorneys in your office dictates material to you without indicating punctuation. He has asked that you give him, as soon as possible, a single copy of a rough draft to be triple-spaced so that he can make corrections.
Of the following, what is the BEST thing for you to do in this situation?

    A. Assume that no punctuation is desired in the material
    B. Insert the punctuation as you type the rough draft
    C. Transcribe the material exactly as dictated, but attach a note to the attorney stating your suggested changes
    D. Before you start to type the draft, tell the attorney you want to read back your notes so that he can indicate punctuation

22.____

23. When it is necessary to type a mailing notation such as CERTIFIED, REGISTERED, or FEDEX on an envelope, the GENERALLY accepted place to type it is

    A. directly above the address
    B. in the area below where the stamp will be affixed
    C. in the lower left-hand corner
    D. in the upper left-hand corner

23.____

24. When taking a citation of a case in shorthand, which of the following should you write FIRST if you are having difficulty keeping up with the dictation?

    A. Volume and page number   B. Title of volume
    C. Name of plaintiff   D. Name of defendant

24.____

25. All of the following abbreviations and their meanings are correctly paired EXCEPT

    A. viz. - namely   B. ibid. - refer
    C. n.b. - note well   D. q.v. - which see

25.____

KEY (CORRECT ANSWERS)

1.	D	11.	D
2.	D	12.	A
3.	B	13.	B
4.	B	14.	D
5.	A	15.	C
6.	C	16.	B
7.	D	17.	A
8.	A	18.	D
9.	A	19.	C
10.	C	20.	A

21.	B
22.	B
23.	B
24.	A
25.	B

EXAMINATION SECTION
TEST 1

DIRECTIONS: Each question or incomplete statement is followed by several suggested answers or completions. Select the one that BEST answers the question or completes the statement. *PRINT THE LETTER OF THE CORRECT ANSWER IN THE SPACE AT THE RIGHT.*

Questions 1-9.

DIRECTIONS: Questions 1 through 9 consist of sentences which may or may not be examples of good English usage. Consider grammar, punctuation, spelling, capitalization, awkwardness, etc. Examine each sentence, and then choose the correct statement about it from the four choices below it. If the English usage in the sentence given is better than it would be with any of the changes suggested in options B, C, and D, choose option A. Do not choose an option that will change the meaning of the sentence.

1. According to Judge Frank, the grocer's sons found guilty of assault and sentenced last Thursday.

    A. This is an example of acceptable writing.
    B. A comma should be placed after the word *sentenced*.
    C. The word *were* should be placed after *sons*
    D. The apostrophe in *grocer's* should be placed after the *s*.

1.____

2. The department heads assistant said that the stenographers should type duplicate copies of all contracts, leases, and bills.

    A. This is an example of acceptable writing.
    B. A comma should be placed before the word *contracts*.
    C. An apostrophe should be placed before the *s* in *heads*.
    D. Quotation marks should be placed before *the stenographers* and after *bills*.

2.____

3. The lawyers questioned the men to determine who was the true property owner?

    A. This is an example of acceptable writing.
    B. The phrase *questioned the men* should be changed to *asked the men questions*.
    C. The word *was* should be changed to *were*.
    D. The question mark should be changed to a period.

3.____

4. The terms stated in the present contract are more specific than those stated in the previous contract.

    A. This is an example of acceptable writing.
    B. The word *are* should be changed to *is*.
    C. The word *than* should be changed to *then*.
    D. The word *specific* should be changed to *specified*.

4.____

5. Of the lawyers considered, the one who argued more skillful was chosen for the job.

    A. This is an example of acceptable writing.
    B. The word *more* should be replaced by the word *most*.
    C. The word *skillful* should be replaced by the word *skillfully,*
    D. The word *chosen* should be replaced by the word *selected.*

5.____

6. Each of the states has a court of appeals; some states have circuit courts. 6.____

    A. This is an example of acceptable writing.
    B. The semi-colon should be changed to a comma.
    C. The word *has* should be changed to *have*.
    D. The word *some* should be capitalized.

7. The court trial has greatly effected the child's mental condition. 7.____

    A. This is an example of acceptable writing.
    B. The word *effected* should be changed to *affected*.
    C. The word *greatly* should be placed after *effected*.
    D. The apostrophe in *child's* should be placed after the *s*.

8. Last week, the petition signed by all the officers was sent to the Better Business Bureau. 8.____

    A. This is an example of acceptable writing.
    B. The phrase *last week* should be placed after *officers*.
    C. A comma should be placed after *petition*.
    D. The word *was* should be changed to *were*.

9. Mr. Farrell claims that he requested form A-12, and three booklets describing court pro- 9.____
cedures.

    A. This is an example of acceptable writing.
    B. The word *that* should be eliminated.
    C. A colon should be placed after *requested*.
    D. The comma after *A-12* should be eliminated.

Questions 10-21.

DIRECTIONS: Questions 10 through 21 contain a word in capital letters followed by four suggested meanings of the word. For each question, choose the BEST meaning
for the word in capital letters.

10. SIGNATORY - A 10.____

    A. lawyer who draws up a legal document
    B. document that must be signed by a judge
    C. person who signs a document
    D. true copy of a signature

11. RETAINER - A 11.____

    A. fee paid to a lawyer for his services
    B. document held by a third party
    C. court decision to send a prisoner back to custody pending trial
    D. legal requirement to keep certain types of files

12. BEQUEATH - To 12.____

    A. receive assistance from a charitable organization
    B. give personal property by will to another
    C. transfer real property from one person to another
    D. receive an inheritance upon the death of a relative

13. RATIFY - To   13._____

   A. approve and sanction   B. forego
   C. produce evidence   D. summarize

14. CODICIL - A   14._____

   A. document introduced in evidence in a civil action
   B. subsection of a law
   C. type of legal action that can be brought by a plaintiff
   D. supplement or an addition to a will

15. ALIAS   15._____

   A. Assumed name   B. In favor of
   C. Against   D. A writ

16. PROXY - A(n)   16._____

   A. phony document in a real estate transaction
   B. opinion by a judge of a civil court
   C. document containing appointment of an agent
   D. summons in a lawsuit

17. ALLEGED   17._____

   A. Innocent   B. Asserted
   C. Guilty   D. Called upon

18. EXECUTE - To   18._____

   A. complete a legal document by signing it
   B. set requirements
   C. render services to a duly elected executive of a municipality
   D. initiate legal action such as a lawsuit

19. NOTARY PUBLIC - A   19._____

   A. lawyer who is running for public office
   B. judge who hears minor cases
   C. public officer, one of whose functions is to administer oaths
   D. lawyer who gives free legal services to persons unable to pay

20. WAIVE - To   20._____

   A. disturb a calm state of affairs
   B. knowingly renounce a right or claim
   C. pardon someone for a minor fault
   D. purposely mislead a person during an investigation

21. ARRAIGN - To   21._____

   A. prevent an escape   B. defend a prisoner
   C. verify a document   D. accuse in a court of law

Questions 22-40.

DIRECTIONS: Questions 22 through 40 each consist of four words which may or may not be
spelled correctly. If you find an error in
only one word, mark your answer A;
any two words, mark your answer B;
any three words, mark your answer C;
none of these words, mark your answer D.

22.	occurrence	Febuary	privilege	similiar	22._____
23.	separate	transferring	analyze	column	23._____
24.	develop	license	bankrupcy	abreviate	24._____
25.	subpoena	arguement	dissolution	foreclosure	25._____
26.	exaggerate	fundamental	significance	warrant	26._____
27.	citizen	endorsed	marraige	appraissal	27._____
28.	precedant	univercity	observence	preliminary	28._____
29.	stipulate	negligence	judgment	prominent	29._____
30.	judisial	whereas	release	guardian	30._____
31.	appeal	larcenny	transcrip	jurist	31._____
32.	petition	tenancy	agenda	insurance	32._____
33.	superfical	premise	morgaged	maintainance	33._____
34.	testamony	publically	installment	possessed	34._____
35.	escrow	decree	eviction	miscelaneous	35._____
36.	securitys	abeyance	adhere	corporate	36._____
37.	kaleidoscope	anesthesia	vermilion	tafetta	37._____
38.	congruant	barrenness	plebescite	vigilance	38._____
39.	picnicing	promisory	resevoir	omission	39._____
40.	supersede	banister	wholly	seize	40._____

KEY (CORRECT ANSWERS)

1.	C	11.	A	21.	D	31.	B
2.	C	12.	B	22.	B	32.	D
3.	D	13.	A	23.	D	33.	C
4.	A	14.	D	24.	B	34.	B
5.	C	15.	A	25.	A	35.	A
6.	A	16.	C	26.	D	36.	A
7.	B	17.	B	27.	B	37.	A
8.	A	18.	A	28.	C	38.	B
9.	D	19.	C	29.	D	39.	C
10.	C	20.	B	30.	A	40.	D

———

PREPARING WRITTEN MATERIAL

EXAMINATION SECTION
TEST 1

DIRECTIONS: The sentences numbered 1 to 10 deal with some phase of police activity. They may be classified most appropriately under one of the following four categories:

A. *Faulty* because of incorrect grammar
B. *Faulty* because of incorrect punctuation
C. *Faulty* because of incorrect use of a word
D. *Correct*

Examine each sentence carefully. Then, in the correspondingly numbered space on the right, print the capital letter preceding the option which is the best of the four suggested above.

(All incorrect sentences contain only one type of error. Consider a sentence correct if it contains none of the types of errors mentioned, even though there may be other correct ways of expressing the same thought.)

1. The Department Medal of Honor is awarded to a member of the Police Force who distinguishes himself inconspicuously in the line of police duty by the performance of an act of gallantry.   1._____

2. Members of the Detective Division are charged with: the prevention of crime, the detection and arrest of criminals, and the recovery of lost or stolen property.   2._____

3. Detectives are selected from the uniformed patrol forces after they have indicated by conduct, aptitude, and performance that they are qualified for the more intricate duties of a detective.   3._____

4. The patrolman, pursuing his assailant, exchanged shots with the gunman and immortally wounded him as he fled into a nearby building.   4._____

5. The members of the Traffic Division has to enforce the Vehicle and Traffic Law, the Traffic Regulations, and ordinances relating to vehicular and pedestrian traffic.   5._____

6. After firing a shot at the gunman, the crowd dispersed from the patrolman's line of fire.   6._____

7. The efficiency of the Missing Persons Bureau is maintained with a maximum of public personnel due to the specialized training given to its members.   7._____

8. Records of persons arrested for violations of Vehicle and Traffic Regulations are transmitted upon request to precincts, courts and other authorized agencies.   8._____

9. The arresting officer done all he could to subdue the perpetrator without physically injuring him.   9._____

10. The Deputy Commissioner is authorized to exercise all of the powers and duties of the Police Commissioner in the latter's absence.   10._____

KEY (CORRECT ANSWERS)

1. C
2. B
3. D
4. C
5. A

6. A
7. C
8. D
9. A
10. D

———

TEST 2

DIRECTIONS: Questions 1 through 4 consist of sentences concerning criminal law. Some of the sentences contain errors in English grammar or usage, punctuation, spelling or capitalization. (A sentence does not contain an error simply because it could be written in a different manner.)

Choose answer
A. if the sentence contains an error in English grammar or usage
B. if the sentence contains an error in punctuation
C. if the sentence contains an error in spelling or capitalization
D. if the sentence does not contain any errors

1. The severity of the sentence prescribed by contemporary statutes - including both the former and the revised New York Penal Laws - do not depend on what crime was intended by the offender.

1.____

2. It is generally recognized that two defects in the early law of *attempt* played a part in the birth of *burglary*: (1) immunity from prosecution for conduct short of the last act before completion of the crime, and (2) the relatively minor penalty imposed for an attempt (its being a common law misdemeanor) vis-à-vis the completed offense.

2.____

3. The first sentence of the statute is applicable to employees who enter their place of employment, invited guests, and all other persons who have an express or implied license or privilege to enter the premises.

3.____

4. Contemporary criminal codes in the United States generally divide burglary into various degrees, differentiating the categories according to place, time and other attendent circumstances.

4.____

KEY (CORRECT ANSWERS)

1. A
2. D
3. D
4. C

TEST 3

DIRECTIONS: For each of the sentences numbered 1 through 10, select from the options
given below the *MOST* applicable choice, and print the letter of the correct
answer in the space at the right.
- A. The sentence is correct
- B. The sentence contains a spelling error only
- C. The sentence contains an English grammar error only
- D. The sentence contains *both* a spelling error and an English grammar error

1. Every person in the group is going to do his share.   1._____

2. The man who we selected is new to Duke University.   2._____

3. She is the older of the four secretaries on the two staffs that are to be combined.   3._____

4. The decision has to be made between him and I.   4._____

5. One of the volunteers are too young for this complecated task, don't you think?   5._____

6. I think your idea is splindid and it will improve this report considerably.   6._____

7. Do you think this is an exagerated account of the behavior you and me observed this   7._____
morning?

8. Our supervisor has a clear idea of excelence.   8._____

9. How many occurences were verified by the observers?   9._____

10. We must complete the typing of the draft of the questionaire by noon tomorrow.   10._____

KEY (CORRECT ANSWERS)

1.	A		6.	B
2.	C		7.	D
3.	C		8.	B
4.	C		9.	B
5.	D		10.	B

———

TEST 4

DIRECTIONS: Questions 1 through 3 are based on the following paragraph, which consists of three numbered sentences.

Edit each sentence to insure clarity of meaning and correctness of grammar without substantially changing the meaning of the sentence.

Examine each sentence and then select the option which changes the sentence to express *BEST* the thought of the sentence.

(1) Unquestionably, a knowledge of business and finance is a good advantage to audit committee members but not essential to all members. (2) Other factors also carry weight; for example, at least one member must have the ability to preside over meetings and to discuss things along constructive lines. (3) In the same way, such factors as the amount of time a member can be able to devote to duties or his rating on the score of motivation, inquisitiveness, persistence, and disposition towards critical analysis are important.

1. In the first sentence, the word   1.____

    A. "good" should be changed to "distinct"
    B. "good" should be omitted
    C. "and" should be changed to "or"
    D. "are" should be inserted between the words "but" and "not"

2. In the second sentence, the   2.____

    A. word "factors" should be changed to "things"
    B. words "preside over" should be changed to "lead at"
    C. phrase "discuss things" should be changed to "direct the discussion"
    D. word "constructive" should be changed to "noteworthy"

3. In the third sentence, the   3.____

    A. word "amount" should be changed to "period"
    B. words "amount of" should be changed to "length of"
    C. word "can" should be changed to "will"
    D. word "same" should be changed to "similar"

KEY (CORRECT ANSWERS)

1. A
2. C
3. C

––––––

TEST 5

DIRECTIONS: Each question or incomplete statement is followed by several suggested answers or completions. Select the one that *BEST* answers the question or completes the statement. Print the letter of the correct answer in the space at the right.

1. Of the following, the *MOST* acceptable close of a business letter would usually be: 1.____

   A. Cordially yours,
   C. Sincerely Yours,
   B. Respectfully Yours,
   D. Yours very truly,

2. When writing official correspondence to members of the armed forces, their titles should be used 2.____

   A. both on the envelope and in the inside address
   B. in the inside address, but not on the envelope
   C. neither on the envelope nor in the inside address
   D. on the envelope but not in the inside address

3. Which one of the following is the *LEAST* important advantage of putting the subject of a letter in the heading to the right of the address? It 3.____

   A. makes filing of the copy easier
   B. makes more space available in the body of the letter
   C. simplifies distribution of letters
   D. simplifies determination of the subject of the letter.

4. Generally, when writing a letter, the use of precise words and concise sentences is 4.____

   A. *good,* because less time will be required to write the letter
   B. *bad,* because it is most likely that the reader will think the letter is unimportant and will not respond favorably
   C. *good,* because it is likely that your desired meaning will be conveyed to the reader
   D. *bad,* because your letter will be too brief to provide adequate information

5. Of the following, it is *MOST* appropriate to use a form letter when it is necessary to answer *many* 5.____

   A. requests or inquiries from a single individual
   B. follow-up letters from individuals requesting additional information
   C. requests or inquiries about a single subject
   D. complaints from individuals that they have been unable to obtain various types of information

KEY (CORRECT ANSWERS)

1. D
2. A
3. B
4. C
5. C

———

TEST 6

DIRECTIONS: Each question or incomplete statement is followed by several suggested answers or completions. Select the one that *BEST* answers the question or completes the statement. Print the letter of the correct answer in the space at the right

1. The one of the following sentences which is *LEAST* acceptable from the viewpoint of correct usage is: 1._____

   A. The police thought the fugitive to be him.
   B. The criminals set a trap for whoever would fall into it.
   C. It is ten years ago since the fugitive fled from the city.
   D. The lecturer argued that criminals are usually cowards.
   E. The police removed four bucketfuls of earth from the scene of the crime.

2. The one of the following sentences which is *LEAST* acceptable from the viewpoint of correct usage is: 2._____

   A. The patrolman scrutinized the report with great care.
   B. Approaching the victim of the assault, two bruises were noticed by the patrolman.
   C. As soon as I had broken down the door, I stepped into the room.
   D. I observed the accused loitering near the building, which was closed at the time.
   E. The storekeeper complained that his neighbor was guilty of violating a local ordinance.

3. The one of the following sentences which is *LEAST* acceptable from the viewpoint of correct usage is: 3._____

   A. I realized immediately that he intended to assault the woman, so I disarmed him.
   B. It was apparent that Mr. Smith's explanation contained many inconsistencies.
   C. Despite the slippery condition of the street, he managed to stop the vehicle before injuring the child.
   D. Not a single one of them wish, despite the damage to property, to make a formal complaint.
   E. The body was found lying on the floor.

———————

KEY (CORRECT ANSWERS)

1. C
2. B
3. D

PREPARING WRITTEN MATERIAL

EXAMINATION SECTION
TEST 1

DIRECTIONS: Each question or incomplete statement is followed by several suggested answers or completions. Select the one that BEST answers the question or completes the statement. *PRINT THE LETTER OF THE CORRECT ANSWER IN THE SPACE AT THE RIGHT.*

Questions 1-4.

DIRECTIONS: Questions 1 through 4 each consist of a sentence which may or may not be an example of good English. The underlined parts of each sentence may be correct or incorrect. Examine each sentence, considering grammar, punctuation, spelling, and capitalization. If the English usage in the underlined parts of the sentence given is better than any of the changes in the underlined words suggested in options B, C, or D, choose option A. If the changes in the underlined words suggested in options B, C, or D would make the sentence correct, choose the correct option. Do not choose an option that will change the meaning of the sentence.

1. This <u>Fall</u>, the office will be closed on <u>Columbus Day, October</u> 9th.   1.____

    A. Correct as is
    B. fall...Columbus Day, October
    C. Fall...columbus day, October
    D. fall...Columbus Day, October

2. There <u>weren't no</u> paper in the supply closet.   2.____

    A. Correct as is   B. weren't any
    C. wasn't any   D. wasn't no

3. The <u>alphabet, or A to Z sequence are</u> the basis of most filing systems.   3.____

    A. Correct as is
    B. alphabet, or A to Z sequence, is
    C. alphabet, or A to Z sequence, are
    D. alphabet, or A too Z sequence, is

4. The Office Aide checked the <u>register and finding</u> the date of the meeting.   4.____

    A. Correct as is   B. regaster and finding
    C. register and found   D. regaster and found

Questions 5-10.

DIRECTIONS: Questions 5 through 10 consist of sentences which contain examples of correct or incorrect English usage. Examine each sentence with reference to grammar, spelling, punctuation, and capitalization. Choose one of the following options that would be BEST for correct English usage:

A. The sentence is correct
B. There is one mistake
C. There are two mistakes
D. There are three mistakes

5. Mrs. Fitzgerald came to the 59th Precinct to retreive her property which were stolen earlier in the week.

5.____

6. The two officer's responded to the call, only to find that the perpatrator and the victim have left the scene.

6.____

7. Mr. Coleman called the 61st Precinct to report that, upon arriving at his store, he discovered that there was a large hole in the wall and that three boxes of radios were missing.

7.____

8. The Administrative Leiutenant of the 62nd Precinct held a meeting which was attended by all the civilians, assigned to the Precinct.

8.____

9. Three days after the robbery occured the detective apprahended two suspects and recovered the stolen items.

9.____

10. The Community Affairs Officer of the 64th Precinct is the liaison between the Precinct and the community; he works closely with various community organizations, and elected officials.

10.____

Questions 11-18.

DIRECTIONS: Questions 11 through 18 are to be answered on the basis of the following paragraph, which contains some deliberate errors in spelling and/or grammar and/or punctuation. Each line of the paragraph is preceded by a number. There are 9 lines and 9 numbers.

Line No.	Paragraph Line
1	The protection of life and proporty are, one of
2	the oldest and most important functions of a city.
3	New York city has it's own full-time police Agency.
4	The police Department has the power an it shall
5	be there duty to preserve the Public piece,
6	prevent crime detect and arrest offenders, supress
7	riots, protect the rites of persons and property, etc.
8	The maintainance of sound relations with the community they
9	serve is an important function of law enforcement officers

11. How many errors are contained in line one?

11.____

    A. One   B. Two   C. Three   D. None

12. How many errors are contained in line two?

12.____

    A. One   B. Two   C. Three   D. None

13. How many errors are contained in line three?

13.____

    A. One   B. Two   C. Three   D. None

14. How many errors are contained in line four?   14.____

    A. One   B. Two   C. Three   D. None

15. How many errors are contained in line five?   15.____

    A. One   B. Two   C. Three   D. None

16. How many errors are contained in line six?   16.____

    A. One   B. Two   C. Three   D. None

17. How many errors are contained in line seven?   17.____

    A. One   B. Two   C. Three   D. None

18. How many errors are contained in line eight?   18.____

    A. One   B. Two   C. Three   D. None

19. In the sentence, *The candidate wants to file his application for preference before it is too*   19.____
late, the word *before* is used as a(n)

    A. preposition   B. subordinating conjunction
    C. pronoun   D. adverb

20. The one of the following sentences which is grammatically PREFERABLE to the others   20.____
is:

    A. Our engineers will go over your blueprints so that you may have no problems in construction.
    B. For a long time he had been arguing that we, not he, are to blame for the confusion.
    C. I worked on this automobile for two hours and still cannot find out what is wrong with it.
    D. Accustomed to all kinds of hardships, fatigue seldom bothers veteran policemen.

KEY (CORRECT ANSWERS)

1.	A	11.	C
2.	C	12.	D
3.	B	13.	C
4.	C	14.	B
5.	C	15.	C
6.	D	16.	B
7.	A	17.	A
8.	C	18.	A
9.	C	19.	B
10.	B	20.	A

TEST 2

DIRECTIONS: Each question or incomplete statement is followed by several suggested answers or completions. Select the one that BEST answers the question or completes the statement. *PRINT THE LETTER OF THE CORRECT ANSWER IN THE SPACE AT THE RIGHT.*

1. The plural of   1.____

   A. turkey is turkies
   B. cargo is cargoes
   C. bankruptcy is bankruptcys
   D. son-in-law is son-in-laws

2. The abbreviation *viz.* means MOST NEARLY   2.____

   A. namely   B. for example
   C. the following   D. see

3. In the sentence, *A man in a light-grey suit waited thirty-five minutes in the ante-room for*   3.____
   the all-important document, the word IMPROPERLY hyphenated is

   A. light-grey   B. thirty-five
   C. ante-room   D. all-important

4. The MOST accurate of the following sentences is: 4.____

   A. The commissioner, as well as his deputy and various bureau heads, were present.
   B. A new organization of employers and employees have been formed.
   C. One or the other of these men have been selected.
   D. The number of pages in the book is enough to discourage a reader.

5. The MOST accurate of the following sentences is: 5.____

   A. Between you and me, I think he is the better man.
   B. He was believed to be me.
   C. Is it us that you wish to see?
   D. The winners are him and her.

Questions 6-13.

DIRECTIONS: The sentences numbered 6 through 13 deal with some phase of police activity. They may be classified most appropriately under one of the following four categories.
   A. Faulty because of incorrect grammar
   B. Faulty because of incorrect punctuation
   C. Faulty because of incorrect use of a word
   D. Correct

Examine each sentence carefully. Then, in the space at the right, print the capital letter preceding the option which is the BEST of the four suggested above. All incorrect sentences contain only one type of error. Consider a sentence correct if it contains none of the types of errors mentioned, even though there may be other correct ways of expressing the same thought.

6. The Department Medal of Honor is awarded to a member of the Police Force who distinguishes himself inconspicuously in the line of police duty by the performance of an act of gallantry.   6.____

7. Members of the Detective Division are charged with the prevention of crime, the detection and arrest of criminals and the recovery of lost or stolen property.   7.____

8. Detectives are selected from the uniformed patrol forces after they have indicated by conduct, aptitude and performance that they are qualified for the more intricate duties of a detective.   8.____

9. The patrolman, pursuing his assailant, exchanged shots with the gunman and immortally wounded him as he fled into a nearby building.   9.____

10. The members of the Traffic Division has to enforce the Vehicle and Traffic Law, the Traffic Regulations and ordinances relating to vehicular and pedestrian traffic.   10.____

11. After firing a shot at the gunman, the crowd dispersed from the patrolman's line of fire.   11.____

12. The efficiency of the Missing Persons Bureau is maintained with a maximum of public personnel due to the specialized training given to its members.   12.____

13. Records of persons arrested for violations of Vehicle and Traffic Regulations are transmitted upon request to precincts, courts and other authorized agencies.   13.____

14. Following are two sentences which may or may not be written in correct English: 14.____
    I. Two clients assaulted the officer.
    II. The van is illegally parked.
Which one of the following statements is CORRECT?

    A. Only Sentence I is written in correct English.
    B. Only Sentence II is written in correct English.
    C. Sentences I and II are both written in correct English.
    D. Neither Sentence I nor Sentence II is written in correct English.

15. Following are two sentences which may or may not be written in correct English: 15.____
    I. Security Officer Rollo escorted the visitor to the patrolroom.
    II. Two entry were made in the facility logbook.
Which one of the following statements is CORRECT?

    A. Only Sentence I is written in correct English.
    B. Only Sentence II is written in correct English.
    C. Sentences I and II are both written in correct English.
    D. Neither Sentence I nor Sentence II is written in correct English.

16. Following are two sentences which may or may not be written in correct English: 16.____
    I. Officer McElroy putted out a small fire in the wastepaper basket.
    II. Special Officer Janssen told the visitor where he could obtained a pass.
Which one of the following statements is CORRECT?

    A. Only Sentence I is written in correct English.
    B. Only Sentence II is written in correct English.
    C. Sentences I and II are both written in correct English.
    D. Neither Sentence I nor Sentence II is written in correct English.

17. Following are two sentences which may or may not be written in correct English: 17.____

    I. Security Officer Warren observed a broken window while he was on his post in Hallway C.

    II. The worker reported that two typewriters had been stoled from the office.

Which one of the following statements is CORRECT?

    A. Only Sentence I is written in correct English.
    B. Only Sentence II is written in correct English.
    C. Sentences I and II are both written in correct English.
    D. Neither Sentence I nor Sentence II is written in correct English.

18. Following are two sentences which may or may not be written in correct English: 18.____

    I. Special Officer Cleveland was attempting to calm an emotionally disturbed visitor.

    II. The visitor did not stops crying and calling for his wife.

Which one of the following statements is CORRECT?

    A. Only Sentence I is written in correct English.
    B. Only Sentence II is written in correct English.
    C. Sentences I and II are both written in correct English.
    D. Neither Sentence I nor Sentence II is written in correct English.

19. Following are two sentences that may or may not be written in correct English: 19.____

    I. While on patrol, I observes a vagrant loitering near the drug dispensary.

    II. I escorted the vagrant out of the building and off the premises.

Which one of the following statements is CORRECT?

    A. Only Sentence I is written in correct English.
    B. Only Sentence II is written in correct English.
    C. Sentences I and II are both written in correct English.
    D. Neither Sentence I nor Sentence II is written in correct English.

20. Following are two sentences which may or may not be written in correct English: 20.____

    I. At 4:00 P.M., Sergeant Raymond told me to evacuate the waiting area immediately due to a bomb threat.

    II. Some of the clients did not want to leave the building.

Which one of the following statements is CORRECT?

    A. Only Sentence I is written in correct English.
    B. Only Sentence II is written in correct English.
    C. Sentences I and II are both written in correct English.
    D. Neither Sentence I nor Sentence II is written in correct English.

KEY (CORRECT ANSWERS)

1.	B	11.	A
2.	A	12.	C
3.	C	13.	D
4.	D	14.	C
5.	A	15.	A
6.	C	16.	D
7.	B	17.	A
8.	D	18.	A
9.	C	19.	B
10.	A	20.	C

PREPARING WRITTEN MATERIAL

EXAMINATION SECTION
TEST 1

DIRECTIONS: Each question or incomplete statement is followed by several suggested answers or completions. Select the one that BEST answers the question or completes the statement. *PRINT THE LETTER OF THE CORRECT ANSWER IN THE SPACE AT THE RIGHT.*

1. The one of the following sentences which is LEAST acceptable from the viewpoint of correct usage is: 1._____

    A. The police thought the fugitive to be him.
    B. The criminals set a trap for whoever would fall into it.
    C. It is ten years ago since the fugitive fled from the city.
    D. The lecturer argued that criminals are usually cowards.
    E. The police removed four bucketfuls of earth from the scene of the crime.

2. The one of the following sentences which is LEAST acceptable from the viewpoint of correct usage is: 2._____

    A. The patrolman scrutinized the report with great care.
    B. Approaching the victim of the assault, two bruises were noticed by the patrolman.
    C. As soon as I had broken down the door, I stepped into the room.
    D. I observed the accused loitering near the building, which was closed at the time.
    E. The storekeeper complained that his neighbor was guilty of violating a local ordinance.

3. The one of the following sentences which is LEAST acceptable from the viewpoint of correct usage is: 3._____

    A. I realized immediately that he intended to assault the woman, so I disarmed him.
    B. It was apparent that Mr. Smith's explanation contained many inconsistencies.
    C. Despite the slippery condition of the street, he managed to stop the vehicle before injuring the child.
    D. Not a single one of them wish, despite the damage to property, to make a formal complaint.
    E. The body was found lying on the floor.

4. The one of the following sentences which contains NO error in usage is: 4._____

    A. After the robbers left, the proprietor stood tied in his chair for about two hours before help arrived.
    B. In the cellar I found the watchmans' hat and coat.
    C. The persons living in adjacent apartments stated that they had heard no unusual noises.
    D. Neither a knife or any firearms were found in the room.
    E. Walking down the street, the shouting of the crowd indicated that something was wrong.

5. The one of the following sentences which contains NO error in usage is: 5.____

   A. The policeman lay a firm hand on the suspect's shoulder.
   B. It is true that neither strength nor agility are the most important requirement for a good patrolman.
   C. Good citizens constantly strive to do more than merely comply the restraints imposed by society.
   D. No decision was made as to whom the prize should be awarded.
   E. Twenty years is considered a severe sentence for a felony.

6. Which of the following is NOT expressed in standard English usage?   6.____

   A. The victim reached a pay-phone booth and manages to call police headquarters.
   B. By the time the call was received, the assailant had left the scene.
   C. The victim has been a respected member of the community for the past eleven years.
   D. Although the lighting was bad and the shadows were deep, the storekeeper caught sight of the attacker.
   E. Additional street lights have since been installed, and the patrols have been strengthened.

7. Which of the following is NOT expressed in standard English usage?   7.____

   A. The judge upheld the attorney's right to question the witness about the missing glove.
   B. To be absolutely fair to all parties is the jury's chief responsibility.
   C. Having finished the report, a loud noise in the next room startled the sergeant.
   D. The witness obviously enjoyed having played a part in the proceedings.
   E. The sergeant planned to assign the case to whoever arrived first.

8. In which of the following is a word misused?   8.____

   A. As a matter of principle, the captain insisted that the suspect's partner be brought for questioning.
   B. The principle suspect had been detained at the station house for most of the day.
   C. The principal in the crime had no previous criminal record, but his closest associate had been convicted of felonies on two occasions.
   D. The interest payments had been made promptly, but the firm had been drawing upon the principal for these payments.
   E. The accused insisted that his high school principal would furnish him a character reference.

9. Which of the following statements is ambiguous?   9.____

   A. Mr. Sullivan explained why Mr. Johnson had been dismissed from his job.
   B. The storekeeper told the patrolman he had made a mistake.
   C. After waiting three hours, the patients in the doctor's office were sent home.
   D. The janitor's duties were to maintain the building in good shape and to answer tenants' complaints.
   E. The speed limit should, in my opinion, be raised to sixty miles an hour on that stretch of road.

10. In which of the following is the punctuation or capitalization faulty?   10.____

    A. The accident occurred at an intersection in the Kew Gardens section of Queens, near the bus stop.
    B. The sedan, not the convertible, was struck in the side.
    C. Before any of the patrolmen had left the police car received an important message from headquarters.
    D. The dog that had been stolen was returned to his master, John Dempsey, who lived in East Village.
    E. The letter had been sent to 12 Hillside Terrace, Rutland, Vermont 05701.

Questions 11-25.

DIRECTIONS: Questions 11 through 25 are to be answered in accordance with correct English usage; that is, standard English rather than nonstandard or substandard. Nonstandard and substandard English includes words or expressions usually classified as slang, dialect, illiterate, etc., which are not generally accepted as correct in current written communication. Standard English also requires clarity, proper punctuation and capitalization and appropriate use of words. Write the letter of the sentence NOT expressed in standard English usage in the space at the right.

11.   A. There were three witnesses to the accident.   11.____
    B. At least three witnesses were found to testify for the plaintiff.
    C. Three of the witnesses who took the stand was uncertain about the defendant's competence to drive.
    D. Only three witnesses came forward to testify for the plaintiff.
    E. The three witnesses to the accident were pedestrians.

12.   A. The driver had obviously drunk too many martinis before leaving for home.   12.____
    B. The boy who drowned had swum in these same waters many times before.
    C. The petty thief had stolen a bicycle from a private driveway before he was apprehended.
    D. The detectives had brung in the heroin shipment they intercepted.
    E. The passengers had never ridden in a converted bus before.

13.   A. Between you and me, the new platoon plan sounds like a good idea.   13.____
    B. Money from an aunt's estate was left to his wife and he.
    C. He and I were assigned to the same patrol for the first time in two months.
    D. Either you or he should check the front door of that store.
    E. The captain himself was not sure of the witness's reliability.

14.   A. The alarm had scarcely begun to ring when the explosion occurred.   14.____
    B. Before the firemen arrived on the scene, the second story had been destroyed.
    C. Because of the dense smoke and heat, the firemen could hardly approach the now-blazing structure.
    D. According to the patrolman's report, there wasn't nobody in the store when the explosion occurred.
    E. The sergeant's suggestion was not at all unsound, but no one agreed with him.

15. A. The driver and the passenger they were both found to be intoxicated.   15._____
     B. The driver and the passenger talked slowly and not too clearly.
     C. Neither the driver nor his passengers were able to give a coherent account of the accident.
     D. In a corner of the room sat the passenger, quietly dozing.
     E. The driver finally told a strange and unbelievable story, which the passenger contradicted.

16. A. Under the circumstances I decided not to continue my examination of the premises.   16._____
     B. There are many difficulties now not comparable with those existing in 1960.
     C. Friends of the accused were heard to announce that the witness had better been away on the day of the trial.
     D. The two criminals escaped in the confusion that followed the explosion.
     E. The aged man was struck by the considerateness of the patrolman's offer.

17. A. An assemblage of miscellaneous weapons lay on the table.   17._____
     B. Ample opportunities were given to the defendant to obtain counsel.
     C. The speaker often alluded to his past experience with youthful offenders in the armed forces.
     D. The sudden appearance of the truck aroused my suspicions.
     E. Her studying had a good affect on her grades in high school.

18. A. He sat down in the theater and began to watch the movie.   18._____
     B. The girl had ridden horses since she was four years old.
     C. Application was made on behalf of the prosecutor to cite the witness for contempt.
     D. The bank robber, with his two accomplices, were caught in the act.
     E. His story is simply not credible.

19. A. The angry boy said that he did not like those kind of friends.   19._____
     B. The merchant's financial condition was so precarious that he felt he must avail himself of any offer of assistance.
     C. He is apt to promise more than he can perform.
     D. Looking at the messy kitchen, the housewife felt like crying.
     E. A clerk was left in charge of the stolen property.

20. A. His wounds were aggravated by prolonged exposure to sub-freezing temperatures.   20._____
     B. The prosecutor remarked that the witness was not averse to changing his story each time he was interviewed.
     C. The crime pattern indicated that the burglars were adapt in the handling of explosives.
     D. His rigid adherence to a fixed plan brought him into renewed conflict with his subordinates.
     E. He had anticipated that the sentence would be delivered by noon.

21.   A. The whole arraignment procedure is badly in need of revision.   21.____
     B. After his glasses were broken in the fight, he would of gone to the optometrist if he could.
     C. Neither Tom nor Jack brought his lunch to work.
     D. He stood aside until the quarrel was over.
     E. A statement in the psychiatrist's report disclosed that the probationer vowed to have his revenge.

22.   A. His fiery and intemperate speech to the striking employees fatally affected any   22.____
       chance of a future reconciliation.
     B. The wording of the statute has been variously construed.
     C. The defendant's attorney, speaking in the courtroom, called the official a demagogue who contempuously disregarded the judge's orders.
     D. The baseball game is likely to be the most exciting one this year.
     E. The mother divided the cookies among her two children.

23.   A. There was only a bed and a dresser in the dingy room.   23.____
     B. John is one of the few students that have protested the new rule.
     C. It cannot be argued that the child's testimony is negligible; it is, on the contrary, of the greatest importance.
     D. The basic criterion for clearance was so general that officials resolved any doubts in favor of dismissal.
     E. Having just returned from a long vacation, the officer found the city unbearably hot.

24.   A. The librarian ought to give more help to small children.   24.____
     B. The small boy was criticized by the teacher because he often wrote careless.
     C. It was generally doubted whether the women would permit the use of her apartment for intelligence operations.
     D. The probationer acts differently every time the officer visits him.
     E. Each of the newly appointed officers has 12 years of service.

25.   A. The North is the most industrialized region in the country.   25.____
     B. L. Patrick Gray 3d, the bureau's acting director, stated that, while "rehabilitation is fine" for some convicted criminals, "it is a useless gesture for those who resist every such effort."
     C. Careless driving, faulty mechanism, narrow or badly kept roads all play their part in causing accidents.
     D. The childrens' books were left in the bus.
     E. It was a matter of internal security; consequently, he felt no inclination to rescind his previous order.

KEY (CORRECT ANSWERS)

1. C	11. C
2. B	12. D
3. D	13. B
4. C	14. D
5. E	15. A
6. A	16. C
7. C	17. E
8. B	18. D
9. B	19. A
10. C	20. C

21. B
22. E
23. B
24. B
25. D

TEST 2

DIRECTIONS: Each question or incomplete statement is followed by several suggested answers or completions. Select the one that BEST answers the question or completes the statement. *PRINT THE LETTER OF THE CORRECT ANSWER IN THE SPACE AT THE RIGHT.*

Questions 1-6.

DIRECTIONS: Each of Questions 1 through 6 consists of a statement which contains a word (one of those underlined) that is either incorrectly used because it is not in keeping with the meaning the quotation is evidently intended to convey, or is misspelled. There is only one INCORRECT word in each quotation. Of the four underlined words, determine if the first one should be replaced by the word lettered A, the second replaced by the word lettered B, the third replaced by the word lettered C, or the fourth replaced by the word lettered D. *PRINT THE LETTER OF THE REPLACEMENT WORD YOU HAVE SELECTED IN THE SPACE AT THE RIGHT.*

1. Whether one depends on <u>fluorescent</u> or artificial light or both, adequate <u>standards</u> should be <u>maintained</u> by means of <u>systematic</u> tests.   1._____

    A. natural   B. safeguards
    C. established   D. routine

2. A police officer has to be <u>prepared</u> to assume his <u>knowledge</u> as a social <u>scientist</u> in the <u>community</u>.   2._____

    A. forced   B. role
    C. philosopher   D. street

3. It is <u>practically</u> impossible to <u>indicate</u> whether a sentence is <u>too</u> long simply by <u>measuring</u> its length.   3._____

    A. almost   B. tell   C. very   D. guessing

4. Strong <u>leaders</u> are <u>required</u> to organize a community for delinquency prevention and for <u>dissemination</u> of organized <u>crime</u> and drug addiction.   4._____

    A. tactics   B. important   C. control   D. meetings

5. The <u>demonstrators</u> who were taken to the Criminal Courts building in <u>Manhattan</u> (because it was large enough to <u>accommodate</u> them), contended that the arrests were <u>unwarrented.</u>   5._____

    A. demonstraters   B. Manhatten
    C. accomodate   D. unwarranted

6. They were <u>guaranteed</u> a calm <u>atmosphere</u>, free from <u>harrassment</u>, which would be conducive to quiet consideration of the <u>indictments</u>.   6._____

    A. guarenteed   B. atmospher
    C. harassment   D. inditements

Questions 7-11.

DIRECTIONS: Each of Questions 7 through 11 consists of a statement containing four words in capital letters. One of these words in capital letters is not in keeping with the meaning which the statement is evidently intended to carry. The four words in capital letters in each statement are reprinted after the statement. Print the capital letter preceding the one of the four words which does MOST to spoil the true meaning of the statement in the space at the right.

7. Retirement and pension systems are essential not only to provide employees with a means of support in the future, but also to prevent longevity and CHARITABLE considerations from UPSETTING the PROMOTIONAL opportunities for RETIRED members of the career service.

   7.____

    A. charitable   B. upsetting
    C. promotional   D. retired

8. Within each major DIVISION in a properly set up public or private organization, provision is made so that each NECESSARY activity is CARED for and lines of authority and responsibility are clear-cut and INFINITE.

   8.____

    A. division   B. necessary   C. cared   D. infinite

9. In public service, the scale of salaries paid must be INCIDENTAL to the services rendered, with due CONSIDERATION for the attraction of the desired MANPOWER and for the maintenance of a standard of living COMMENSURATE with the work to be performed.

   9.____

    A. incidental   B. consideration
    C. manpower   D. commensurate

10. An understanding of the AIMS of an organization by the staff will AID greatly in increasing the DEMAND of the correspondence work of the office, and will to a large extent DETERMINE the nature of the correspondence.

   10.____

    A. aims   B. aid   C. demand   D. determine

11. BECAUSE the Civil Service Commission strongly feels that the MERIT system is a key factor in the MAINTENANCE of democratic government, it has adopted as one of its major DEFENSES the progressive democratization of its own procedures in dealing with candidates for positions in the public service.

   11.____

    A. Because   B. merit
    C. maintenance   D. defenses

Questions 12-14.

DIRECTIONS: Questions 12 through 14 consist of one sentence each. Each sentence contains an incorrectly used word. First, decide which is the incorrectly used word. Then, from among the options given, decide which word, when substituted for the incorrectly used word, makes the meaning of the sentence clear.

EXAMPLE:
The U.S. national income exhibits a pattern of long term deflection.
A. reflection   B. subjection
C. rejoicing   D. growth

The word *deflection* in the sentence does not convey the meaning the sentence evidently intended to convey. The word *growth* (Answer D), when substituted for the word *deflection,* makes the meaning of the sentence clear. Accordingly, the answer to the question is D.

12. The study commissioned by the joint committee fell compassionately short of the mark and would have to be redone.   12.____

  A. successfully   B. insignificantly
  C. experimentally   D. woefully

13. He will not idly exploit any violation of the provisions of the order.   13.____

  A. tolerate   B. refuse   C. construe   D. guard

14. The defendant refused to be virile and bitterly protested service.   14.____

  A. irked   B. feasible   C. docile   D. credible

Questions 15-25.

DIRECTIONS: Questions 15 through 25 consist of short paragraphs. Each paragraph contains one word which is INCORRECTLY used because it is NOT in keeping with the meaning of the paragraph. Find the word in each paragraph which is INCORRECTLY used and then select as the answer the suggested word which should be substituted for the incorrectly used word.

SAMPLE QUESTION:
In determining who is to do the work in your unit, you will have to decide just who does what from day to day. One of your lowest responsibilities is to assign work so that everybody gets a fair share and that everyone can do his part well.
  A. new   B. old   C. important   D. performance

EXPLANATION:
The word which is NOT in keeping with the meaning of the paragraph is *lowest.* This is the INCORRECTLY used word. The suggested word *important* would be in keeping with the meaning of the paragraph and should be substituted for *lowest.* Therefore, the CORRECT answer is choice C.

15. If really good practice in the elimination of preventable injuries is to be achieved and held in any establishment, top management must refuse full and definite responsibility and must apply a good share of its attention to the task.   15.____

  A. accept   B. avoidable   C. duties   D. problem

16. Recording the human face for identification is by no means the only service performed by the camera in the field of investigation. When the trial of any issue takes place, a word picture is sought to be distorted to the court of incidents, occurrences, or events which are in dispute.   16.____

A. appeals   B. description
C. portrayed   D. deranged

17. In the collection of physical evidence, it cannot be emphasized too strongly that a hap-   17.____
hazard systematic search at the scene of the crime is vital. Nothing must be overlooked.
Often the only leads in a case will come from the results of this search.

     A. important   B. investigation
     C. proof   D. thorough

18. If an investigator has reason to suspect that the witness is mentally stable, or a habitual   18.____
drunkard, he should leave no stone unturned in his investigation to determine if the witness was under the influence of liquor or drugs, or was mentally unbalanced either at the
time of the occurrence to which he testified or at the time of the trial.

     A. accused   B. clue   C. deranged   D. question

19. The use of records is a valuable step in crime investigation and is the main reason every   19.____
department should maintain accurate reports. Crimes are not committed through the use
of departmental records alone but from the use of all records, of almost every type, wherever they may be found and whenever they give any incidental information regarding the
criminal.

     A. accidental   B. necessary
     C. reported   D. solved

20. In the years since passage of the Harrison Narcotic Act of 1914, making the possession   20.____
of opium amphetamines illegal in most circumstances, drug use has become a subject of
considerable scientific interest and investigation. There is at present a voluminous litera-
ture on drug use of various kinds.

     A. ingestion   B. derivatives
     C. addiction   D. opiates

21. Of course, the fact that criminal laws are extremely patterned in definition does not mean   21.____
that the majority of persons who violate them are dealt with as criminals. Quite the contrary, for a great many forbidden acts are voluntarily engaged in within situations of pri-
vacy and go unobserved and unreported.

     A. symbolic   B. casual
     C. scientific   D. broad-gauged

22. The most punitive way to study punishment is to focus attention on the pattern of punitive   22.____
action: to study how a penalty is applied, to study what is done to or taken from an
offender.

     A. characteristic   B. degrading
     C. objective   D. distinguished

23. The most common forms of punishment in times past have been death, physical torture,   23.____
mutilation, branding, public humiliation, fines, forfeits of property, banishment, transportation, and imprisonment. Although this list is by no means differentiated, practically every
form of punishment has had several variations and applications.

     A. specific   B. simple
     C. exhaustive   D. characteristic

24. There is another important line of inference between ordinary and professional criminals, and that is the source from which they are recruited. The professional criminal seems to be drawn from legitimate employment and, in many instances, from parallel vocations or pursuits.

24.____

   A. demarcation
   C. superiority
   B. justification
   D. reference

25. He took the position that the success of the program was insidious on getting additional revenue.

25.____

   A. reputed
   C. failure
   B. contingent
   D. indeterminate

KEY (CORRECT ANSWERS)

1.	A	11.	D
2.	B	12.	D
3.	B	13.	A
4.	C	14.	C
5.	D	15.	A
6.	C	16.	C
7.	D	17.	D
8.	D	18.	C
9.	A	19.	D
10.	C	20.	B

21.	D
22.	C
23.	C
24.	A
25.	B

TEST 3

DIRECTIONS: Each question or incomplete statement is followed by several suggested answers or completions. Select the one that BEST answers the question or completes the statement. *PRINT THE LETTER OF THE CORRECT ANSWER IN THE SPACE AT THE RIGHT.*

Questions 1-5.

DIRECTIONS: Question 1 through 5 are to be answered on the basis of the following:

You are a supervising officer in an investigative unit. Earlier in the day, you directed Detectives Tom Dixon and Sal Mayo to investigate a reported assault and robbery in a liquor store within your area of jurisdiction.

Detective Dixon has submitted to you a preliminary investigative report containing the following information:

- At 1630 hours on 2/20, arrived at Joe's Liquor Store at 350 SW Avenue with Detective Mayo to investigate A & R.
- At store interviewed Rob Ladd, store manager, who stated that he and Joe Brown (store owner) had been stuck up about ten minutes prior to our arrival.
- Ladd described the robbers as male whites in their late teens or early twenties. Further stated that one of the robbers displayed what appeared to be an automatic pistol as he entered the store, and said, *Give us the money or we'll kill you.* Ladd stated that Brown then reached under the counter where he kept a loaded .38 caliber pistol. Several shots followed, and Ladd threw himself to the floor.
- The robbers fled, and Ladd didn't know if any money had been taken.
- At this point, Ladd realized that Brown was unconscious on the floor and bleeding from a head wound.
- Ambulance called by Ladd, and Brown was removed by same to General Hospital.
- Personally interviewed John White, 382 Dartmouth Place, who stated he was inside store at the time of occurrence. White states that he hid behind a wine display upon hearing someone say, *Give us the money.* He then heard shots and saw two young men run from the store to a yellow car parked at the curb. White was unable to further describe auto. States the taller of the two men drove the car away while the other sat on passenger side in front.
- Recovered three spent .38 caliber bullets from premises and delivered them to Crime Lab.
- To General Hospital at 1800 hours but unable to interview Brown, who was under sedation and suffering from shock and a laceration of the head.
- Alarm #12487 transmitted for car and occupants.
- Case Active.

Based solely on the contents of the preliminary investigation submitted by Detective Dixon, select one sentence from the following groups of sentences which is MOST accurate and is grammatically correct.

1. A. Both robbers were armed.   1.____
    B. Each of the robbers were described as a male white.
    C. Neither robber was armed.
    D. Mr. Ladd stated that one of the robbers was armed.

2. A. Mr. Brown fired three shots from his revolver.   2.____
    B. Mr. Brown was shot in the head by one of the robbers.
    C. Mr. Brown suffered a gunshot wound of the head during the course of the
       robbery.
    D. Mr. Brown was taken to General Hospital by ambulance.

3. A. Shots were fired after one of the robbers said, *Give us* the money or we'll kill you.   3.____
    B. After one of the robbers demanded the money from Mr. Brown, he fired a shot.
    C. The preliminary investigation indicated that although Mr. Brown did not have a
       license for the gun, he was justified in using deadly physical force.
    D. Mr. Brown was interviewed at General Hospital.

4. A. Each of the witnesses were customers in the store at the time of occurrence.   4.____
    B. Neither of the witnesses interviewed was the owner of the liquor store.
    C. Neither of the witnesses interviewed were the owner of the store.
    D. Neither of the witnesses was employed by Mr. Brown.

5. A. Mr. Brown arrived at General Hospital at about 5:00 P.M.   5.____
    B. Neither of the robbers was injured during the robbery.
    C. The robbery occurred at 3:30 P.M. on February 10.
    D. One of the witnesses called the ambulance.

Questions 6-10.

DIRECTIONS: Each of Questions 6 through 10 consists of information given in outline form
               and four sentences labelled A, B, C, and D. For each question, choose the one
               sentence which CORRECTLY expresses the information given in outline form
               and which also displays PROPER English usage.

6. Client's Name - Joanna Jones   6.____
    Number of Children - 3
    Client's Income - None
    Client's Marital Status - Single

    A. Joanna Jones is an unmarried client with three children who have no income.
    B. Joanna Jones, who is single and has no income, a client she has three children.
    C. Joanna Jones, whose three children are clients, is single and has no income.
    D. Joanna Jones, who has three children, is an unmarried client with no income.

7. Client's Name - Bertha Smith   7.____
    Number of Children - 2
    Client's Rent - $105 per month
    Number of Rooms - 4

A. Bertha Smith, a client, pays $105 per month for her four rooms with two children.
B. Client Bertha Smith has two children and pays $105 per month for four rooms.
C. Client Bertha Smith is paying $105 per month for two children with four rooms.
D. For four rooms and two children client Bertha Smith pays $105 per month.

8. Name of Employee - Cynthia Dawes
Number of Cases Assigned - 9
Date Cases were Assigned - 12/16
Number of Assigned Cases Completed - 8

A. On December 16, employee Cynthia Dawes was assigned nine cases; she has completed eight of these cases.
B. Cynthia Dawes, employee on December 16, assigned nine cases, completed eight.
C. Being employed on December 16, Cynthia Dawes completed eight of nine assigned cases.
D. Employee Cynthia Dawes, she was assigned nine cases and completed eight, on December 16.

9. Place of Audit - Broadway Center
Names of Auditors - Paul Cahn, Raymond Perez
Date of Audit - 11/20
Number of Cases Audited - 41

A. On November 20, at the Broadway Center 41 cases was audited by auditors Paul Cahn and Raymond Perez.
B. Auditors Raymond Perez and Paul Cahn has audited 41 cases at the Broadway Center on November 20.
C. At the Broadway Center, on November 20, auditors Paul Cahn and Raymond Perez audited 41 cases.
D. Auditors Paul Cahn and Raymond Perez at the Broadway Center, on November 20, is auditing 41 cases.

10. Name of Client - Barbra Levine
Client's Monthly Income - $210
Client's Monthly Expenses - $452

A. Barbra Levine is a client, her monthly income is $210 and her monthly expenses is $452.
B. Barbra Levine's monthly income is $210 and she is a client, with whose monthly expenses are $452.
C. Barbra Levine is a client whose monthly income is $210 and whose monthly expenses are $452.
D. Barbra Levine, a client, is with a monthly income which is $210 and monthly expenses which are $452.

Questions 11-13.

DIRECTIONS: Questions 11 through 13 involve several statements of fact presented in a very simple way. These statements of fact are followed by 4 choices which attempt to incorporate all of the facts into one logical sentence which is properly constructed and grammatically correct.

11.   I.   Mr. Brown was sweeping the sidewalk in front of his house.   11.____
       II.   He was sweeping it because it was dirty.
       III. He swept the refuse into the street
       IV. Police Officer Green gave him a ticket.

Which one of the following BEST presents the information given above?

    A. Because his sidewalk was dirty, Mr. Brown received a ticket from Officer Green when he swept the refuse into the street.
    B. Police Officer Green gave Mr. Brown a ticket because his sidewalk was dirty and he swept the refuse into the street.
    C. Police Officer Green gave Mr. Brown a ticket for sweeping refuse into the street because his sidewalk was dirty.
    D. Mr. Brown, who was sweeping refuse from his dirty sidewalk into the street, was given a ticket by Police Officer Green.

12.   I.   Sergeant Smith radioed for help.   12.____
       II.   The sergeant did so because the crowd was getting larger.
       III. It was 10:00 A.M. when he made his call.
       IV. Sergeant Smith was not in uniform at the time of occurrence.

Which one of the following BEST presents the information given above?

    A. Sergeant Smith, although not on duty at the time, radioed for help at 10 o'clock because the crowd was getting uglier.
    B. Although not in uniform, Sergeant Smith called for help at 10:00 A.M. because the crowd was getting uglier.
    C. Sergeant Smith radioed for help at 10:00 A.M. because the crowd was getting larger.
    D. Although he was not in uniform, Sergeant Smith radioed for help at 10:00 A.M. because the crowd was getting larger.

13.   I.   The payroll office is open on Fridays.   13.____
       II.   Paychecks are distributed from 9:00 A.M. to 12 Noon.
       III. The office is open on Fridays because that's the only day the payroll staff is available.
       IV. It is open for the specified hours in order to permit employees to cash checks at the bank during lunch hour.

The choice below which MOST clearly and accurately presents the above idea is:

    A. Because the payroll office is open on Fridays from 9:00 A.M. to 12 Noon, employees can cash their checks when the payroll staff is available.
    B. Because the payroll staff is only available on Fridays until noon, employees can cash their checks during their lunch hour.
    C. Because the payroll staff is available only on Fridays, the office is open from 9:00 A.M. to 12 Noon to allow employees to cash their checks.
    D. Because of payroll staff availability, the payroll office is open on Fridays. It is open from 9:00 A.M. to 12 Noon so that distributed paychecks can be cashed at the bank while employees are on their lunch hour.

Questions 14-16.

DIRECTIONS: In each of Questions 14 through 16, the four sentences are from a paragraph in a report. They are not in the right order. Which of the following arrangements is the BEST one?

14.   I.   An executive may answer a letter by writing his reply on the face of the letter itself instead of having a return letter typed.
      II. This procedure is efficient because it saves the executive's time, the typist's time, and saves office file space.
      III. Copying machines are used in small offices as well as large offices to save time and money in making brief replies to business letters.
      IV. A copy is made on a copying machine to go into the company files, while the original is mailed back to the sender.
      The CORRECT answer is:

      A.   I, II, IV, III   B.   I, IV, II, III
      C.   III, I, IV, II   D.   III, IV, II, I

15.   I.   Most organizations favor one of the types but always include the others to a lesser degree.
      II. However, we can detect a definite trend toward greater use of symbolic control.
      III. We suggest that our local police agencies are today primarily utilizing material control.
      IV. Control can be classified into three types: physical, material, and symbolic.
      The CORRECT answer is:

      A.   IV, II, III, I   B.   II, I, IV, III
      C.   III, IV, II, I   D.   IV, I, III, II

16.   I.   They can and do take advantage of ancient political and geographical boundaries, which often give them sanctuary from effective police activity.
      II. This country is essentially a country of small police forces, each operating independently within the limits of its jurisdiction.
      III. The boundaries that define and limit police operations do not hinder the movement of criminals, of course.
      IV. The machinery of law enforcement in America is fragmented, complicated, and frequently overlapping.
      The CORRECT answer is:

      A.   III, I, II, IV   B.   II, IV, I, III
      C.   IV, II, III, I   D.   IV, III, II, I

17.   Examine the following sentence, and then choose from below the words which should be inserted in the blank spaces to produce the best sentence.
      The unit has exceeded _____ goals and the employees are satisfied with _____ accomplishments.

      A.   their, it's   B.   it's, it's
      C.   its, there   D.   its, their

14._____

15._____

16._____

17._____

18. Examine the following sentence, and then choose from below the words which should be   18.____
inserted in the blank spaces to produce the best sentence.
Research indicates that employees who _____ no opportunity for close social relationships often find their work unsatisfying, and this _____ of satisfaction often
reflects itself in low production.

    A. have, lack   B. have, excess
    C. has, lack   D. has, excess

19. Words in a sentence must be arranged properly to make sure that the intended meaning   19.____
of the sentence is clear. The sentence below that does NOT make sense because a
clause has been separated from the word on which its meaning depends is:

    A. To be a good writer, clarity is necessary.
    B. To be a good writer, you must write clearly.
    C. You must write clearly to be a good writer.
    D. Clarity is necessary to good writing.

Questions 20-21.

DIRECTIONS: Each of Questions 20 and 21 consists of a statement which contains a word
(one of those underlined) that is either incorrectly used because it is not in
keeping with the meaning the quotation is evidently intended to convey, or is
misspelled. There is only one INCORRECT word in each quotation. Of the four
underlined words, determine if the first one should be replaced by the word lettered A, the second one replaced by the word lettered B, the third one
replaced by the word lettered C, or the fourth one replaced by the word lettered D. *PRINT THE LETTER OF THE REPLACEMENT WORD YOU HAVE
SELECTED IN THE SPACE AT THE RIGHT.*

20. The alleged killer was occasionally permitted to excercise in the corridor.   20.____

    A. alledged   B. ocasionally
    C. permited   D. exercise

21. Defense counsel stated, in affect, that their conduct was permissible under the First   21.____
Amendment.

    A. council   B. effect
    C. there   D. permissable

Question 22.

DIRECTIONS: Question 22 consists of one sentence. This sentence contains an incorrectly
used word. First, decide which is the incorrectly used word. Then, from among
the options given, decide which word, when substituted for the incorrectly used
word, makes the meaning of the sentence clear.

22. As today's violence has no single cause, so its causes have no single scheme.   22.____

    A. deference   B. cure   C. flaw   D. relevance

23. In the sentence, *A man in a light-grey suit waited thirty-five minutes in the ante-room for the all-important document,* the word IMPROPERLY hyphenated is   23._____

    A. light-grey   B. thirty-five
    C. ante-room   D. all-important

24. In the sentence, *The candidate wants to file his application for preference before it is too late,* the word *before* is used as a(n)   24._____

    A. preposition   B. subordinating conjunction
    C. pronoun   D. adverb

25. In the sentence, *The perpetrators ran from the scene,* the word *from* is a   25._____

    A. preposition   B. pronoun
    C. verb   D. conjunction

KEY (CORRECT ANSWERS)

1.	D		11.	D
2.	D		12.	D
3.	A		13.	D
4.	B		14.	C
5.	D		15.	D
6.	D		16.	C
7.	B		17.	D
8.	A		18.	A
9.	C		19.	A
10.	C		20.	D

21.	B
22.	B
23.	C
24.	B
25.	A

PREPARING WRITTEN MATERIAL

PARAGRAPH REARRANGEMENT
COMMENTARY

The sentences which follow are in scrambled order. You are to rearrange them in proper order and indicate the letter choice containing the correct answer at the space at the right.

Each group of sentences in this section is actually a paragraph presented in scrambled order. Each sentence in the group has a place in that paragraph; no sentence is to be left out. You are to read each group of sentences and decide upon the best order in which to put the sentences so as to form as well-organized paragraph.

The questions in this section measure the ability to solve a problem when all the facts relevant to its solution are not given.

More specifically, certain positions of responsibility and authority require the employee to discover connections between events sometimes, apparently, unrelated. In order to do this, the employee will find it necessary to correctly infer that unspecified events have probably occurred or are likely to occur. This ability becomes especially important when action must be taken on incomplete information.

Accordingly, these questions require competitors to choose among several suggested alternatives, each of which presents a different sequential arrangement of the events. Competitors must choose the MOST logical of the suggested sequences.

In order to do so, they may be required to draw on general knowledge to infer missing concepts or events that are essential to sequencing the given events. Competitors should be careful to infer only what is essential to the sequence. The plausibility of the wrong alternatives will always require the inclusion of unlikely events or of additional chains of events which are NOT essential to sequencing the given events.

It's very important to remember that you are looking for the best of the four possible choices, and that the best choice of all may not even be one of the answers you're given to choose from.

There is no one right way to solve these problems. Many people have found it helpful to first write out the order of the sentences, as they would have arranged them, on their scrap paper before looking at the possible answers. If their optimum answer is there, this can save them some time. If it isn't, this method can still give insight into solving the problem. Others find it most helpful to just go through each of the possible choices, contrasting each as they go along. You should use whatever method feels comfortable, and works, for you.

While most of these types of questions are not that difficult, we've added a higher percentage of the difficult type, just to give you more practice. Usually there are only one or two questions on this section that contain such subtle distinctions that you're unable to answer confidently, and you then may find yourself stuck deciding between two possible choices, neither of which you're sure about.

———

EXAMINATION SECTION
TEST 1

DIRECTIONS: Each question consists of several sentences which can be arranged in a logical sequence. For each question, select the choice which places the numbered sentences in the MOST logical sequence. *PRINT THE LETTER OF THE CORRECT ANSWER IN THE SPACE AT THE RIGHT.*

1.
   I. A body was found in the woods.
   II. A man proclaimed innocence.
   III. The owner of a gun was located.
   IV. A gun was traced.
   V. The owner of a gun was questioned.
   The CORRECT answer is:

   A. IV, III, V, II, I
   B. II, I, IV, III, V
   C. I, IV, III, V, II
   D. I, III, V, II, IV
   E. I, II, IV, III, V

   1.____

2.
   I. A man was in a hunting accident.
   II. A man fell down a flight of steps.
   III. A man lost his vision in one eye.
   IV. A man broke his leg.
   V. A man had to walk with a cane.
   The CORRECT answer is:

   A. II, IV, V, I, III
   B. IV, V, I, III, II
   C. III, I, IV, V, II
   D. I, III, V, II, IV
   E. I, III, II, IV, V

   2.____

3.
   I. A man is offered a new job.
   II. A woman is offered a new job.
   III. A man works as a waiter.
   IV. A woman works as a waitress.
   V. A woman gives notice.
   The CORRECT answer is:

   A. IV, II, V, III, I
   B. IV, II, V, I, III
   C. II, IV, V, III, I
   D. III, I, IV, II, V
   E. IV, III, II, V, I

   3.____

4.
   I. A train left the station late.
   II. A man was late for work.
   III. A man lost his job.
   IV. Many people complained because the train was late.
   V. There was a traffic jam.
   The CORRECT answer is:

   A. V, II, I, IV, III
   B. V, I, IV, II, III
   C. V, I, II, IV, III
   D. I, V, IV, II, III
   E. II, I, IV, V, III

   4.____

5. I.   The burden of proof as to each issue is determined before trial and remains upon the same party throughout the trial.
    II. The jury is at liberty to believe one witness' testimony as against a number of contradictory witnesses.
    III. In a civil case, the party bearing the burden of proof is required to prove his contention by a fair preponderance of the evidence.
    IV. However, it must be noted that a fair preponderance of evidence does not necessarily mean a greater number of witnesses.
    V.   The burden of proof is the burden which rests upon one of the parties to an action to persuade the trier of the facts, generally the jury, that a proposition he asserts is true.
    VI. If the evidence is equally balanced, or if it leaves the jury in such doubt as to be unable to decide the controversy either way, judgment must be given against the party upon whom the burden of proof rests.

The CORRECT answer is:

5.____

A. III, II, V, IV, I, VI
C. III, IV, V, I, II, VI
E. I, V, III, VI, IV, II
B. I, II, VI, V, III, IV
D. V, I, III, VI, IV, II

6. I.   If a parent is without assets and is unemployed, he cannot be convicted of the crime of non-support of a child.
    II. The term *sufficient ability* has been held to mean sufficient financial ability.
    III. It does not matter if his unemployment is by choice or unavoidable circumstances.
    IV. If he fails to take any steps at all, he may be liable to prosecution for endangering the welfare of a child.
    V.   Under the penal law, a parent is responsible for the support of his minor child only if the parent is of *sufficient ability*.
    VI. An indigent parent may meet his obligation by borrowing money or by seeking aid under the provisions of the Social Welfare Law.

The CORRECT answer is:

6.____

A. VI, I, V, III, II, IV
C. V, II, I, III, VI, IV
E. II, V, I, III, VI, IV
B. I, III, V, II, IV, VI
D. I, VI, IV, V, II, III

7. I.   Consider, for example, the case of a rabble rouser who urges a group of twenty people to go out and break the windows of a nearby factory.
    II. Therefore, the law fills the indicated gap with the crime of *inciting to riot*.
    III. A person is considered guilty of inciting to riot when he urges ten or more persons to engage in tumultuous and violent conduct of a kind likely to create public alarm.
    IV. However, if he has not obtained the cooperation of at least four people, he cannot be charged with unlawful assembly.
    V.   The charge of inciting to riot was added to the law to cover types of conduct which cannot be classified as either the crime of *riot* or the crime of *unlawful assembly*.
    VI. If he acquires the acquiescence of at least four of them, he is guilty of unlawful assembly even if the project does not materialize.

The CORRECT answer is:

7.____

A. III, V, I, VI, IV, II   B. V, I, IV, VI, II, III
C. III, IV, I, V, II, VI   D. V, I, IV, VI, III, II
E. V, III, I, VI, IV, II

8.   I.   If, however, the rebuttal evidence presents an issue of credibility, it is for the jury to   8.____
determine whether the presumption has, in fact, been destroyed.
    II.   Once sufficient evidence to the contrary is introduced, the presumption disappears from the trial.
   III.   The effect of a presumption is to place the burden upon the adversary to come
forward with evidence to rebut the presumption.
   IV.   When a presumption is overcome and ceases to exist in the case, the fact or
facts which gave rise to the presumption still remain.
    V.   Whether a presumption has been overcome is ordinarily a question for the court.
   VI.   Such information may furnish a basis for a logical inference.
The CORRECT answer is:

A. IV, VI, II, V, I, III   B. III, II, V, I, IV, VI
C. V, III, VI, IV, II, I   D. V, IV, I, II, VI, III
E. II, III, V, I, IV, VI

9.   I.   An executive may answer a letter by writing his reply on the face of the letter itself   9.____
instead of having a return letter typed.
    II.   This procedure is efficient because it saves the executive's time, the typist's time,
and saves office file space.
   III.   Copying machines are used in small offices as well as large offices to save time
and money in making brief replies to business letters.
   IV.   A copy is made on a copying machine to go into the company files, while the
original is mailed back to the sender.
The CORRECT answer is:

A. I, II, IV, III   B. I, IV, II, III
C. III, I, IV, II   D. III, IV, II, I

10.   I.   Most organizations favor one of the types but always include the others to a lesser   10.____
degree.
    II.   However, we can detect a definite trend toward greater use of symbolic control.
   III.   We suggest that our local police agencies are today primarily utilizing material
control.
   IV.   Control can be classified into three types: physical, material, and symbolic.
The CORRECT answer is:

A. IV, II, III, I   B. II, I, IV, III
C. III, IV, II, I   D. IV, I, III, II

11.   I.   Project residents had first claim to this use, followed by surrounding neighborhood   11.____
children.
    II.   By contrast, recreation space within the project's interior was found to be used
more often by both groups.
   III.   Studies of the use of project grounds in many cities showed grounds left open for
public use were neglected and unused, both by residents and by members of the
surrounding community.

IV. Project residents had clearly laid claim to the play spaces, setting up and enforcing unwritten rules for use.

V. Each group, by experience, found their activities easily disrupted by other groups, and their claim to the use of space for recreation difficult to enforce.

The CORRECT answer is:

A. IV, V, I, II, III
C. I, IV, III, II, V
B. V, II, IV, III, I
D. III, V, II, IV, I

12. I. They do not consider the problems correctable within the existing subsidy formula and social policy of accepting all eligible applicants regardless of social behavior and lifestyle.

II. A recent survey, however, indicated that tenants believe these problems correctable by local housing authorities and management within the existing financial formula.

III. Many of the problems and complaints concerning public housing management and design have created resentment between the tenant and the landlord.

IV. This same survey indicated that administrators and managers do not agree with the tenants.

The CORRECT answer is: 12.____

A. II, I, III, IV
C. III, II, IV, I
B. I, III, IV, II
D. IV, II, I, III

13. I. In single-family residences, there is usually enough distance between tenants to prevent occupants from annoying one another.

II. For example, a certain small percentage of tenant families has one or more members addicted to alcohol.

III. While managers believe in the right of individuals to live as they choose, the manager becomes concerned when the pattern of living jeopardizes others' rights.

IV. Still others turn night into day, staging lusty entertainments which carry on into the hours when most tenants are trying to sleep.

V. In apartment buildings, however, tenants live so closely together that any misbehavior can result in unpleasant living conditions.

VI. Other families engage in violent argument.

The CORRECT answer is: 13.____

A. III, II, V, IV, VI, I
C. II, V, IV, I, III, VI
B. I, V, II, VI, IV, III
D. IV, II, V, VI, III, I

14. I. Congress made the commitment explicit in the Housing Act of 1949, establishing as a national goal the realization of *a decent home and suitable environment for every American family.*

II. The result has been that the goal of decent home and suitable environment is still as far distant as ever for the disadvantaged urban family.

III. In spite of this action by Congress, federal housing programs have continued to be fragmented and grossly underfunded.

IV. The passage of the National Housing Act signalled a new federal commitment to provide housing for the nation's citizens.

The CORRECT answer is: 14.____

A. I, IV, III, II
C. IV, I, II, III
B. IV, I, III, II
D. II, IV, I, III

144

15.   I.   The greater expense does not necessarily involve *exploitation,* but it is often per-   15.____
           ceived as exploitative and unfair by those who are aware of the price differences
           involved, but unaware of operating costs.
     II.   Ghetto residents believe they are *exploited* by local merchants, and evidence
           substantiates some of these beliefs.
    III.   However, stores in low-income areas were more likely to be small independents,
           which could not achieve the economies available to supermarket chains and
           were, therefore, more likely to charge higher prices, and the customers were
           more likely to buy smaller-sized packages which are more expensive per unit of
           measure.
    IV.   A study conducted in one city showed that distinctly higher prices were charged
           for goods sold in ghetto stores than in other areas.
    The CORRECT answer is:

    A.   IV, II, I, III   B.   IV, I, III, II
    C.   II, IV, III, I   D.   II, III, IV, I

KEY (CORRECT ANSWERS)

1.	C	6.	C
2.	E	7.	A
3.	B	8.	B
4.	B	9.	C
5.	D	10.	D

11.	D
12.	C
13.	B
14.	B
15.	C

EXAMINATION SECTION
TEST 1

DIRECTIONS: Each group of sentences in this section is actually a paragraph presented in scrambled order. Each sentence in the group has a place in that paragraph; no sentence is to be left out. You are to read each group of sentences, so as to form a well-organized paragraph. Before trying to answer the questions which follow each group of sentences, jot down the correct order of the sentences. Then answer each of the questions by printing the letter of the correct answer in the space at the right. Remember that you will receive credit only for answers marked.

P. American divorce statutes derive principally from ecclesiastical law and embody certain moral concepts.

Q. Divorces are granted under such statutes only to an innocent spouse where the other spouse has been guilty of statutorily-defined misconduct.

R. All the states and territories of the United States grant divorces.

S. If, therefore, both parties are guilty, there can be no divorce.

T. The statutes of each territory and state determine the permissible grounds for the divorces granted in that territory and state.

1. Which sentence did you put after Sentence R?　　　　　　　　　　　　　　1.____

    A. P
    B. Q
    C. S
    D. T
    E. None of the above. Sentence R is last.

2. Which sentence did you put before Sentence Q?　　　　　　　　　　　　2.____

    A. P
    B. R
    C. S
    D. T
    E. None of the above. Sentence Q is first.

3. Which sentence did you put after Sentence S?　　　　　　　　　　　　3.____

    A. P
    B. Q
    C. R
    D. T
    E. None of the above. Sentence S is last.

4. Which sentence did you put last?　　　　　　　　　　　　　　　　　　4.____

    A. P　　　　　B. Q　　　　　C. R　　　　　D. S　　　　　E. T

5. Which sentence did you put before Sentence R?

    A. P
    B. Q
    C. S
    D. T
    E. None of the above. Sentence R is first.

5.____

KEY (CORRECT ANSWERS)

1. D
2. A
3. E
4. D
5. E

TEST 2

DIRECTIONS: Each group of sentences in this section is actually a paragraph presented in scrambled order. Each sentence in the group has a place in that paragraph; no sentence is to be left out. You are to read each group of sentences, so as to form a well-organized paragraph. Before trying to answer the questions which follow each group of sentences, jot down the correct order of the sentences. Then answer each of the questions by printing the letter of the correct answer in the space at the right. Remember that you will receive credit only for answers marked.

P. Sporting dogs include pointers, setters, and retrievers.
Q. Terriers include airedales, fox terriers, and schnauzers.
R. Hounds include bloodhounds, greyhounds, and wolfhounds.
S. Working dogs include collies, sheep dogs, and boxers.
T. Four of the major classifications of dogs are sporting dogs, hounds, terriers, and working dogs.

1. Which sentence did you put before Sentence R?   1.____

   A. P
   B. Q
   C. S
   D. T
   E. None of the above. Sentence R is first.

2. Which sentence did you put after Sentence S?   2.____

   A. P
   B. Q
   C. R
   D. T
   E. None of the above. Sentence S is last.

3. Which sentence did you put before Sentence Q?   3.____

   A. P
   B. R
   C. S
   D. T
   E. None of the above. Sentence Q is first.

4. Which sentence did you put last?   4.____
   A. P   B. Q   C. R   D. S   E. T

5. Which sentence did you put after Sentence T?   5.____

   A. P
   B. Q
   C. R
   D. S
   E. None of the above. Sentence T is last.

KEY (CORRECT ANSWERS)

1. A
2. E
3. B
4. D
5. A

TEST 3

DIRECTIONS: Each group of sentences in this section is actually a paragraph presented in scrambled order. Each sentence in the group has a place in that paragraph; no sentence is to be left out. You are to read each group of sentences, so as to form a well-organized paragraph. Before trying to answer the questions which follow each group of sentences, jot down the correct order of the sentences. Then answer each of the questions by printing the letter of the correct answer in the space at the right. Remember that you will receive credit only for answers marked.

P. Dostoevsky came to be regarded as the most promising of Russia's young novelists.
Q. He continued, however, to write prolifically for the next three years, producing three novels in that period.
R. Unlike his later works, too, they betray intense interest in problems of form and show originality of verbal expression.
S. But his second novel, THE DOUBLE, disappointed critics, and his success began to wane.
T. These early works display the strong influence of Gogol.

1. Which sentence did you put before Sentence P?   1.____

    A. Q
    B. R
    C. S
    D. T
    E. None of the above. Sentence P is first.

2. Which sentence did you put third?   2.____

    A. P   B. Q   C. R   D. S   E. T

3. Which sentence did you put after Sentence Q?   3.____

    A. P
    B. R
    C. S
    D. T
    E. None of the above. Sentence Q is last.

4. Which sentence did you put last?   4.____

    A. P   B. Q   C. R   D. S   E. T

5. Which sentence did you put before Sentence S?   5.____

    A. P
    B. Q
    C. R
    D. T
    E. None of the above. Sentence S is first.

―――――――

KEY (CORRECT ANSWERS)

1. E
2. B
3. D
4. C
5. A

TEST 4

DIRECTIONS: Each group of sentences in this section is actually a paragraph presented in scrambled order. Each sentence in the group has a place in that paragraph; no sentence is to be left out. You are to read each group of sentences, so as to form a well-organized paragraph. Before trying to answer the questions which follow each group of sentences, jot down the correct order of the sentences. Then answer each of the questions by printing the letter of the correct answer in the space at the right. Remember that you will receive credit only for answers marked.

P. Not every state of awareness in sleep is classifiable as a dream state.
Q. Dreams are ordinarily defined as states of consciousness taking place during sleep.
R. For example, people often hear a telephone ringing while asleep, and awaken to find that a telephone is, indeed, ringing.
S. And sleep is not invariably necessary to the manifestation of dream consciousness.
T. This definition is hardly adequate.

1. Which sentence did you put after Sentence T?   1.____

    A. P
    B. Q
    C. R
    D. S
    E. None of the above. Sentence T is last.

2. Which sentence did you put after Sentence R?   2.____

    A. P
    B. Q
    C. S
    D. T
    E. None of the above. Sentence R is last.

3. Which sentence did you put after Sentence Q?   3.____

    A. P
    B. R
    C. S
    D. T
    E. None of the above. Sentence Q is last.

4. Which sentence did you put after Sentence P?   4.____

    A. Q
    B. R
    C. S
    D. T
    E. None of the above. Sentence P is last.

5. Which sentence did you put before Sentence Q?   5.____

    A. P
    B. R
    C. S
    D. T
    E. None of the above. Sentence Q is first.

KEY (CORRECT ANSWERS)

1. A
2. C
3. D
4. B
5. E

TEST 5

DIRECTIONS: Each group of sentences in this section is actually a paragraph presented in scrambled order. Each sentence in the group has a place in that paragraph; no sentence is to be left out. You are to read each group of sentences, so as to form a well-organized paragraph. Before trying to answer the questions which follow each group of sentences, jot down the correct order of the sentences. Then answer each of the questions by printing the letter of the correct answer in the space at the right. Remember that you will receive credit only for answers marked.

P. Yet the long history of disarmament proposals and counterproposals is discouraging.

Q. It is also a wasteful mode of international competition.

R. Only those, therefore, who despair of the West's ability to compete constructively put their trust in the arms race.

S. It is now generally accepted that the arms race is too dangerous for any nation to continue pursuing without restraint or inhibition.

T. The fears and tensions it generates prevent East and West from competing constructively.

1. Which sentence did you put next to last?   1._____

    A. P   B. Q   C. R   D. S   E. T

2. Which sentence did you put before Sentence T?   2._____

    A. P
    B. Q
    C. R
    D. S
    E. None of the above. Sentence T is first.

3. Which sentence did you put before Sentence Q?   3._____

    A. P
    B. R
    C. S
    D. T
    E. None of the above. Sentence Q is first.

4. Which sentence did you put after Sentence R?   4._____

    A. P
    B. Q
    C. S
    D. T
    E. None of the above. Sentence R is last.

5. Which sentence did you put before Sentence S?   5.____

    A. P

    B. Q

    C. R

    D. T

    E. None of the above. Sentence S is first.

KEY (CORRECT ANSWERS)

1. C
2. B
3. C
4. A
5. E

PREPARING WRITTEN MATERIAL
EXAMINATION SECTION
TEST 1

DIRECTIONS: The following groups of sentences need to be arranged in an order that makes sense. Select the letter preceding the sequence that represents the *BEST sentence order. PRINT THE LETTER OF THE CORRECT ANSWER IN THE SPACE AT THE RIGHT.*

1.

    I.   A large Naval station on Alameda Island, near Oakland, held many warships in port, and the War Department was worried that if the bridge were to be blown up by the enemy, passage to and from the bay would be hopelessly blocked.

    II.   Though many skeptics were opposed to the idea of building such an enormous bridge, the most vocal opposition came from a surprising source: the United States War Department.

    III. The War Department's concerns led to a showdown at San Francisco City Hall between Strauss and the Secretary of War, who demanded to know what would happen if a military enemy blew up the bridge.

    IV. In 1933, by submitting a construction cost estimate of $17 million, an engineer named Joseph Strauss won the contract to build the Golden Gate Bridge of San Francisco, which would then become one of the world's largest bridges.

    V.   Strauss quickly ended the debate by explaining that the Golden Gate Bridge was to be a suspension bridge, whose roadway would hang in the air from cables strung between two huge towers, and would immediately sink into three hundred feet of water if it were destroyed.

The best order is
A.   II, III, I, IV, V
B.   I, II, III, V, IV
C.   IV, II, I, III, V
D.   IV, I, III, V, II

1._____

2.

I. Plastic surgeons have already begun to use virtual reality to map out the complex nerve and tissue structures of a particular patient's face, in order to prepare for delicate surgery.

II. A virtual reality program responds to these movements by adjusting the Images that a person sees on a screen or through goggles, thereby creating an "interactive" world in which a person can see and touch three-dimensional graphic objects.

III. No more than a computer program that is designed to build and display graphic images, the virtual reality program takes graphic programs a step further by sensing a person's head and body movements.

IV. The computer technology known as virtual reality, now in its very first stages of development, is already revolutionizing some aspects of contemporary life.

V. Virtual reality computers are also being used by the space program, most recently to simulate conditions for the astronauts who were launched on a repair mission to the Hubble telescope.

The best order is
A. IV, II, I, V, III
B. III, I, V, II, IV
C. IV, III, II, I, V
D. III, I, II, IV, V

3.

I. Before you plant anything, the soil in your plant bed should be carefully raked level, a small section at a time, and any clods or rocks that can't be broken up should be removed.

II. Your plant should be placed in a hole that will position it at the same level it was at the nursery, and a small indentation should be pressed into the soil around the plant in order to hold water near it roots.

III. Before placing the plant in the soil, lightly separate any roots that may have been matted together in the container, cutting away any thick masses that can't be separated, so that the remaining roots will be able to grow outward.

IV. After the bed is ready, remove your plant from its container by turning it upside down and tapping or pushing on the bottom — never remove it by pulling on the plant.

V. When you bring home a small plant in an individual container from the nursery, there are several things to remember while preparing to plant it in your own garden.

The best order is
A. V, IV, III, II, I
B. V, I, IV, III, II
C. I, IV, II, III, V
D. I, IV, V, II, III

4.   4._____

    I.   The motte and its tower were usually built first, so that sentries could use it as a lookout to warn the castle workers of any danger that might approach the castle.

    II.   Though the moat and palisade offered the bailey a good deal of protection, it was linked to the motte by a set of stairs that led to a retractable drawbridge at the motte's gate, to enable people to evacuate and retreat onto the motte in case of an attack.

    III.   The *motte* of these early castles was a fortified hill, sometimes as high as one hundred feet, on which stood a palisade and tower.

    IV.   The *bailey* was a clear, level spot below the motte, also enclosed by a palisade, which in turn was surrounded by a large trench or moat.

    V.   The earliest castles built in Europe were not the magnificent stone giants that still tower over much of the European landscape, but simpler wooden constructions called motte-and-bailey castles.

The best order is
A. V, III, I, IV, II
B. V, IV, I, II, III
C. I, IV, IIII, II, V
D. I, III, II, IV, V

5.   5._____

    I.   If an infant is left alone or abandoned for a short while, its immediate response is to cry loudly, accompanying its screams with aggressive flailing of its legs and limbs.

    II.   If a child has been abandoned for a longer period of time, it becomes completely still and quiet, as if realizing that now its only chance for survival is to shut its mouth and remain motionless.

    III.   Along with their intense fear of the dark, the crying behavior of human infants offers insights into how prehistoric newborn children might have evolved instincts that would prevent them from becoming victims of predators.

    IV.   This behavior often surprises people who enter a hospital's maternity ward for the first time and encounter total silence from a roomful of infants.

    V.   This violent screaming response is quite different from an infant's cries of discomfort or hunger, and seems to serve as either the child's first line of defense against an unwanted intruder, or a desperate attempt to communicate its position to the mother.

The best order is
A. III, II, IV, I, V
B. III, I, V, II, IV
C. I, V, IV, II, III
D. II, IV, I, V, III

6.

I. When two cats meet who are strangers, their first actions and gestures determine who the "dominant" cat will be, at least for the time being.

II. Unlike dogs, cats are typically a solitary animal species who avoid social interaction, but they do display specific social responses to each other upon meeting.

III. This is unlikely, however; before such a point of open hostility is reached, one of the cats will usually take the "submissive" position of crouching down while looking away from the other cat.

IV. If a cat desires dominance or sees the other cat as a threat to its territory, it will stare directly at the intruder with a lowered tail.

V. If the other cat responds with a similar gesture, or with the strong defensive posture of an arched back, laid-back ears and raised tail, a fight or chase is likely if neither cat gives in.

The best order is
A. IV, II, I, V, III
B. I, II, IV, V, III
C. I, IV, V, III, II
D. II, I, IV, V, III

7.

I. A star or planet's gravitational force can best be explained in this way: anything passing through this "dent" in space will veer toward the star or planet as if it were rolling into a hole.

II. Objects that are massive or heavy, such as stars or planets, "sink" into this surface, creating a sort of dent or concavity in the surrounding space.

III. Black holes, the most massive objects known to exist in space, create dents so large and deep that the space surrounding them actually folds in on itself, preventing anything that falls in — even light — from ever escaping again.

IV. The sort of dent a star or planet makes depends on how massive it is; planets generally have weak gravitational pulls, but stars, which are larger and heavier, make a bigger "dent" that will attract more matter.

V. In outer space, the force of gravity works as if the surrounding space is a soft, flat surface.

The best order is
A. III, V, II, I, IV
B. III, IV, I, V, II
C. V, II, I, IV, III
D. I, V, II, IV, III

8.

   I.   Eventually, the society of Kyoto gave the world one of its first and greatest novels when Japan's most prominent writer, Lady Murasaki Shikibu, wrote her chronicle of Kyoto's society, *The Tale of Genji*, which preceded the first European novels by more than 500 years.

   II.   The society of Kyoto was dedicated to the pleasures of art; the courtiers experimented with new and colorful methods of sculpture, painting, writing, decorative gardening, and even making clothes.

   III.   Japanese culture began under the powerful authority of Chinese Buddhism, which influenced every aspect of Japanese life from religion to politics and art.

   IV.   This new, vibrant culture was so sophisticated that all the people in Kyoto's imperial court considered themselves poets, and the line between life and art hardly existed — lovers corresponded entirely through written verses, and even government officials communicated by writing poems to each other.

   V.   In the eighth century, when the emperor established the town of Kyoto as the capital of the Japanese empire, Japanese society began to develop its own distinctive style.

The best order is
A. V, II, IV, I, III
B. II, I, V, IV, III
C. V, III, IV, I, II
D. III, V, II, IV, I

9.

   I.   Instead of wheels, the HSST uses two sets of magnets, one which sits on the track, and another that is carried by the train; these magnets generate an identical magnetic field which forces the two sets apart.

   II.   In the last few decades, railway travel has become less popular throughout the world, because it is much slower than travel by airplane, and not much less expensive.

   III.   The HSST's designers say that the train can take passengers from one town to another as quickly as a jet plane — while consuming less than half the energy.

   IV.   This repellent effect is strong enough to lift the entire train above the trackway, and the train, literally traveling on air, rockets along at speeds of up to 300 miles per hour.

   V.   The revolutionary technology of magnetic levitation, currently being tested by Japan's experimental HSST (High Speed Surface Transport), may yet bring passenger trains back from the dead.

The best order is
A. II, V, I, IV, III
B. II, I, IV, III, V
C. V, II, III, I, IV
D. V, I, III, IV, II

10.

I. When European countries first began to colonize the African continent, their impression of the African people was of a vast group of loosely organized tribal societies, without any great centralized source of power or wealth.

II. The legend of Timbuktu persisted until the nineteenth century, when a French adventurer visited Timbuktu and found that raids by neighboring tribesmen had made the city a shadow of its former self.

III. In the fifteenth century, when the stories of travelers who had traveled Africa's Sudan region began circulating around Europe, this impression began to change.

IV. In 1470, an Italian merchant named Benedetto Dei traveled to Timbuktu and confirmed these rumors, describing a thriving metropolis where rich and poor people worshipped together in the city's many ornate mosques — there was even a university in Timbuktu, much like its European counterparts, where African scholars pursued their studies in the arts and sciences.

V. The travelers' legends told of an enormous city in the western Sudan, Timbuktu, where the streets were crowded with goods brought by faraway caravans, and where there was a stone palace as large as any in Europe.

The best order is
A. III, V, I, IV, II
B. I, II, IV, III, V
C. I, III, V, IV, II
D. II, I, III, IV, V

11.

I. Also, our reference points in sighting the moon may make us believe that its size is changing; when the moon is rising through the trees, it seems huge, because our brains unconsciously compare the size of the moon with the size of the trees in the foreground.

II. To most people, the sky itself appears more distant at the horizon than directly overhead, and if the moon's size — which remains constant — is projected from the horizon, the apparent distance of the horizon makes the moon look bigger.

III. Up higher in the sky, the moon is set against tiny stars in the background, which will make the moon seem smaller.

IV. People often wonder why the moon becomes bigger when it approaches the horizon, but most scientists agree that this is a complicated optical illusion, produced by at least three factors.

V. The moon illusion may also be partially explained by a phenomenon that has nothing to do with errors in our perception — light that enters the earth's atmosphere is sometimes refracted, and so the atmosphere may act as a kind of magnifying glass for the moon's image.

The best order is
A. IV, III, V, II, I
B. IV, II, I, III, V
C. V, II, I, III, IV
D. II, I, III, IV, V

12.

12._____

I.   When the Native Americans were introduced to the horses used by white explorers, they were amazed at their new alternative — here was an animal that was strong and swift, would patiently carry a person or other loads on its back, and, they later discovered, was right at home on the plains.

II. Before the arrival of European explorers to North America, the natives of the American plains used large dogs to carry their travois-long lodgepoles loaded with clothing, gear, and food.

III. These horses, it is now known, were not really strangers to North America; the very first horses originated here, on this continent, tens of thousands of years ago, and migrated into Asia across the Bering Land Bridge, a strip of land that used to link our continent with the Eastern world.

IV. At first, the natives knew so little about horses that at least one tribe tried to feed their new animals pieces of dried meat and animal fat, and were surprised when the horses turned their heads away and began to eat the grass of the prairie.

V.   The American horse eventually became extinct, but its Asian cousins were reintroduced to the New World when the European explorers brought them to live among the Native Americans.

The best order is
A. II, I, IV, III, V
B. II, IV, I, III, V
C. I, II, IV, III, V
D. I, III, V, II, IV

13.

13._____

I.   The dress worn by the dancer is believed to have been adorned in the past by shells which would strike each other as the dancer performed, creating a lovely sound.

II. Today's jingle-dress is decorated with the tin lids of snuff cans, which are rolled into cones and sewn onto the dress.

III. During the jingle-dress dance, the dancer must blend complicated footwork with a series of gentle hops that cause the cones to jingle in rhythm to a drumbeat.

IV. When contemporary Native American tribes meet for a pow-wow, one of the most popular ceremonies to take place is the women's jingle-dress dance.

V.   Besides being more readily available than shells, the lids are thought by many dancers to create a softer, more subtle sound.

The best order is
A. II, IV, V, I, III
B. IV, II, I, III, V
C. II, I, III, V, IV
D. IV, I, II, V, III

14.

   I.   If a homeowner lives where seasonal climates are extreme, deciduous shade trees — which will drop their leaves in the winter and allow sunlight to pass through the windows — should be planted near the southern exposure in order to keep the house cool during the summer.

   II.   This trajectory is shorter and lower in the sky than at any other time of year during the winter, when a house most requires heating; the northern-facing parts of a house do not receive any direct sunlight at all.

   III.   In designing an energy-efficient house, especially in colder climates, it is important to remember that most of the house's windows should face south.

   IV.   Though the sun always rises in the east and sets in the west, the sun of the northern hemisphere is permanently situated in the southern portion of the sky.

   V.   The explanation for why so many architects and builders want this "southern exposure" is related to the path of the sun in the sky.

The best order is
A. III, I, V, IV, II
B. III, V, IV, II, I
C. I, III, IV, II, V
D. I, II, V, IV, III

15.

   I.   His journeying lasted twenty-four years and took him over an estimated 75,000 miles, a distance that would not be surpassed by anyone other than Magellan — who sailed around the world — for another six hundred years.

   II.   Perhaps the most far-flung of these lesser-known travelers was Ibn Batuta, an African Moslem who left his birthplace of Tangier in the summer of 1325.

   III.   Ibn Batuta traveled all over Africa and Asia, from Niger to Peking, and to the islands of Maldive and Indonesia.

   IV.   However, a few explorers of the Eastern world logged enough miles and adventures to make Marco Polo's voyage look like an evening stroll.

   V.   In America, the most well-known of the Old World's explorers are usually Europeans such as Marco Polo, the Italian who brought many elements of Chinese culture to the Western world.

The best order is
A. V, IV, II, III, I
B. V, IV, III, II, I
C. III, II, I, IV, V
D. II, III, I, IV, V

16.   16._____

   I.   In the rain forests of South America, a rare species of frog practices a repro-
        ductive method that is entirely different from this standard process.
  II.   She will eventually carry each of the tadpoles up into the canopy and drop
        each into its own little pool, where it will be easy to locate and safe from most
        predators.
 III.   After fertilization, the female of the species, who lives almost entirely on the
        forest floor, lays between 2 and 16 eggs among the leaf litter at the base of a
        tree, and stands watch over these eggs until they hatch.
 IV.   Most frogs are pond-dwellers who are able to deposit hundreds of eggs in
        the water and then leave them alone, knowing that enough eggs have been
        laid to insure the survival of some of their offspring.
  V.   Once the tadpoles emerge, the female backs in among them, and a tadpole
        will wriggle onto her back to be carried high into the forest canopy, where the
        female will deposit it in a little pool of water cupped in the leaf of a plant.

The best order is
A. I, IV, III, II, V
B. I, III, V, II, IV
C. IV, III, II, V, I
D. IV, I, III, V, II

17.   17._____

   I.   Eratosthenes had heard from travelers that at exactly noon on June 21, in the
        ancient city of Aswan, Egypt, the sun cast no shadow in a well, which meant
        that the sun must be directly overhead.
  II.   He knew the sun always cast a shadow in Alexandria, and so he figured that if
        he could measure the length of an Alexandria shadow at the time when there
        was no shadow in Aswan, he could calculate the angle of the sun, and therefore
        the circumference of the earth.
 III.   The evidence for a round earth was not new in 1492; in fact, Eratosthenes, an
        Alexandrian geographer who lived nearly sixteen centuries before Columbus's
        voyage (275-195 B.C.), actually developed a method for calculating the circum-
        ference of the earth that is still in use today.
 IV.   Eratosthenes's method was correct, but his result — 28,700 miles — was about
        15 percent too high, probably because of the inaccurate ancient methods of
        keeping time, and because Aswan was not due south of Alexandria, as
        Eratosthenes had believed.
  V.   When Christopher Columbus sailed across the Atlantic Ocean for the first time in
        1492, there were still some people in the world who ignored scientific evidence
        and believed that the earth was flat, rather than round.

The best order is
A. I, II, V, III, IV
B. V, III, IV, I, II
C. V, III, I, II, IV
D. III, V, I, II, IV

18.

I.   The first name for the child is considered a trial naming, often impersonal and neutral, such as the Ngoni name *Chabwera*, meaning "it has arrived."

II.   This sort of name is not due to any parental indifference to the child, but is a kind of silent recognition of Africa's sometimes high infant death rate; most parents ease the pain of losing a child with the belief that it is not really a person until it has been given a final name.

III.   In many tribal African societies, families often give two different names to their children, at different periods in time.

IV.   After the trial naming period has subsided and it is clear that the child will survive, the parents choose a final name for the child, an act that symbolically completes the act of birth.

V.   In fact, some African first-given names are explicitly uncomplimentary, translating as "I am dead" or "I am ugly," in order to avoid the jealousy of ancestral spirits who might wish to take a child that is especially healthy or attractive.

The best order is
A. III, I, II, V, IV
B. III, IV, II, I, V
C. IV, III, I, II, V
D. IV, V, III, I, II

19.

I.   Though uncertain of the definite reasons for this behavior, scientists believe the birds digest the clay in order to counteract toxins contained in the seeds of certain fruits that are eaten by macaws.

II.   For example, all macaws flock to riverbanks at certain times of the year to eat the clay that is found in river mud.

III.   The macaws of South America are not only among the largest and most beautifully colored of the world's flying birds, but they are also one of the smartest.

IV.   It is believed that macaws are forced to resort to these toxic fruits during the dry season, when foods are more scarce.

V.   The macaw's intelligence has led to intense study by scientists, who have discovered some macaw behaviors that have not yet been explained.

The best order is
A. III, IV, I, II, V
B. III, V, II, I, IV
C. V, II, I, IV, III
D. IV, I, II, III, V

20.

20._____

    I.   Although Maggie Kuhn has since passed away, the Gray Panthers are still waging a campaign to reinstate the historical view of the elderly as people whose experience allows them to make their greatest contribution in their later years.

    II.   In 1972, an elderly woman named Maggie Kuhn responded to this sort of treatment by forming a group called the Gray Panthers, an organization of both old and young adults with the common goal of creating change.

    III. This attitude is reflected strongly in the way elderly people are treated by our society; many are forced into early retirement, or are placed in rest homes in which they are isolated from their communities.

    IV. Unlike most other cultures around the world, Americans tend to look upon old age with a sense of dread and sadness.

    V.   Kuhn believed that when the elderly are forced to withdraw into lives that lack purpose, society loses one of its greatest resources: people who have a lifetime of experience and wisdom to offer their communities.

The best order is
A. IV, III, II, V, I
B. IV, II, I, III, V
C. II, IV, III, V, I
D. II, I, IV, III, V

21.

21._____

    I.   The current theory among most anthropologists is that humans evolved from apes who lived in trees near the grasslands of Africa.

    II.   Still, some anthropologists insist that such an invention was necessary for the survival of early humans, and point to the Kung Bushmen of central Africa as a society in which the sling is still used in this way.

    III. Two of these inventions — fire, and weapons such as spears and clubs — were obvious defenses against predators, and there is archaeological evidence to support the theory of their use.

    IV. Once people had evolved enough to leave the safety of trees and walk upright, they needed the protection of several inventions in order to survive.

    V.   But another invention, a leather or fiber sling that allowed mothers to carry children while leaving their hands free to gather roots or berries, would certainly have decomposed and left behind no trace of itself.

The best order is
A. I, II, III, V, IV
B. IV, I, II, III, V
C. I, IV, III, V, II
D. IV, III, V, II, I

22.

I. The person holding the bird should keep it in hot water up to its neck, and the person cleaning should work a mild solution of dishwashing liquid into the bird's plumage, paying close attention to the head and neck.

II. When rinsing the bird, after all the oil has been removed, the running water should be directed against the lay of its feathers, until water begins to bead off the surface of the feathers — a sign that all the detergent has been rinsed out.

III. If you have rescued a sea bird from an oil spill and want to restore it to clean and normal living, you need a large sink, a constant supply of running hot water (a little over 100° F), and regular dishwashing liquid.

IV. This cleaning with detergent solution should be repeated as many times as it takes to remove all traces of oil from the bird's feathers, sometimes over a period of several days.

V. But before you begin to clean the bird, you must first find a partner, because cleaning an oiled bird is a two-person job.

The best order is
A. III, I, II, IV, V
B. III, V, I, IV, II
C. III, I, IV, V, II
D. III, IV, V, I, II

23.

I. The most difficult time of year for the Tsaatang is the spring calving, when the reindeer leave their wintering ground and rush to their accustomed calving place, without stopping by night or by day.

II. Reindeer travel in herds, and though some animals are tamed by the Tsaatang for riding or milking, the herds are allowed to roam free.

III. This journey is hard for the Tsaatang, who carry all their possessions with them, but once it's over it proves worthwhile; the Tsaatang can immediately begin to gather milk from reindeer cows who have given birth.

IV. The Tsaatang, a small tribe who live in the far northwest corner of Mongolia, practice a lifestyle that is completely dependent on the reindeer, their main resource for food, clothing, and transport.

V. The people must follow their yearly migrations, living in portable shelters that resemble Native American tepees.

The best order is
A. I, III, II, V, IV
B. I, IV, II, V, III
C. IV, I, III, V, II
D. IV, II, V, I, III

24.   24._____

    I.   The Romans later improved this system by installing these heated pipe networks throughout walls and ceilings, supplying heat to even the uppermost floors of a building — a system that, to this day, hasn't been much improved.

    II.   Air-conditioning, the method by which humans control indoor temperatures, was practiced much earlier than most people think.

    III.   The earliest heating devices other than open fires were used in 350 B.C. by the ancient Greeks, who directed air that had been heated by underground fires into baked clay pipes that ran under the floor.

    IV.   Ironically, the first successful cooling system, patented in England in 1831, used fire as its main energy source — fires were lit in the attic of a building, creating an updraft of air that drew cool air into the building through ducts that had underground openings near the river Thames.

    V.   Cooling buildings was more of a challenge, and wasn't attempted until 1500: a water-based system, designed by Leonardo da Vinci, does not appear to have been successful, since it was never used again.

The best order is
A. III, V, IV, I, II
B. III, I, II, V, IV
C. II, III, I, V, IV
D. IV, II, III, I, V

25.   25._____

    I.   Cold, dry air from Canada passes over the Rocky Mountains and sweeps down onto the plains, where it collides with warm, moist air from the waters of the Gulf of Mexico, and when the two air masses meet, the resulting disturbance sometimes forms a violent funnel cloud that strikes the earth and destroys virtually everything in its path.

    II.   Hurricanes, storms which are generally not this violent and last much longer, are usually given names by meteorologists, but this tradition cannot be applied to tornados, which have a life span measured in minutes and disappear in the same way as they are born — unnamed.

    III.   A tornado funnel forms rotating columns of air whose speed reaches three hundred miles an hour — a speed that can only be estimated, because no wind-measuring devices in the direct path of a storm have ever survived.

    IV.   The natural phenomena known as tornados occur primarily over the mid-western grasslands of the United States.

    V.   It is here, meteorologists tell us, that conditions for the formation of tornados are sometimes perfect during the spring months.

The best order is
A. II, IV, V, I, III
B. II, III, I, V, IV
C. IV, V, I, III, II
D. IV, III, I, V, II

KEY (CORRECT ANSWERS)

1.	C		11.	B
2.	C		12.	A
3.	B		13.	D
4.	A		14.	B
5.	B		15.	A
6.	D		16.	D
7.	C		17.	C
8.	D		18.	A
9.	A		19.	B
10.	C		20.	A

21.	C
22.	B
23.	D
24.	C
25.	C

READING COMPREHENSION
UNDERSTANDING AND INTERPRETING WRITTEN MATERIAL
STRATEGIES

Surveying Passages, Sentences as Cues

While individual readers develop unique reading styles and skills, there are some known strategies which can assist any reader in improving his or her reading comprehension and performance on the reading subtest. These strategies include understanding how single paragraphs and entire passages are structured, how the ideas in them are ordered, and how the author of the passage has connected these ideas in a logical and sequential way for the reader.

The section that follows highlights the importance of reading a passage through once for meaning, and provides instruction on careful reading for context cues within the sentences before and after the missing word.

SURVEY THE ENTIRE PASSAGE

To get a sense of the topic and the organization of ideas in a passage, it is important to survey each passage initially in its entirety and to identify the main idea. (The first sentence of a paragraph usually states the main idea.) Do not try to fill in the blanks initially. The purpose of surveying a passage is to prepare for the more careful reading which will follow. You need a sense of the big picture before you start to fill in the details; for example, a quick survey of the passage on page 11, indicates that the topic is the early history of universities. The paragraphs are organized to provide information on the origin of the first universities, the associations formed by teachers and students, the early curriculum, and graduation requirements.

READ PRECEDING SENTENCES CAREFULLY

The missing words in a passage cannot be determined by reading and understanding only the sentences in which the deletions occur. Information from the sentences which precede or follow can provide important cues to determine the correct choice. For example, if you read the first sentence from the passage about universities which contains a blank, you will notice that all the alternatives make sense if this one sentence is read in isolation:

Nobody actually _____ them.

A. started
C. blamed
E. remembered

B. guarded
D. compared

The only way that you can make the correct word choice is to read the preceding sentences. In the excerpt below, notice that the first sentence tells the reader what the passage will be about: how universities developed. A key word in the first sentence is *emerged,* which is closely related in meaning to one of the five choices for the first blank. The second sentence explains the key word, *emerged,* by pointing out that we have no historical record of a decree or a date indicating when the first university was established. Understanding the ideas in the first two sentences makes it possible to select the correct word for the blank. Look at the sentence with the deleted word in the context of the preceding sentences and think about why you are now able to make the correct choice.

The first universities emerged at the end of the 11th century and beginning of the 12th. These institutions were not founded on any particular date or created by any formal action. Nobody actually _____ them.

A. started
C. blamed
E. remembered

B. guarded
D. compared

Started is the best choice because it fits the main idea of the passage and is closely related to the key word *emerged*.

READ THE SENTENCE WHICH FOLLOWS TO VERIFY YOUR CHOICE

The sentences which follow the one from which a word has been deleted may also provide cues to the correct choice. For example, look at an excerpt from the passage about universities again, and consider how the sentence which follows the one with the blank helps to reinforce the choice of the word, *started*.

The first universities emerged at the end of the llth century and the beginning of the 12th. These institutions were not founded on any particular date or created by any formal action. Nobody actually _____ them. Instead, they developed gradually in places like Paris, Oxford, and Bologna, where scholars had long been teaching students.

A. started
C. blamed
E. remembered

B. guarded
D. compared

The words, *developed gradually,* mean the same as the key word, *emerged.* The signal word, *instead,* helps to distinguish the difference between starting on a specific date as a result of some particular act or event and emerging over a period of time as a result of various factors.

Here is another example of how the sentence which follows the one from which a word is deleted might help you decide which of two good alternatives is the correct choice. This excerpt is from the practice passage about bridges (page 11).

Bridges are built to allow a continuous flow of highway and railway traffic across water lying in their paths. But engineers cannot forget that river traffic, too, is essential to our economy. The role of _____ is important. To keep these vessels moving freely, bridges are built big enough, when possible, to let them pass underneath.

A. wind
C. weight
E. experiences

B. boats
D. wires

After the first two sentences, the reader may be uncertain about the direction the writer intended to take in the rest of the paragraph. If the writer intended to continue the paragraph with information concerning how engineers make choices about the relative importance and requirements of land traffic and river traffic, *experience* might be the appropriate choice for the missing word. However, the sentence following the one in which the deletion occurs makes it clear that *boats* is the correct choice. It provides the synonym *vessels*, which in the noun phrase *these vessels* must refer back to the previous sentence or sentences. The phrase *to let them pass underneath* also helps make it clear that *boats* is the appropriate choice. *Them* refers back to *these vessels* which, in turn, refers back to *boats* when the word *boats* is placed in the previous sentence. Thus, the reader may use these cohesive ties (the pronoun referents) to verify the final choice.

Even when the text following a sentence with a deletion is not necessary to choose the best alternative, it may be helpful in other ways. Specifically, complete sentences provide important transitions into a related topic which is developed in the rest of the paragraph or in the next paragraph of the same passage. For example, the first paragraph in the passage about universities ends with a sentence which introduces the term *guilds*: *But, over time, they joined together to form guilds.* Prior to this sentence, information about the slow emergence of universities and about how independently scholars had acted was introduced. The next paragraph begins with two sentences about guilds in general. Someone who had not read the last sentence in the first paragraph might have missed the link between guilds and scholars and universities and, thus, might have been unnecessarily confused.

Cohesive Ties As Cues

Sentences in a paragraph may be linked together by several devices called cohesive ties. Attention to these ties may provide further cues about missing words. This section will describe the different types of cohesive ties and show how attention to them can help you to select the correct word.

PERSONAL PRONOUNS

Personal pronouns (e.g., he, she, they, it, its) are often used in adjoining sentences to refer back to an already mentioned person, place, thing, or idea. The word to which the pronoun refers is called the antecedent.

Tools used in farm work changed very slowly from ancient times to the eighteenth century, and the changes were minor. Since the eighteenth century *they* have changed quickly and dramatically.

The word *they* refers back to *tools* in the example above.

In the examination reading subtest, a deleted word sometimes occurs in a sentence in which the sentence subject is a pronoun that refers back to a previously mentioned noun. You must correctly identify the referent for the particular pronoun in order to interpret the sentence and select the correct answer. Here is an example from the passage about bridges.

An ingenious engineer designed the bridge so that it did not have to be raised above traffic. Instead it was _____.

A.	burned	B.	emptied
C.	secured	D.	shared
E.	lowered		

Q. What is the antecedent of *it* in both cases in the example?

A. The antecedent, of course, is *bridge.*

DEMONSTRATIVE PRONOUNS

Demonstrative pronouns (e.g., this, that, these) are also used to refer to a specific, previously mentioned noun. They may occur alone as noun replacements, or they may accompany and modify nouns.

I like jogging, swimming, and tennis. *These* are the only sports I enjoy.

In the sentence above, the word *these* is a replacement noun. However, demonstrative pronouns may also occur as adjectives modifying nouns.

I like jogging, swimming, and tennis. *These* sports are the only ones I enjoy.

The word *these* in the example above is an adjective modifier. The word *these* in each of the two previous examples refers to *jogging, swimming,* and *tennis.*

Here is an example from the passage about universities on page 12.

Undergraduates took classes in Greek philosophy, Latin grammar, arithmetic, music, and astronomy. These were the only _____ available.

A. rooms   B. subjects
C. clothes   D. pens
E. company

Q. Which word is a noun replacement?
A. The word *these* is the replacement noun for *Greek philosophy, Latin grammar, arithmetic, music,* and *astronomy.*

Here is another example from the same passage.

The concept of a fixed program of study leading to a degree first evolved in Medieval Europe. This _____ had not appeared before.

A. idea   B. desk
C. library   D. capital

Q. What is the antecedent of *this*?

A. The antecedent is *the concept of a fixed program of study leading to a degree.*

COMPARATIVE ADJECTIVES AND ADVERBS

When comparative adjectives or adverbs (e.g., so, such, better, more) occur, they refer to something else in the passage, otherwise a comparison could not be made.

The hotels in the city were all full; so were the motels and boarding houses.

Q. To what in the first sentence does the word *so* refer?
A. *So* tells us to compare the *motels* and *boarding houses* to the *hotels in the city.*

Q. In what way are the *hotels, motels,* and *boarding houses* similar to each other?

A. The *hotels, motels,* and *boarding houses* are similar in that they were all *full.*

Look at an example from the passage about universities.

Guilds were groups of tradespeople, somewhat akin to modern trade unions. In the Middle Ages, all the crafts had such

A. taxes
C. products
E. organizations

B. secrets
D. problems

Q. To what in the first sentence does the word *such* refer?
A. *Such* refers to *groups of tradespeople.*

SUBSTITUTIONS

Substitution is another form of cohesive tie. A substitution occurs when one linguistic item (e.g., a noun) is replaced by another. Sometimes the substitution provides new or contrasting information. The substitution is not identical to the original, or antecedent, idea. A frequently occurring substitution involves the use of *one.* A noun substitution may involve another member of the same class as the original one.

My car is falling apart. I need a new one.

Q. What in the first sentence is replaced in the second sentence with *one?*
A. *One* is a substitute for the specific car mentioned in the first sentence. The contrast comes from the fact that the *new one* isn't the writer's current car.

The substitution may also pinpoint a specific member of a general class.

1. There are many unusual courses available at the university this summer. The *one* I am taking is called *Death and Dying.*
2. There are many unusual courses available at the university this summer. *Some* have never been offered before.

Q. In these examples, what is the general class in the first sentence that is replaced by *one* and by *some?*
A. In both cases the words *one* and *some* replace *many unusual* courses.

SYNONYMS

Synonyms are words that have similar meaning. In the examination reading subtest, a synonym of a deleted word is sometimes found in one of the sentences before and/or after the sentence with the deletion. Examine the following excerpt from the passage about bridges again.

But engineers cannot forget that river traffic, too, is essential to our economy. The role of _____ is important. To keep these vessels moving freely, bridges are built high enough, when possible, to let them pass underneath.

A. wind   B. boats
C. weight   D. wires
E. experience

Q   Can you identify synonyms in the sentences, before and after the sentence containing the deletion, which are cues to the correct deleted word?

A. If you identified the correct words, you probably noticed that *river traffic* is not exactly a synonym, since it is a slightly more general term than the word *boats* (the correct choice). But the word *vessels* is a direct synonym. Demonstrative pronouns (this, that, these, those) are sometimes used as modifiers for synonymous nouns in sentences which follow those containing deletions. The word *these* in *these vessels* is the demonstrative pronoun (modifier) for the synonymous noun *vessels*.

ANTONYMS

Antonyms are words of opposite meaning. In the examination reading subtest passages, antonyms may be cues for missing words. A contrasting relationship, which calls for the use of an antonym, is often signaled by the connective words *instead, however, but,* etc. Look at an excerpt from the passage about bridges.

An ingenious engineer designed the bridge so that it did not have to be raised above traffic. Instead it was _____.

A. burned   B. emptied
C. secured   D. shared
E. lowered

Q. Can you identify an antonym in the first sentence for one of the five alternatives?
A. The word *raised* is an antonym for the word *lowered*.

SUPERORDINATE-SUBORDINATE WORDS

In the examination reading subtest, a passage sometimes contains a general term which provides a cue that a more specific term is the appropriate alternative. At other times, the passage may contain a specific term which provides cues that a general term is the appropriate alternative for a particular deletion. The general and more specific words are said to have superordinate-subordinate relationships.

Look at example 1 below. The more specific word *boy* in the first sentence serves as the antecedent for the more general word *child* in the second sentence. In example 2, the relationship is reversed. In both examples, the words *child* and *boy* reflect a superordinate-subordinate relationship.
   1. The *boy* climbed the tree. Then the *child* fell.
   2. The *child* climbed the tree. Then the *boy* fell.

In the practice passage about bridges on page 11, the phrase *river traffic* is a general term that is superordinate to the alternative *boats* (item 1). Later in the passage about bridges the following sentences also contain superordinate-subordinate words:

A lift bridge was desired, but there were wartime shortages of steel and machinery needed for the towers. It was hard to find enough _____.

A. work
C. time
E. space

B. material
D. power

Q. Can you identify two words in the first sentence that are specific examples for the correct response in the second sentence?

A. Of course, the words *steel* and *machinery* are the specific examples for the more general term *material*.

WORDS ASSOCIATED BY ENTAILMENT

Sometimes the concept described by one word within the context of the passage entails, or implies, the concept described by another word. For example, consider again item 7 in the practice passage about bridges. Notice how the follow-up sentence to item 7 provides a cue to the correct response.

An ingenious engineer designed the bridge so that it did not have to be raised above traffic. Instead it was _____. It could be submerged seven meters below the surface of the river.

A. burned
C. secured
E. lowered

B. emptied
D. shared

Q. What word in the sentence after the blank implies the concept of an alternative?

A. *Submerged* implies *lowered*. The concept of submerging something implies the idea of lowering the object beneath the surface of the water.

WORDS ASSOCIATED BY PART-WHOLE RELATIONSHIPS

Words may be related because they involve part of a whole and the whole itself; for example, *nose* and *face*. Words may also be related because they involve two parts of the same whole; for example, *radiator* and *muffler* both refer to parts of a car.

The captain of the ship was nervous. The storm was becoming worse and worse. The hardened man paced the _____.

A. floor
C. deck

B. hall
D. court

Q. Which choice has a part-whole relationship with a word in the sentences above?

A. A *deck* is a part of a *ship*. Therefore, *deck* has a part-whole relationship with *ship*.

CONJUNCTIVE AND CONNECTIVE WORDS AND PHRASES

Conjunctions or connectives are words or phrases that connect parts of sentences or parts of a passage to each other. Their purpose is to help the reader understand the logical and conceptual relationships between ideas and events within a passage. Examples of these words and phrases include coordinate conjunctions (e.g., and, but, yet), subordinate conjunctions (e.g., because, although, since, after), and other connective words and phrases (e,g, too, also, on the other hand, as a result).

Listed below are types of logical relationships expressed by conjunctive, or connective words. Also listed are examples of words used to cue relationships to the reader.

Additive and comparative words and phrases: and, in addition to, too, also, furthermore, similarly

Adversative and contrastive words and phrases: yet, though, only, but, however, instead, rather, on the other hand, in contrast, conversely

Causal words or phrases: so, therefore, because, as a result, if...then, unless, except, in that case, under the circumstances

Temporal words and phrases: before, after, when, while, initially, lastly, finally, until.

Examples

1. I enjoy fast-paced sports like tennis and volleyball, but my brother prefers _____ sports.

    A. running   B. slower
    C. team   D. active

Q. What is the connective word that tells you to look for a contrast relationship between the two clauses?
A The connective word *but* signals that a contrast relationship exists between the two parts of the sentence.

Q. Of the four options, what is the best choice for the blank?
A The word *slower* is the best response here.

2. The child stepped to close to the edge of the brook. As a result, he _____ in.

    A. fell   B. waded
    C. ran   D. jumped

Q. What is the connective phrase that links the two sentences?
A. The connective phrase *as a result* links the two sentences.

Q. Of the four relationships of words and phrases listed previously, what kind of relationship between the two sentences does the connective phrase in the example signal to the reader?
A. The phrase *as a result* signals that a cause and effect relationship exists between the two sentences.

Q. Identify the correct response which makes the second sentence reflect the cause and effect relationship.
A. The correct response is *fell*.

Understanding connectives is very important to success on the examination reading sub-test. Sentences with deletions are often very closely related to adjacent sentences in meaning, and the relationship is often signaled by connective words or phrases. Here is an example from the practice passage about universities.

> At first, these tutors had not been associated with one another. Rather, they had been _____. But, over time, they joined together to form guilds.

>   A. curious   B. poor
>   C. religious   D. ready
>   E. independent

Q. Identify the connective and contrastive words and phrases in the example.

A. *At first* and *over time* are connective phrases that set up temporal progression. *Rather* and *but* are contrastive items. The use of *rather* in the sentence with the deletion tells the reader that the missing word has to convey a meaning in contrast to *associated with one another*. (Notice also that *rather* occurs after a negative statement.) The use of *but* in the sentence after the one with the deletion indicates that the deleted word in the previous sentence has to reflect a meaning that contrasts with *joined together*. Thus, the reader is given two substantial cues to the meaning of the missing word. *Independent* is the only choice that meets the requirement for contrastive meaning.

SAMPLE QUESTIONS

DIRECTIONS: There are two passages on the following pages. In each passage some words are missing. Wherever a word is missing, there is a blank line with a number on it. Below the passage you will find the same number and five words. Choose the word that makes the best sense in the blank. You may not be sure of the answer to a question until you read the sentences that come after the blank, so be sure to read enough to answer the questions. As you work on these passages, you will find that the second passage is harder to read than the first. Answer as many questions as you can.

Bridges are built to allow a continuous flow of highway and railway traffic across water lying in their paths. But engineers cannot forget that river traffic, too, is essential to our economy. The role of ___1___ is important. To keep these vessels moving freely, bridges are built high enough, when possible, to let them pass underneath. Sometimes, however, channels must accommodate very tall ships. It may be uneconomical to build a tall enough bridge. The ___2___ would be too high. To save money, engineers build movable bridges.

In the swing bridge, the middle part pivots or swings open. When the bridge is closed, this section joins the two ends of the bridge, blocking tall vessels. But this section ___3___ . When swung open, it is perpendicular to the ends of the bridge, creating two free channels for river traffic. With swing bridges channel width is limited by the bridge's piers. The largest swing bridge provides only a 75-meter channel. Such channels are sometimes too ___4___ . In such cases, a bascule bridge may be built.

Bascule bridges are drawbridges with two arms that swing upward. They provide an opening as wide as the span. They are also versatile. These bridges are not limited to being fully opened or fully closed. They can be ___5___ in many ways. They can be fixed at different angles to accommodate different vessels.

In vertical lift bridges, the center remains horizontal. Towers at both ends allow the center to be lifted like an elevator. One interesting variation of this kind of bridge was built during World War II. A lift bridge was desired, but there were wartime shortages of the steel and machinery needed for the towers. It was hard to find enough ___6___ . An ingenious engineer designed the bridge so that it did not have to be raised above traffic. Instead it was ___7___ . It could be submerged seven meters below the surface of the river. Ships sailed over it.

1. A. wind   B. boats   C. experience
    D. wires   E. experience

2.   A.   levels   B.   cost   C.   standards
       D.   waves   E.   deck

3.   A.   stands   B.   floods   C.   wears
       D.   turns   E.   supports

4.   A.   narrow   B.   rough   C.   long
       D.   deep   E.   straight

5.   A.   crossed   B.   approached   C.   lighted
       D.   planned   E.   positioned

6.   A.   work   B.   material   C.   time
       D.   power   E.   space

7.   A.   burned   B.   emptied   C.   secured
       D.   shared   E.   lowered

The first universities emerged at the end of the 11th century and beginning of the 12th. These institutions were not founded on any particular date or created by any formal action.

Nobody actually ____8____ them. Instead, they developed gradually in places like Paris, Oxford, and Bologna, where scholars had long been teaching students. At first, these tutors

had not been associated with one another. Rather, they had been ____9____ . But, over time, they joined together to form guilds.

Guilds were groups of tradespeople, somewhat akin to modern unions. In the Middle

Ages, all the crafts had such ____10____ . The scholars' guilds built school buildings and evolved an administration which charged fees and set standards for the curriculum. It set prices for members' services and fixed requirements for entering the profession.

Professors were not the only schoolpeople forming associations. In Italy, students joined guilds to which teachers had to swear obedience. The students set strict rules, fining professors for beginning class a minute late. Teachers had to seek their students' permission to

marry, and such permission was not always granted. Sometimes the students ____11____ . Even if they said yes, the teacher got only one day's honeymoon.

Undergraduates took classes in Greek philosophy, Latin grammar, arithmetic, music, and

astronomy. These were the only ____12____ available. More advanced study was possible in law, medicine, and theology, but one could not earn such postgraduate degrees quickly. It

took a long time to ____13____ . Completing the requirements in theology, for example, took at least 13 years.

The concept of a fixed program of study leading to a degree first evolved in medieval

Europe. This ____14____ had not appeared before. In earlier academic settings, notions about *meeting requirements* and *graduating* had been absent. Since the Middle Ages, though, we have continued to view education as a set curriculum culminating in a degree.

8.   A. started   B. guarded   C. blamed
      D. compared   E. remembered

9.   A. curious   B. poor   C. religious
      D. curious   E. independent

10.   A. taxes   B. secrets   C. products
      D. problems   E. organizations

11.   A. left   B. copied   C. refused
      D. paid   E. prepared

12.   A. rooms   B. subjects   C. clothes
      D. pens   E. markets

13.   A. add   B. answer   C. forget
      D. finish   E. travel

14.   A. idea   B. desk   C. library
      D. capital   E. company

KEY (CORRECT ANSWERS)

1.	B	6.	B
2.	B	7.	E
3.	D	8.	A
4.	A	9.	E
5.	E	10.	E

11.	C
12.	B
13.	D
14.	A

READING COMPREHENSION
UNDERSTANDING AND INTERPRETING WRITTEN MATERIAL

EXAMINATION SECTION
TEST 1

Questions 1-40.

DIRECTIONS: Read the following passages, and select the most appropriate word from the five alternatives provided for each deleted word. Print the letter of the correct answer in the space at the right.

PASSAGE I

Bridges are built to allow a continuous flow of highway and railway traffic across water lying in their paths. But engineers cannot forget the fact that river traffic, too, is essential to our economy. The role of 1 is important. To keep these vessels moving freely, bridges are built high enough, when possible, to let them pass underneath. Sometimes, however, channels must accommodate very tall ships. It may be uneconomical to build a tall enough bridge. The 2 would be too high. To save money, engineers build movable bridges.

1. A. wind   B. boats   C. weight   1.____
    D. wires   E. experience

2. A. levels   B. cost   C. standards   2.____
    D. waves   E. deck

In the swing bridge, the middle part pivots or swings open. When the bridge is closed, this section joins the two ends of the bridge, blocking tall vessels. But this section 3. When swung open, it is perpendicular to the ends of the bridge, creating two free channels for river traffic. With swing bridges, channel width is limited by the bridge's piers. The largest swing bridge provides only a 75-meter channel. Such channels are sometimes too 4. In such cases, a bascule bridge may be built.

3. A. stands   B. floods   C. wears   3.____
    D. turns   E. supports

4. A. narrow   B. rough   C. long   4.____
    D. deep   E. straight

Bascule bridges are drawbridges with two arms that swing upward. They provide an opening as wide as the span. They are also versatile. These bridges are not limited to being fully opened or fully closed. They can be 5 in many ways. They can be fixed at different angles to accommodate different vessels.

5. A. approached   B. crossed   C. lighted   5.____
    D. planned   E. positioned

In vertical lift bridges, the center remains horizontal. Towers at both ends allow the center to be lifted like an elevator. One interesting variation of this kind of bridge was built during World War II. A lift bridge was desired, but there were wartime shortages of the steel and machinery needed for the towers. It was hard to find enough 6. An ingenious engineer designed the bridge so that it did not have to be raised above traffic. Instead it was <u>7</u>. It could be submerged seven meters below the river surface. Ships sailed over it.

6.   A.   work   B.   material   C.   time   6._____
       D.   power   E.   space

7.   A.   burned   B.   emptied   C.   secured   7._____
       D.   shared   E.   lowered

PASSAGE II

Before anesthetics were discovered, surgery was carried out under very severe time restrictions. Patients were awake, tossing and screaming in terrible pain. Surgeons were forced to hurry in order to constrain suffering and minimize shock. <u>8</u> was essential. Haste, however, did not make for good outcomes in surgery. No surprise, then, that the <u>9</u> were often poor.

8.   A.   Blood   B.   Silence   C.   Speed   8._____
       D.   Water   E.   Money

9.   A.   quarters   B.   teeth   C.   results   9._____
       D.   materials   E.   families

The discovery of anesthetics happened, in part, by accident. During the early 1800' s, nitrous oxide and ether were used for entertainment. At "ether frolics" in theaters, volunteers would breathe these gases, become lightheaded, and run around the stage laughing and dancing. By chance, a Connecticut dentist saw such a <u>10</u>. One volunteer banged his leg against a sharp edge. But he did not <u>11</u>. He paid no attention to his wound, as though he felt nothing. This gave the dentist the idea of using gas to kill pain.

10.   A.   show   B.   machine   C.   face   10._____
       D.   source   E.   growth

11.   A.   dream   B.   recover   C.   succeed   11._____
       D.   agree   E.   notice

At first, using the "open drip method," ether and chloroform were filtered through a cotton pad placed over the mouth and nose. This direct dose was difficult to regulate and irritating to the nose and throat. Patients would hold their breath, cough, or gag. This made it impossible for them to relax, let alone sleep. Consequently, surgery was often <u>12</u>. It couldn't begin until the patient had quieted and the anesthesia had taken hold.

12.   A.   delayed   B.   required   C.   blamed   12._____
       D.   observed   E.   repeated

Today's procedures are safer and more accurate. In the "closed method," a fixed amount of gas is released from sealed bottles into an inhalator bag when the patient exhales. He inhales this gas through tubes with his next breath. In this way, the gas is <u>13</u>. The system carefully regulates how much gas reaches the patient.

13.   A.   heated   B.   controlled   C.   cleaned   13._____
       D.   selected   E.   wasted

For dentistry and minor operations, patients need not be asleep. Newer anesthetics can be used which deaden nerves only in the affected part of the body. These <u>14</u> anesthetics offer several advantages. For instance, since the anesthesia is fairly light and patients remain awake, they can cooperate with their doctors.

14. A. local   B. natural   C. ancient   14.____
     D. heavy   E. thyee

PASSAGE III

An indispensable element in the development of telephony was the continual improvement of telephone station instruments, those operating units located at the client's premises. Modern units normally consist of a transmitter, receiver, and transformer. They also contain a bell or equivalent summoning device, a mechanism for controlling the unit's connection to the client's line, and various associated items, like dials. All of these 15 have changed over the years. The transmitter, especially, has undergone enormous refinement during the last century.

15. A. parts   B. costs   C. services   15.____
     D. models   E. routes

Bell's original electromagnetic transmitter functioned likewise as receiver, the same instrument being held alternately to mouth and ear. But having to 16 the instrument this way was inconvenient. Suggestions understandably emerged for mounting the transmitter and receiver onto a common handle, thereby creating what are now known as handsets. Transmitter and receiver were, in fact, later 17 his way. Combination handsets were produced for commercial utilization late in the nineteenth century, but prospects for their acceptance were uncertain as the initial quality of transmissions with the handsets was disappointing. But 18 transmissions followed. With adequately high transmission standards attained, acceptance of handsets was virtually assured.

16. A. store   B. use   C. test   16.____
     D. strip   E. clean

17. A. grounded   B. marked   C. covered   17.____
     D. priced   E. coupled

18. A. shorter   B. fewer   C. better   18.____
     D. faster   E. cheaper

Among the most significant improvements in transmitters has been the enormous amplification (up to a thousandfold) of speech sounds. This increased 19 has benefited telecommunications enormously. Nineteenth century telephone conversations frequently were only marginally audible, whereas nowadays even murmured conversations can be transmitted successfully, barring unusual atmospheric or electronic disturbances.

19. A. distance   B. speed   C. market   19.____
     D. volume   E. number

Vocal quality over nineteenth century instruments was distorted, the speaker not readily identifiable. By comparison, current sound is characterized by considerably greater naturalism. Modern telephony produces speech sounds more nearly resembling an individual's actual voice. Thus it is easier to 20 the speaker. A considerable portion of this improvement is attributable to practical applications of laboratory investigations concerning the mechanisms of human speech and audition. These 21 have exerted a profound influence. Their results prompted technical innovations in modern transmitter design which contributed appreciably to the excellent communication available nowadays.

20. A. time   B. help   C. bill   20.____
     D. stop   E. recognize

21. A. studies   B. rates   C. materials   21.____
     D. machines   E. companies

PASSAGE IV

The dramatic events of December 7, 1941, plunged this nation into war. The full 22 of the war we cannot even now comprehend, but one of the effects stands out in sharp relief — the coming of the air age. The airplane, which played a relatively 23 part in World War I, has already soared to heights undreamed of save by the few with mighty vision.

In wartime the airplane is the 24 on wings and the battleship that flies. To man in his need it symbolizes deadly, extremes; friend or foe; deliverance or 25.

It is a powerful instrument of war revolutionizing military strategy, but its peacetime role is just as 26. This new master of time and space, fruit of man's inventive genius, has come to stay, smalling the earth and smoothing its surface.

To all of us, then, to youth, and to 27 alike. comes the winged challenge to get ourselves ready–to 28 ourselves for living in an age which the airplane seems destined to mold.

22. A. destruction   B. character   C. history   22.____
     D. import   E. picture

23. A. important   B. dull   C. vast   D. unknown   E. minor   23.____

24. A. giant   B. ant   C. monster   D. artillery   E. robot   24.____

25. A. ecstasy   B. bombardment   C. death   25.____
     D. denial   E. survival

26. A. revolting   B. revolutionary   C. residual   26.____
     D. reliable   E. regressive

27. A. animals   B. nations   C. women   D. men   E. adult   27.____

28. A. distract   B. engage   C. determine   D. deter   E. orient   28.____

PASSAGE V

Let us consider how voice training may contribute to 29 development and an improved social 30.

In the first place, it has been fairly well established that individuals tend to become what they believe 31 people think them to be.

When people react more favorably toward us because our voices 32 the impression that we are friendly, competent, and interesting, there is a strong tendency for us to develop those 33 in our personality.

If we are treated with respect by others, we soon come to have more respect for 34.

Then, too, one's own consciousness of having a pleasant, effective voice of which he does not need to be ashamed contributes materially to a feeling of poise, self-confidence, and a just pride in himself.

A good voice, like good clothes, can do much for an 35 that otherwise might be inclined to droop.

29. A. facial   B. material   C. community   29.____
     D. personality   E. physical

30. A. adjustment   B. upheaval   C. development   30.____
     D. bias   E. theories

31. A. some   B. hostile   C. jealous   D. inferior   E. other   31.____

32. A. betray   B. imply   C. destroy   32.____
     D. transfigure   E. convey

33. A. defects   B. qualities   C. techniques   33.____
     D. idiosyncrasies   E. quirks

34. A. others   B. their children   C. their teachers   34.____
     D. ourselves   E. each other

35. A. mind   B. heart   C. brain   D. feeling   E. ego.   35.____

PASSAGE VI

How are symphony orchestras launched, kept going, and built up in smaller communities? Recent reports from five of them suggest that, though the 36 changes, certain elements are fairly common. One thing shines out; 37 is essential.

Also, aside from the indispensable, instrumentalists who play, the following personalities, either singly, or preferably in 38. seem to be the chief needs; a conductor who wants to conduct so badly he will organize his own orchestra if it is the only way he can get one; a manager with plenty of resourcefulness in rounding up audiences and finding financial support; an energetic community leader, generally a woman, who will take up locating the orchestra as a 39; and generous visiting soloists who will help draw those who are 40 that anything local can be used.

36. A. world   B. pattern   C. reason   D. scene   E. cast   36.____

37. A. hatred   B. love   C. enthusiasm   37.____
     D. participation   E. criticism

38. A. combination   B. particular   C. isolation   38.____
     D. sympathy   E. solitary

39. A. chore   B. duty   C. hobby   D. delight   E. career   39.____

40. A. convinced   B. skeptical   C. happy   40.____
     D. unhappy   E. unsure

KEY (CORRECT ANSWERS)

1.	B	11.	E	21.	A	31.	E
2.	B	12.	A	22.	D	32.	E
3.	D	13.	B	23.	E	33.	B
4.	A	14.	A	24.	D	34.	D
5.	E	15.	A	25.	C	35.	E
6.	B	16.	B	26.	B	36.	B
7.	E	17.	E	27.	E	37.	C
8.	C	18.	C	28.	E	38.	A
9.	C	19.	D	29.	D	39.	C
10.	A	20.	E	30.	A	40.	B

READING COMPREHENSION
UNDERSTANDING AND INTERPRETING WRITTEN MATERIAL

COMMENTARY

The ability to read and understand written materials – texts, publications, newspapers, orders, directions, expositions – is a skill basic to a functioning democracy and to an efficient business or viable government.

That is why almost all examinations – for beginning, middle, and senior levels – test reading comprehension, directly or indirectly.

The reading test measures how well you understand what you read. This is how it is done: You read a short paragraph and five statements. From the five statements, you choose the one statement, or answer, that is BEST supported by, or best matches, what is said in the paragraph.

SAMPLE QUESTIONS

DIRECTIONS: Each question has five suggested answers, lettered A, B, C, D, and E. Decide which one is the BEST answer. *PRINT THE LETTER OF THE CORRECT ANSWER IN THE SPACE AT THE RIGHT.*

1. The prevention of accidents makes it necessary not only that safety devices be used to guard exposed machinery but also that mechanics be instructed in safety rules which they must follow for their own protection and that the light in the plant be adequate. The paragraph BEST supports the statement that industrial accidents

    1.____

A.   are always avoidable
B.   may be due to ignorance
C.   usually result from inadequate machinery
D.   cannot be entirely overcome
E.   result in damage to machinery

ANALYSIS

Remember what you have to do–
    First   - Read the paragraph.
    Second - Decide what the paragraph means.
    Third   - Read the five suggested answers.
    Fourth   - Select the one answer which BEST matches what the paragraph says or is BEST supported by something in the paragraph. (Sometimes you may have to read the paragraph again in order to be sure which suggested answer is best.)

This paragraph is talking about three steps that should be taken to prevent industrial accidents–

1.   use safety devices on machines
2.   instruct mechanics in safety rules
3.   provide adequate lighting.

SELECTION

With this in mind let's look at each suggested answer. Each one starts with "Industrial accidents..."

SUGGESTED ANSWER A.

Industrial accidents (A) are always avoidable.
(The paragraph talks about how to avoid accidents, but does not say that accidents are always avoidable.)

SUGGESTED ANSWER B.

Industrial accidents (b) may be due to ignorance.
(One of the steps given in the paragraph to prevent accidents is to instruct mechanics on safety rules. This suggests that lack of knowledge or ignorance of safety rules causes accidents. This suggested answer sounds like a good possibility for being the right answer.)

SUGGESTED ANSWER C.

Industrial accidents (C) usually result from inadequate machinery.
(The paragraph does suggest that exposed machines cause accidents, but it doesn't say that it is the usual cause of accidents. The word usually makes this a wrong answer.)

SUGGESTED ANSWER D.

Industrial accidents (D) cannot be entirely overcome.
(You may know from your own experience that this is a true statement. But that is not what the paragraph is talking about. Therefore it is NOT the correct answer.)

SUGGESTED ANSWER E.

Industrial accidents (E) result in damage to machinery.
(This is a statement that may or may not be true, but in any case it is NOT covered by the paragraph.)

_____

Looking back, you see that the one suggested answer of the five given that BEST matches what the paragraph says is—

Industrial accidents (B) may be due to ignorance.

The CORRECT answer then is B.

Be sure you read ALL the possible answers before you make your choice. You may think that none of the five answers is really good, but choose the BEST one of the five.

_____

2. Probably few people realize, as they drive on a concrete road, that steel is used to keep the surface flat in spite of the weight of the busses and trucks. Steel bars, deeply embedded in the concrete, provide sinews to take the stresses so that the stresses cannot crack the slab or make it wavy.

2.____

The paragraph BEST supports the statement that a concrete road

   A. is expensive to build
   B. usually cracks under heavy weights
   C. looks like any other road
   D. is used only for heavy traffic
   E. is reinforced with other material

ANALYSIS

This paragraph is commenting on the fact that—
   1. few people realize, as they drive on a concrete road, that steel is deeply embedded
   2. steel keeps the surface flat
   3. steel bars enable the road to take the stresses without cracking or becoming wavy.

SELECTION

Now read and think about the possible answers:
   A. A concrete road is expensive to build. (Maybe so but that is not what the paragraph is about.)
   B. A concrete road usually cracks under heavy weights. (The paragraph talks about using steel bars to prevent heavy weights from cracking concrete roads. It says nothing about how usual it is for the roads to crack. The word *usually* makes this suggested answer wrong.)
   C. A concrete road looks like any other road. (This may or may not be true. The important thing to note is that it has nothing to do with what the paragraph is about.)
   D. A concrete road is used only for heavy traffic. (This answer at least has something to do with the paragraph-concrete roads are used with heavy traffic but it does not say "used only.")
   E. A concrete road is reinforced with other material. (This choice seems to be the correct one on two counts: First, the paragraph does suggest that concrete roads are made stronger by embedding steel bars in them. This is another way of saying "concrete roads are reinforced with steel bars." Second, by the process of elimination, the other four choices are ruled out as correct answers simply because they do not apply.)

You can be sure that not all the reading questions will be so easy as these.

———————

HINTS FOR ANSWERING READING QUESTIONS

1. Read the paragraph carefully. Then read each suggested answer carefully. Read every word, because often one word can make the difference between a right and a wrong answer.

2. Choose that answer which is supported in the paragraph itself. Do not choose an answer which is a correct statement unless it is based on information in the paragraph.

3. Even though a suggested answer has many of the words used in the paragraph, it may still be wrong.

4. Look out for words — such as *always, never, entirely, or only* — which tend to make a suggested answer wrong.

5. Answer first those questions which you can answer most easily. Then work on the other questions.

6. If you can't figure out the answer to the question, guess.

———

READING COMPREHENSION
UNDERSTANDING AND INTERPRETING WRITTEN MATERIAL

EXAMINATION SECTION
TEST 1

DIRECTIONS: Each question or incomplete statement is followed by several suggested answers or completions. Select the one that BEST answers the question or completes the statement. *PRINT THE LETTER OF THE CORRECT ANSWER IN THE SPACE AT THE RIGHT.*

Questions 1-5.

DIRECTIONS: Questions 1 through 5 are to be answered on the basis of the following passage.

The laws with which criminal courts are concerned contain threats of punishment for infraction of specified rules. Consequently, the courts are organized primarily for implementation of the punitive societal reaction of crime. While the informal organization of most courts allows the judge to use discretion as to which guilty persons actually are to be punished, the threat of punishment for all guilty persons always is present. Also, in recent years a number of formal provisions for the use of non-punitive and treatment methods by the criminal courts have been made, but the threat of punishment remains, even for the recipients of the treatment and non-punitive measures. For example, it has become possible for courts to grant probation, which can be non-punitive, to some offenders, but the probationer is constantly under the threat of punishment, for, if he does not maintain the conditions of his probation, he may be imprisoned. As the treatment reaction to crime becomes more popular, the criminal courts may have as their sole function the determination of the guilt or innocence of the accused persons, leaving the problem of correcting criminals entirely to outsiders. Under such conditions, the organization of the court system, the duties and activities of court personnel, and the nature of the trial all would be decidedly different.

1. Which one of the following is the BEST description of the subject matter of the above passage?
   The

   A. value of non-punitive measures for criminals
   B. effect of punishment on guilty individuals
   C. punitive functions of the criminal courts
   D. success of probation as a deterrent of crime

1.____

2. It may be INFERRED from the above passage that the present traditional organization of the criminal court system is a result of

   A. the nature of the laws with which these courts are concerned
   B. a shift from non-punitive to punitive measures for correctional purposes
   C. an informal arrangement between court personnel and the government
   D. a formal decision made by court personnel to increase efficiency

2.____

3. All persons guilty of breaking certain specified rules, according to the above passage, are subject to the threat of   3.____

    A. treatment   B. punishment
    C. probation   D. retrial

4. According to the above passage, the decision whether or not to punish a guilty person is a function USUALLY performed by   4.____

    A. the jury   B. the criminal code
    C. the judge   D. corrections personnel

5. According to the above passage, which one of the following is a possible effect of an increase in the *treatment reactions to crime?*   5.____

    A. A decrease in the number of court personnel
    B. An increase in the number of criminal trials
    C. Less reliance on probation as a non-punitive treatment measure
    D. A decrease in the functions of the court following determination of guilt

Questions 6-8.

DIRECTIONS: Questions 6 through 8 are to be answered on the basis of the following passage.

A glaring exception to the usual practice of the judicial trial as a means of conflict resolution is the utilization of administrative hearings. The growing tendency to create administrative bodies with rule-making and quasi-judicial powers has shattered many standard concepts. A comprehensive examination of the legal process cannot neglect these newer patterns.

In the administrative process, the legislative, executive, and judicial functions are mixed together, and many functions, such as investigating, advocating, negotiating, testifying, rule making, and adjudicating, are carried out by the same agency. The reason for the breakdown of the separation-of-powers formula is not hard to find. It was felt by Congress, and state and municipal legislatures, that certain regulatory tasks could not be performed efficiently, rapidly, expertly, and with due concern for the public interest by the traditional branches of government. Accordingly, regulatory agencies were delegated powers to consider disputes from the earliest stage of investigation to the final stages of adjudication entirely within each agency itself, subject only to limited review in the regular courts.

6. The above passage states that the usual means for conflict resolution is through the use of   6.____

    A. judicial trial   B. administrative hearing
    C. legislation   D. regulatory agencies

7. The above passage IMPLIES that the use of administrative hearing in resolving conflict is a(n) _____ approach.   7.____

    A. traditional   B. new
    C. dangerous   D. experimental

8. The above passage states that the reason for the breakdown of the separation-of-powers formula in the administrative process is that   8.____

A. Congress believed that certain regulatory tasks could be better performed by separate agencies
B. legislative and executive functions are incompatible in the same agency
C. investigative and regulatory functions are not normally reviewed by the courts
D. state and municipal legislatures are more concerned with efficiency than with legality

Questions 9-10.

DIRECTIONS: Questions 9 and 10 are to be answered SOLELY on the basis of the information given in the following paragraph.

An assumption commonly made in regard to the reliability of testimony is that when a number of persons report upon the same matter, those details upon which there is an agreement may, in general, be considered as substantiated. Experiments have shown, however, that there is a tendency for the same errors to appear in the testimony of different individuals, and that, quite apart from any collusion, agreement of testimony is no proof of dependability.

9. According to the above paragraph, it is commonly assumed that details of an event are substantiated when   9.____

   A. a number of persons report upon them
   B. a reliable person testifies to them
   C. no errors are apparent in the testimony of different individuals
   D. several witnesses are in agreement about them

10. According to the above paragraph, agreement in the testimony of different witnesses to the same event is   10.____

   A. evaluated more reliably when considered apart from collusion
   B. not the result of chance
   C. not a guarantee of the accuracy of the facts
   D. the result of a mass reaction of the witnesses

Questions 11-12.

DIRECTIONS: Questions 11 and 12 are to be answered SOLELY on the basis of the information given in the following paragraph.

The accuracy of the information about past occurrence obtainable in an interview is so low that one must take the stand that the best use to be made of the interview in this connection is a means of finding clues and avenues of access to more reliable sources of information. On the other hand, feelings and attitudes have been found to be clearly and correctly revealed in a properly conducted personal interview.

11. According to the above paragraph, information obtained in a personal interview   11.____

   A. can be corroborated by other clues and more reliable sources of information revealed at the interview
   B. can be used to develop leads to other sources of information about past events
   C. is not reliable
   D. is reliable if it relates to recent occurrences

12. According to the above paragraph, the personal interview is suitable for obtaining 12.____

    A. emotional reactions to a given situation
    B. fresh information on factors which may be forgotten
    C. revived recollection of previous events for later use as testimony
    D. specific information on material already reduced to writing

Questions 13-15.

DIRECTIONS: Questions 13 through 15 are to be answered on the basis of the following paragraph.

Admissibility of handwriting standards (samples of handwriting for the purpose of comparison) as a basis for expert testimony is frequently necessary when the authenticity of disputed documents may be at issue. Under the older rules of common law, only that writing relating to the issues in the case could be used as a basis for handwriting testimony by an expert. Today, most jurisdictions admit irrelevant writings as standards for comparison. However, their genuineness, in all instances, must be established to the satisfaction of the court. There are a number of types of documents, however, not ordinarily relevant to the issues which are seldom acceptable to the court as handwriting standards, such as bail bonds, signatures on affidavits, depositions, etc. These are usually already before the court as part of the record in a case. Exhibits written in the presence of a witness or prepared voluntarily for a law enforcement officer are readily admissible in most jurisdictions. Testimony of a witness who is considered familiar with the writing is admissible in some jurisdictions. In criminal cases, it is possible that the signature on the fingerprint card obtained in connection with the arrest of the defendant for the crime currently charged may be admitted as a handwriting standard. In order to give the defendant the fairest possible treatment, most jurisdictions do not admit the signatures on fingerprint cards pertaining to prior arrests. However, they are admitted sometimes. In such instances, the court usually requires that the signature be photographed or removed from the card and no reference be made to the origin of the signature.

13. Of the following, the types of handwriting standards MOST likely to be admitted in evidence by most jurisdictions are those 13.____

    A. appearing on depositions and bail bonds
    B. which were written in the presence of a witness or voluntarily given to a law enforcement officer
    C. identified by witnesses who claim to be familiar with the handwriting
    D. which are in conformity with the rules of common law only

14. The PRINCIPAL factor which generally determines the acceptance of handwriting standards by the courts is 14.____

    A. the relevance of the submitted documents to the issues of the case
    B. the number of witnesses who have knowledge of the submitted documents
    C. testimony that the writing has been examined by a handwriting expert
    D. acknowledgment by the court of the authenticity of the submitted documents

15. The MOST logical reason for requiring the removal of the signature of a defendant from fingerprint cards pertaining to prior arrests, before admitting the signature in court as a handwriting standard, is that 15.____

A. it simplifies the process of identification of the signature as a standard for comparison
B. the need for identifying the fingerprints is eliminated
C. mention of prior arrests may be prejudicial to the defendant
D. a handwriting expert does not need information pertaining to prior arrests in order to make his identification

Questions 16-20.

DIRECTIONS: Questions 16 through 20 are to be answered SOLELY on the basis of the information contained in the following paragraph.

A statement which is offered in an attempt to prove the truth of the matters therein stated, but which is not made by the author as a witness before the court at the particular trial in which it is so offered, is hearsay. This is so whether the statement consists of words (oral or written), of symbols used as a substitute for words, or of signs or other conduct offered as the equivalent of a statement. Subject to some well-established exceptions, hearsay is not generally acceptable as evidence, and it does not become competent evidence just because it is received by the court without objection. One basis for this rule is simply that a fact cannot be proved by showing that somebody stated it was a fact. Another basis for the rule is the fundamental principle that in a criminal prosecution the testimony of the witness shall be taken before the court, so that at the time he gives the testimony offered in evidence he will be sworn and subject to cross-examination, the scrutiny of the court, and confrontation by the accused.

16.   Which of the following is hearsay?   16.____
       A(n)

       A.   written statement by a person not present at the court hearing where the statement is submitted as proof of an occurrence
       B.   oral statement in court by a witness of what he saw
       C.   written statement of what he saw by a witness present in court
       D.   re-enactment by a witness in court of what he saw

17.   In a criminal case, a statement by a person not present in court is   17.____

       A.   *acceptable* evidence if not objected to by the prosecutor
       B.   *acceptable* evidence if not objected to by the defense lawyer
       C.   *not acceptable* evidence except in certain well-settled circumstances
       D.   *not acceptable* evidence under any circumstances

18.   The rule on hearsay is founded on the belief that   18.____

       A.   proving someone said an act occurred is not proof that the act did occur
       B.   a person who has knowledge about a case should be willing to appear in court
       C.   persons not present in court are likely to be unreliable witnesses
       D.   permitting persons to testify without appearing in court will lead to a disrespect for law

19. One reason for the general rule that a witness in a criminal case must give his testimony in court is that   19.____

    A. a witness may be influenced by threats to make untrue statements
    B. the opposite side is then permitted to question him
    C. the court provides protection for a witness against unfair questioning
    D. the adversary system is designed to prevent a miscarriage of justice

20. Of the following, the MOST appropriate title for the above passage would be   20.____

    A. WHAT IS HEARSAY?   B. RIGHTS OF DEFENDANTS
    C. TRIAL PROCEDURES   D. TESTIMONY OF WITNESSES

21. A person's statements are independent of who he is or what he is. Statements made by   21.____
a person are not proved true or false by questioning his character or his position. A statement should stand or fall on its merits, regardless of who makes the statement. Truth is determined by evidence only. A person's character or personality should not be the determining factor in logic. Discussions should not become incidents of name calling. According to the above, whether or not a statement is true depends on the

    A. recipient's conception of validity
    B. maker's reliability
    C. extent of support by facts
    D. degree of merit the discussion has

Question 22-25.

DIRECTIONS: Questions 22 through 25 are to be answered on the basis of the following passage.

The question, whether an act, repugnant to the Constitution, can become the law of the land, is a question deeply interesting to the United States; but, happily, not of an intricacy proportioned to its interest. It seems only necessary to recognize certain principles, supposed to have been long and well-established, to decide it. That the people have an original right to establish, for their future government, such principles as, in their opinion, shall most conduce to their own happiness, is the basis on which the whole American fabric has been erected. The exercise of this original right is a very great exertion; nor can it, nor ought it, to be frequently repeated. The principles, therefore, so established are deemed fundamental; and as the authority from which they proceed is supreme, and can seldom act, they are designed to be permanent.

22. The BEST title for the above passage would be   22.____

    A. PRINCIPLES OF THE CONSTITUTION
    B. THE ROOT OF CONSTITUTIONAL CHANGE
    C. ONLY PEOPLE CAN CHANGE THE CONSTITUTION
    D. METHODS OF CONSTITUTIONAL CHANGE

23. According to the above passage, original right is   23.____

    A. fundamental to the principle that the people may choose their own form of government
    B. established by the Constitution

C. the result of a very great exertion and should not often be repeated
D. supreme, can seldom act, and is designed to be permanent

24. Whether an act not in keeping with Constitutional principles can become law is, according to the above passage,   24._____

    A. an intricate problem requiring great thought and concentration
    B. determined by the proportionate interests of legislators
    C. determined by certain long established principles, fundamental to Constitutional Law
    D. an intricate problem, but less intricate than it would seem from the interest shown in it

25. According to the above passage, the phrase *and can seldom act* refers to the   25._____

    A. principle enacted early into law by Americans when they chose their future form of government
    B. original rights of the people as vested in the Constitution
    C. original framers of the Constitution
    D. established, fundamental principles of government

KEY (CORRECT ANSWERS)

1.	C		11.	B
2.	A		12.	A
3.	B		13.	B
4.	C		14.	D
5.	D		15.	C
6.	A		16.	A
7.	B		17.	C
8.	A		18.	A
9.	D		19.	B
10.	C		20.	A

21.	C
22.	B
23.	A
24.	D
25.	A

TEST 2

DIRECTIONS: Each question or incomplete statement is followed by several suggested answers or completions. Select the one that BEST answers the question or completes the statement. *PRINT THE LETTER OF THE CORRECT ANSWER IN THE SPACE AT THE RIGHT.*

Questions 1-3.

DIRECTIONS: Questions 1 through 3 are to be answered SOLELY on the basis of the following paragraph.

The police laboratory performs a valuable service in crime investigation by assisting in the reconstruction of criminal action and by aiding in the identification of persons and things. When studied by a technician, physical things found at crime scenes often reveal facts useful in identifying the criminal and in determining what has occurred. The nature of substances to be examined and the character of the examination to be made vary so widely that the services of a large variety of skilled scientific persons are needed in crime investigations. To employ such a complete staff and to provide them with equipment and standards needed for all possible analysis and comparisons is beyond the means and the needs of any but the largest police departments. The search of crime scenes for physical evidence also calls for the services of specialists supplied with essential equipment and assigned to each tour of duty so as to provide service at any hour.

1. If a police department employs a large staff of technicians of various types in its laboratory, it will affect crime investigations to the extent that   1._____

    A. most crimes will be speedily solved
    B. identification of criminals will be aided
    C. search of crime scenes for physical evidence will become of less importance
    D. investigation by police officers will not usually be required

2. According to the above paragraph, the MOST complete study of objects found at the scenes of crimes is   2._____

    A. always done in all large police departments
    B. based on assigning one technician to each tour of duty
    C. probably done only in large police departments
    D. probably done in police departments of communities with low crime rates

3. According to the above paragraph, a large variety of skilled technicians is useful in criminal investigations because   3._____

    A. crimes cannot be solved without their assistance as part of the police team
    B. large police departments need large staffs
    C. many different kinds of tests on various substances can be made
    D. the police cannot predict what methods may be tried by wily criminals

Questions 4-6.

DIRECTIONS: Questions 4 through 6 are to be answered SOLELY on the basis of the following passage.

Probably the most important single mechanism for bringing the resources of science and technology to bear on the problems of crime would be the establishment of a major prestigious science and technology research program within a research institute. The program would create interdisciplinary teams of mathematicians, computer scientists, electronics engineers, physicists, biologists, and other natural scientists, psychologists, sociologists, economists, and lawyers. The institute and the program must be significant enough to attract the best scientists available, and, to this end, the director of this institute must himself have a background in science and technology and have the respect of scientists. Because it would be difficult to attract such a staff into the Federal government, the institute should be established by a university, a group of universities, or an independent nonprofit organization, and should be within a major metropolitan area. The institute would have to establish close ties with neighboring criminal justice agencies that would receive the benefit of serving as experimental laboratories for such an institute. In fact, the proposal for the institute might be jointly submitted with the criminal justice agencies. The research program would require, in order to bring together the necessary *critical mass* of competent staff, an annual budget which might reach 5 million dollars, funded with at least three years of lead time to assure continuity. Such a major scientific and technological research institute should be supported by the Federal government.

4. Of the following, the MOST appropriate title for the foregoing passage is   4._____

    A. RESEARCH - AN INTERDISCIPLINARY APPROACH TO FIGHTING CRIME
    B. A CURRICULUM FOR FIGHTING CRIME
    C. THE ROLE OF THE UNIVERSITY IN THE FIGHT AGAINST CRIME
    D. GOVERNMENTAL SUPPORT OF CRIMINAL RESEARCH PROGRAMS

5. According to the above passage, in order to attract the best scientists available, the   5._____
research institute should

    A. provide psychologists and sociologists to counsel individual members of interdisciplinary teams
    B. encourage close ties with neighboring criminal justice agencies
    C. be led by a person who is respected in the scientific community
    D. be directly operated and funded by the Federal government

6. The term *critical mass,* as used in the above passage, refers MAINLY to   6._____

    A. a staff which would remain for three years of continuous service to the institute
    B. staff members necessary to carry out the research program of the institute successfully
    C. the staff necessary to establish relations with criminal justice agencies which will serve as experimental laboratories for the institute
    D. a staff which would be able to assist the institute in raising adequate funds

Questions 7-9.

DIRECTIONS: Questions 7 through 9 are to be answered SOLELY on the basis of the following paragraph.

The use of modern scientific methods in the examination of physical evidence often provides information to the investigator which he could not otherwise obtain. This applies particularly to small objects and materials present in minute quantities or trace evidence because the quantities here are such that they may be overlooked without methodical searching, and often special means of detection are needed. Whenever two objects come in contact with one another, there is a transfer of material, however slight. Usually, the softer object will transfer to the harder, but the transfer may be mutual. The quantity of material transferred differs with the type of material involved and the more violent the contact the greater the degree of transference. Through scientific methods of determining physical properties and chemical composition, we can add to the facts observable by the investigator's unaided senses, and thereby increase the chances of identification.

7. According to the above paragraph, the amount of material transferred whenever two objects come in contact with one another

    7.____

    A. varies directly with the softness of the objects involved
    B. varies directly with the violence of the contact of the objects
    C. is greater when two soft, rather than hard, objects come into violent contact with each other
    D. is greater when coarse-grained, rather than smooth-grained, materials are involved

8. According to the above paragraph, the PRINCIPAL reason for employing scientific methods in obtaining trace evidence is that

    8.____

    A. other methods do not involve a methodical search of the crime scene
    B. scientific methods of examination frequently reveal physical evidence which did not previously exist
    C. the amount of trace evidence may be so sparse that other methods are useless
    D. trace evidence cannot be properly identified unless special means of detection are employed

9. According to the above paragraph, the one of the following statements which BEST describes the manner in which scientific methods of analyzing physical evidence assists the investigator is that such methods

    9.____

    A. add additional valuable information to the investigator's own knowledge of complex and rarely occurring materials found as evidence
    B. compensate for the lack of important evidential material through the use of physical and chemical analyses
    C. make possible an analysis of evidence which goes beyond the ordinary capacity of the investigator's senses
    D. identify precisely those physical characteristics of the individual which the untrained senses of the investigator are unable to discern

Questions 10-13.

DIRECTIONS: Questions 10 through 13 are to be answered SOLELY on the basis of the information contained in the following paragraph.

Under the provisions of the Bank Protection Act of 1968, enacted July 8, 1968, each Federal banking supervisory agency, as of January 7, 1969, had to issue rules establishing minimum standards with which financial institutions under their control must comply with respect to the installation, maintenance, and operation of security devices and procedures, reasonable in cost, to discourage robberies, burglaries, and larcenies, and to assist in the identification and apprehension of persons who commit such acts. The rules set the time limits within which the affected banks and savings and loan associations must comply with the standards, and the rules require the submission of periodic reports on the steps taken. A violator of a rule under this Act is subject to a civil penalty not to exceed $100 for each day of the violation. The enforcement of these regulations rests with the responsible banking supervisory agencies.

10. The Bank Protection Act of 1968 was designed to   10.____

    A. provide Federal police protection for banks covered by the Act
    B. have organizations covered by the Act take precautions against criminals
    C. set up a system for reporting all bank robberies to the FBI
    D. insure institutions covered by the Act from financial loss due to robberies, burglaries, and larcenies

11. Under the provisions of the Bank Protection Act of 1968, each Federal banking supervi-   11.____
sory agency was required to set up rules for financial institutions covered by the Act governing the

    A. hiring of personnel
    B. punishment of burglars
    C. taking of protective measures
    D. penalties for violations

12. Financial institutions covered by the Bank Protection Act of 1968 were required to   12.____

    A. file reports at regular intervals on what they had done to prevent theft
    B. identify and apprehend persons who commit robberies, burglaries, and larcenies
    C. draw up a code of ethics for their employees
    D. have fingerprints of their employees filed with the FBI

13. Under the provisions of the Bank Protection Act of 1968, a bank which is subject to the   13.____
rules established under the Act and which violates a rule is liable to a penalty of NOT
_____ than $100 for each _____.

    A. more; violation   B. less; day of violation
    C. less; violation   D. more; day of violation

Questions 14-17.

DIRECTIONS: Questions 14 through 17 are to be answered SOLELY on the basis of the following passage.

    Specific measures for prevention of pilferage will be based on careful analysis of the conditions at each agency. The most practical and effective method to control casual pilferage is the establishment of psychological deterrents.

    One of the most common means of discouraging casual pilferage is to search individuals leaving the agency at unannounced times and places. These spot searches may occasionally detect attempts at theft, but greater value is realized by bringing to the attention of individuals the fact that they may be apprehended if they do attempt the illegal removal of property.

    An aggressive security education program is an effective means of convincing employees that they have much more to lose than they do to gain by engaging in acts of theft. It is important for all employees to realize that pilferage is morally wrong no matter how insignificant the value of the item which is taken. In establishing any deterrent to casual pilferage, security officers must not lose sight of the fact that most employees are honest and disapprove of thievery. Mutual respect between security personnel and other employees of the agency must be maintained if the facility is to be protected from other more dangerous forms of human hazards. Any security measure which infringes on the human rights or dignity of others will jeopardize, rather than enhance, the overall protection of the agency.

14. The $100,000 yearly inventory of an agency revealed that $50 worth of goods had been stolen; the only individuals with access to the stolen materials were the employees. Of the following measures, which would the author of the above passage MOST likely recommend to a security officer?   14.____

    A. Conduct an intensive investigation of all employees to find the culprit.
    B. Make a record of the theft, but take no investigative or disciplinary action against any employee.
    C. Place a tight security check on all future movements of personnel.
    D. Remove the remainder of the material to an area with much greater security.

15. What does the passage imply is the percentage of employees whom a security officer should expect to be honest?   15.____

    A. No employee can be expected to be honest all of the time
    B. Just 50%
    C. Less than 50%
    D. More than 50%

16. According to the above passage, the security officer would use which of the following methods to minimize theft in buildings with many exits when his staff is very small?   16.____

    A. Conduct an inventory of all material and place a guard near that which is most likely to be pilfered
    B. Inform employees of the consequences of legal prosecution for pilfering
    C. Close off the unimportant exits and have all his men concentrate on a few exits
    D. Place a guard at each exit and conduct a casual search of individuals leaving the premises

17. Of the following, the title BEST suited for this passage is   17.____

    A. CONTROL MEASURES FOR CASUAL PILFERING
    B. DETECTING THE POTENTIAL PILFERER
    C. FINANCIAL LOSSES RESULTING FROM PILFERING
    D. THE USE OF MORAL PERSUASION IN PHYSICAL SECURITY

Questions 18-24.

DIRECTIONS: Questions 18 through 24 are to be answered SOLELY on the basis of the following passage.

Burglar alarms are designed to detect intrusion automatically. Robbery alarms enable a victim of a robbery or an attack to signal for help. Such devices can be located in elevators, hallways, homes and apartments, businesses and factories, and subways, as well as on the street in high-crime areas. Alarms could deter some potential criminals from attacking targets so protected. If alarms were prevalent and not visible, then they might serve to suppress crime generally. In addition, of course, the alarms can summon the police when they are needed.

All alarms must perform three functions: sensing or initiation of the signal, transmission of the signal and annunciation of the alarm. A burglar alarm needs a sensor to detect human presence or activity in an unoccupied enclosed area like a building or a room. A robbery victim would initiate the alarm by closing a foot or wall switch, or by triggering a portable transmitter which would send the alarm signal to a remote receiver. The signal can sound locally as a loud noise to frighten away a criminal, or it can be sent silently by wire to a central agency. A centralized annunciator requires either private lines from each alarmed point, or the transmission of some information on the location of the signal.

18. A conclusion which follows LOGICALLY from the above passage is that   18.____

    A. burglar alarms employ sensor devices; robbery alarms make use of initiation devices
    B. robbery alarms signal intrusion without the help of the victim; burglar alarms require the victim to trigger a switch
    C. robbery alarms sound locally; burglar alarms are transmitted to a central agency
    D. the mechanisms for a burglar alarm and a robbery alarm are alike

19. According to the above passage, alarms can be located   19.____

    A. in a wide variety of settings
    B. only in enclosed areas
    C. at low cost in high-crime areas
    D. only in places where potential criminals will be deterred

20. According to the above passage, which of the following is ESSENTIAL if a signal is to be received in a central office?   20.____

    A. A foot or wall switch
    B. A noise-producing mechanism
    C. A portable reception device
    D. Information regarding the location of the source

21. According to the above passage, an alarm system can function WITHOUT a   21.____

    A. centralized annunciating device
    B. device to stop the alarm
    C. sensing or initiating device
    D. transmission device

22. According to the above passage, the purpose of robbery alarms is to   22.____

    A. find out automatically whether a robbery has taken place
    B. lower the crime rate in high-crime areas
    C. make a loud noise to frighten away the criminal
    D. provide a victim with the means to signal for help

23. According to the above passage, alarms might aid in lessening crime if they were   23.____

    A. answered promptly by police
    B. completely automatic
    C. easily accessible to victims
    D. hidden and widespread

24. Of the following, the BEST title for the above passage is   24.____

    A. DETECTION OF CRIME BY ALARMS
    B. LOWERING THE CRIME RATE
    C. SUPPRESSION OF CRIME
    D. THE PREVENTION OF ROBBERY

25. Although the rural crime reporting area is much less developed than that for cities and   25.____
    towns, current data are collected in sufficient volume to justify the generalization that
    rural crime rates are lower than those or urban communities.
    According to this statement,

    A. better reporting of crime occurs in rural areas than in cities
    B. there appears to be a lower proportion of crime in rural areas than in cities
    C. cities have more crime than towns
    D. crime depends on the amount of reporting

KEY (CORRECT ANSWERS)

1.	B	11.	C
2.	C	12.	A
3.	C	13.	D
4.	A	14.	B
5.	C	15.	D
6.	B	16.	B
7.	B	17.	A
8.	C	18.	A
9.	C	19.	A
10.	B	20.	D

21.	A
22.	D
23.	D
24.	A
25.	B

CLERICAL ABILITIES

EXAMINATION SECTION
TEST 1

DIRECTIONS: Each question or incomplete statement is followed by several suggested answers or completions. Select the one that BEST answers the question or completes the statement. *PRINT THE LETTER OF THE CORRECT ANSWER IN THE SPACE AT THE RIGHT.*

Questions 1-4.

DIRECTIONS: Questions 1 through 4 are to be answered on the basis of the information given below.

The most commonly used filing system and the one that is easiest to learn is alphabetical filing. This involves putting records in an A to Z order, according to the letters of the alphabet. The name of a person is filed by using the following order: first, the surname or last name; second, the first name; third, the middle name or middle initial. For example, *Henry C. Young* is filed under *Y* and thereafter under *Young, Henry C.* The name of a company is filed in the same way. For example, *Long Cabinet Co.* is filed under *L,* while *John T. Long Cabinet Co.* is filed under *L* and thereafter under *Long., John T. Cabinet Co.*

1. The one of the following which lists the names of persons in the CORRECT alphabetical order is:

    A. Mary Carrie, Helen Carrol, James Carson, John Carter
    B. James Carson, Mary Carrie, John Carter, Helen Carrol
    C. Helen Carrol, James Carson, John Carter, Mary Carrie
    D. John Carter, Helen Carrol, Mary Carrie, James Carson

1._____

2. The one of the following which lists the names of persons in the CORRECT alphabetical order is:

    A. Jones, John C.; Jones, John A.; Jones, John P.; Jones, John K.
    B. Jones, John P.; Jones, John K.; Jones, John C.; Jones, John A.
    C. Jones, John A.; Jones, John C.; Jones, John K.; Jones, John P.
    D. Jones, John K.; Jones, John C.; Jones, John A.; Jones, John P.

2._____

3. The one of the following which lists the names of the companies in the CORRECT alphabetical order is:

    A. Blane Co., Blake Co., Block Co., Blear Co.
    B. Blake Co., Blane Co., Blear Co., Block Co.
    C. Block Co., Blear Co., Blane Co., Blake Co.
    D. Blear Co., Blake Co., Blane Co., Block Co.

3._____

4. You are to return to the file an index card on *Barry C. Wayne Materials and Supplies Co.* Of the following, the CORRECT alphabetical group that you should return the index card to is

    A. A to G   B. H to M   C. N to S   D. T to Z

4._____

Questions 5-10.

DIRECTIONS: In each of Questions 5 through 10, the names of four people are given. For
each question, choose as your answer the one of the four names given which
should be filed FIRST according to the usual system of alphabetical filing of
names, as described in the following paragraph.

In filing names, you must start with the last name. Names are filed in order of the first letter of the last name, then the second letter, etc. Therefore, BAILY would be filed before
BROWN, which would be filed before COLT. A name with fewer letters of the same type
comes first; i.e., Smith before Smithe. If the last names are the same, the names are filed
alphabetically by the first name. If the first name is an initial, a name with an initial would
come before a first name that starts with the same letter as the initial. Therefore, I. BROWN
would come before IRA BROWN. Finally, if both last name and first name are the same, the
name would be filed alphabetically by the middle name, once again an initial coming before a
middle name which starts with the same letter as the initial. If there is no middle name at all,
the name would come before those with middle initials or names.

Sample Question;   A.   Lester Daniels
                     B.   William Dancer
                     C.   Nathan Danzig
                     D.   Dan Lester

The last names beginning with D are filed before the last name beginning with L. Since
DANIELS, DANCER, and DANZIG all begin with the same three letters, you must look at the
fourth letter of the last name to determine which name should be filed first. C comes before I
or Z in the alphabet, so DANCER is filed before DANIELS or DANZIG. Therefore, the answer
to the above sample question is B.

5.   A.   Scott Biala   5._____
      B.   Mary Byala
      C.   Martin Baylor
      D.   Francis Bauer

6.   A.   Howard J. Black   6._____
      B.   Howard Black
      C.   J. Howard Black
      D.   John H. Black

7.   A.   Theodora Garth Kingston   7._____
      B.   Theadore Barth Kingston
      C.   Thomas Kingston
      D.   Thomas T. Kingston

8.   A.   Paulette Mary Huerta   8._____
      B.   Paul M. Huerta
      C.   Paulette L. Huerta
      D.   Peter A. Huerta

9. A. Martha Hunt Morgan
    B. Martin Hunt Morgan
    C. Mary H. Morgan
    D. Martine H. Morgan

9._____

10. A. James T. Meerschaum
    B. James M. Mershum
    C. James F. Mearshaum
    D. James N. Meshum

10._____

Questions 11-14.

DIRECTIONS: Questions 11 through 14 are to be answered SOLELY on the basis of the following information.

You are required to file various documents in file drawers which are labeled according to the following pattern:

DOCUMENTS

MEMOS		LETTERS	
File	Subject	File	Subject
84PM1 - (A-L)		84PC1 - (A-L)	
84PM2 - (M-Z)		84PC2 - (M-Z)	

REPORTS		INQUIRIES	
File	Subject	File	Subject
84PR1 - (A-L)		84PQ1 - (A-L)	
84PR2 - (M-Z)		84PQ2 - (M-Z)	

11. A letter dealing with a burglary should be filed in the drawer labeled

    A. 84PM1   B. 84PC1   C. 84PR1   D. 84PQ2

11._____

12. A report on Statistics should be found in the drawer labeled

    A. 84PM1   B. 84PC2   C. 84PR2   D. 84PQ2

12._____

13. An inquiry is received about parade permit procedures. It should be filed in the drawer labeled

    A. 84PM2   B. 84PC1   C. 84PR1   D. 84PQ2

13._____

14. A police officer has a question about a robbery report you filed.
    You should pull this file from the drawer labeled

    A. 84PM1   B. 84PM2   C. 84PR1   D. 84PR2

14._____

Questions 15-22.

DIRECTIONS: Each of Questions 15 through 22 consists of four or six numbered names. For each question, choose the option (A, B, C, or D) which indicates the order in which the names should be filed in accordance with the following filing instructions:
- File alphabetically according to last name, then first name, then middle initial.
- File according to each successive letter within a name.

- When comparing two names in which, the letters in the longer name are identical to the corresponding letters in the shorter name, the shorter name is filed first.
- When the last names are the same, initials are always filed before names beginning with the same letter.

15.   I.   Ralph Robinson   15._____
            II. Alfred Ross
           III. Luis Robles
           IV. James Roberts

The CORRECT filing sequence for the above names should be

  A. IV, II, I, III   B. I, IV, III, II
  C. III, IV, I, II   D. IV, I, III, II

16.   I.   Irwin Goodwin   16._____
            II. Inez Gonzalez
           III. Irene Goodman
           IV. Ira S. Goodwin
            V. Ruth I. Goldstein
           VI. M.B. Goodman

The CORRECT filing sequence for the above names should be

  A. V, II, I, IV, III, VI   B. V, II, VI, III, IV, I
  C. V, II, III, VI, IV, I   D. V, II, III, VI, I, IV

17.   I.   George Allan   17._____
            II. Gregory Allen
           III. Gary Allen
           IV. George Allen

The CORRECT filing sequence for the above names should be

  A. IV, III, I, II   B. I, IV, II, III
  C. III, IV, I, II   D. I, III, IV, II

18.   I.   Simon Kauffman   18._____
            II. Leo Kaufman
           III. Robert Kaufmann
           IV. Paul Kauffmann

The CORRECT filing sequence for the above names should be

  A. I, IV, II, III   B. II, IV, III, I
  C. III, II, IV, I   D. I, II, III, IV

19.   I.   Roberta Williams   19._____
            II. Robin Wilson
           III. Roberta Wilson
           IV. Robin Williams

The CORRECT filing sequence for the above names should be

  A. III, II, IV, I   B. I, IV, III, II
  C. I, II, III, IV   D. III, I, II, IV

20.
    I.   Lawrence Shultz
    II.   Albert Schultz
    III.   Theodore Schwartz
    IV.   Thomas Schwarz
    V.   Alvin Schultz
    VI.   Leonard Shultz

The CORRECT filing sequence for the above names should be

  A. II, V, III, IV, I, VI   B. IV, III, V, I, II, VI
  C. II, V, I, VI, III, IV   D. I, VI, II, V, III, IV

20.____

21.
    I.   McArdle
    II.   Mayer
    III.   Maletz
    IV.   McNiff
    V.   Meyer
    VI.   MacMahon

The CORRECT filing sequence for the above names should be

  A. I, IV, VI, III, II, V   B. II, I, IV, VI, III, V
  C. VI, III, II, I, IV, V   D. VI, III, II, V, I, IV

21.____

22.
    I.   Jack E. Johnson
    II.   R.H. Jackson
    III.   Bertha Jackson
    IV.   J.T. Johnson
    V.   Ann Johns
    VI.   John Jacobs

The CORRECT filing sequence for the above names should be

  A. II, III, VI, V, IV, I   B. III, II, VI, V, IV, I
  C. VI, II, III, I, V, IV   D. III, II, VI, IV, V, I

22.____

Questions 23-30.

DIRECTIONS: The code table below shows 10 letters with matching numbers. For each question, there are three sets of letters. Each set of letters is followed by a set of numbers which may or may not match their correct letter according to the code table. For each question, check all three sets of letters and numbers and mark your answer:
    A. if no pairs are correctly matched
    B. if only one pair is correctly matched
    C. if only two pairs are correctly matched
    D. if all three pairs are correctly matched

CODE TABLE

T	M	V	D	S	P	R	G	B	H
1	2	3	4	5	6	7	8	9	0

Sample Question: TMVDSP - 123456
                         RGBHTM - 789011
                         DSPRGB - 256789

In the sample question above, the first set of numbers correctly matches its set of letters. But the second and third pairs contain mistakes. In the second pair, M is incorrectly matched with number 1. According to the code table, letter M should be correctly matched with number 2. In the third pair, the letter D is incorrectly matched with number 2. According to the code table, letter D should be correctly matched with number 4. Since only one of the pairs is correctly matched, the answer to this sample question is B.

23. RSBMRM 759262
    GDSRVH 845730
    VDBRTM 349713

    23.____

24. TGVSDR 183247
    SMHRDP 520647
    TRMHSR 172057

    24.____

25. DSPRGM 456782
    MVDBHT 234902
    HPMDBT 062491

    25.____

26. BVPTRD 936184
    GDPHMB 807029
    GMRHMV 827032

    26.____

27. MGVRSH 283750
    TRDMBS 174295
    SPRMGV 567283

    27.____

28. SGBSDM 489542
    MGHPTM 290612
    MPBMHT 269301

    28.____

29. TDPBHM 146902
    VPBMRS 369275
    GDMBHM 842902

    29.____

30. MVPTBV 236194
    PDRTMB 647128
    BGTMSM 981232

    30.____

KEY (CORRECT ANSWERS)

1.	A	11.	B	21.	C
2.	C	12.	C	22.	B
3.	B	13.	D	23.	B
4.	D	14.	D	24.	B
5.	D	15.	D	25.	C
6.	B	16.	C	26.	A
7.	B	17.	D	27.	D
8.	B	18.	A	28.	A
9.	A	19.	B	29.	D
10.	C	20.	A	30.	A

TEST 2

DIRECTIONS: Each question or incomplete statement is followed by several suggested answers or completions. Select the one that BEST answers the question or completes the statement. PRINT THE LETTER OF THE CORRECT ANSWER IN THE SPACE AT THE RIGHT.

Questions 1-10.

DIRECTIONS: Questions 1 through 10 each consists of two columns, each containing four lines of names, numbers and/or addresses. For each question, compare the lines in Column I with the lines in Column II to see if they match exactly, and mark your answer A, B, C, or D, according to the following instructions:
   A. all four lines match exactly
   B. only three lines match exactly
   C. only two lines match exactly
   D. only one line matches exactly

		COLUMN I	COLUMN II	
1.	I. II. III. IV.	Earl Hodgson 1409870 Shore Ave. Macon Rd.	Earl Hodgson 1408970 Schore Ave. Macon Rd.	1.____
2.	I. II. III. IV.	9671485 470 Astor Court Halprin, Phillip Frank D. Poliseo	9671485 470 Astor Court Halperin, Phillip Frank D. Poliseo	2.____
3.	I. II. III. IV.	Tandem Associates 144-17 Northern Blvd. Alberta Forchi Kings Park, NY 10751	Tandom Associates 144-17 Northern Blvd. Albert Forchi Kings Point, NY 10751	3.____
4.	I. II. III. IV.	Bertha C. McCormack Clayton, MO. 976-4242 New City, NY 10951	Bertha C. McCormack Clayton, MO. 976-4242 New City, NY 10951	4.____
5.	I. II. III. IV.	George C. Morill Columbia, SC 29201 Louis Ingham 3406 Forest Ave.	George C. Morrill Columbia, SD 29201 Louis Ingham 3406 Forest Ave.	5.____
6.	I. II. III. IV.	506 S. Elliott Pl. Herbert Hall 4712 Rockaway Pkway 169 E. 7 St.	506 S. Elliott Pl. Hurbert Hall 4712 Rockaway Pkway 169 E. 7 St.	6.____

		COLUMN I	COLUMN II	
7.	I.	345 Park Ave.	345 Park Pl.	7.____
	II.	Colman Oven Corp.	Coleman Oven Corp.	
	III.	Robert Conte	Robert Conti	
	IV.	6179846	6179846	
8.	I.	Grigori Schierber	Grigori Schierber	8.____
	II.	Des Moines, Iowa	Des Moines, Iowa	
	III.	Gouverneur Hospital	Gouverneur Hospital	
	IV.	91-35 Cresskill Pl.	91-35 Cresskill Pl.	
9.	I.	Jeffery Janssen	Jeffrey Janssen	9.____
	II.	8041071	8041071	
	III.	40 Rockefeller Plaza	40 Rockafeller Plaza	
	IV.	407 6 St.	406 7 St.	
10.	I.	5971996	5871996	10.____
	II.	3113 Knickerbocker Ave.	3113 Knickerbocker Ave.	
	III.	8434 Boston Post Rd.	8424 Boston Post Rd.	
	IV.	Penn Station	Penn Station	

Questions 11-14.

DIRECTIONS: Questions 11 through 14 are to be answered by looking at the four groups of names and addresses listed below (I, II, III, and IV) and then finding out the number of groups that have their corresponding numbered lines exactly the same.

GROUP I
Line 1. Richmond General Hospital
Line 2. Geriatric Clinic
Line 3. 3975 Paerdegat St.
Line 4 Loudonville, New York 11538

GROUP II
Richman General Hospital
Geriatric Clinic
3975 Peardegat St.
Londonville, New York 11538

GROUP III
Line 1. Richmond General Hospital
Line 2. Geriatric Clinic
Line 3. 3795 Paerdegat St.
Line 4. Loudonville, New York 11358

GROUP IV
Richmend General Hospital
Geriatric Clinic
3975 Paerdegat St.
Loudonville, New York 11538

11. In how many groups is line one exactly the same?   11.____

    A. Two   B. Three   C. Four   D. None

12. In how many groups is line two exactly the same?   12.____

    A. Two   B. Three   C. Four   D. None

13. In how many groups is line three exactly the same?   13.____

    A. Two   B. Three   C. Four   D. None

14. In how many groups is line four exactly the same?   14.____

    A. Two   B. Three   C. Four   D. None

Questions 15-18.

DIRECTIONS: Each of Questions 15 through 18 has two lists of names and addresses. Each list contains three sets of names and addresses. Check each of the three sets in the list on the right to see if they are the same as the corresponding set in the list on the left. Mark your answers:
- A. if none of the sets in the right list are the same as those in the left list
- B. if only one of the sets in the right list is the same as those in the left list
- C. if only two of the sets in the right list are the same as those in the left list
- D. if all three sets in the right list are the same as those in the left list

15.
Mary T. Berlinger	Mary T. Berlinger	15.____
2351 Hampton St.	2351 Hampton St.	
Monsey, N.Y. 20117	Monsey, N.Y. 20117	

Eduardo Benes   Eduardo Benes
473 Kingston Avenue   473 Kingston Avenue
Central Islip, N.Y. 11734   Central Islip, N.Y. 11734

Alan Carrington Fuchs   Alan Carrington Fuchs
17 Gnarled Hollow Road   17 Gnarled Hollow Road
Los Angeles, CA 91635   Los Angeles, CA 91685

16.
David John Jacobson	David John Jacobson	16.____
178 35 St. Apt. 4C	178 53 St. Apt. 4C	
New York, N.Y. 00927	New York, N.Y. 00927	

Ann-Marie Calonella   Ann-Marie Calonella
7243 South Ridge Blvd.   7243 South Ridge Blvd.
Bakersfield, CA 96714   Bakersfield, CA 96714

Pauline M. Thompson   Pauline M. Thomson
872 Linden Ave.   872 Linden Ave.
Houston, Texas 70321   Houston, Texas 70321

17.
Chester LeRoy Masterton	Chester LeRoy Masterson	17.____
152 Lacy Rd.	152 Lacy Rd.	
Kankakee, Ill. 54532	Kankakee, Ill. 54532	

William Maloney   William Maloney
S. LaCrosse Pla.   S. LaCross Pla.
Wausau, Wisconsin 52146 Wausau, Wisconsin 52146

Cynthia V. Barnes   Cynthia V. Barnes
16 Pines Rd.   16 Pines Rd.
Greenpoint, Miss. 20376 Greenpoint, Miss. 20376

18. Marcel Jean Frontenac   Marcel Jean Frontenac   18.____
     8 Burton On The Water   6 Burton On The Water
     Calender, Me. 01471   Calender, Me. 01471

     J. Scott Marsden   J. Scott Marsden
     174 S. Tipton St.   174 Tipton St.
     Cleveland, Ohio   Cleveland, Ohio

     Lawrence T. Haney   Lawrence T. Haney
     171 McDonough St.   171 McDonough St.
     Decatur, Ga. 31304   Decatur, Ga. 31304

Questions 19-26.

DIRECTIONS: Each of Questions 19 through 26 has two lists of numbers. Each list contains
             three sets of numbers. Check each of the three sets in the list on the right to
             see if they are the same as the corresponding set in the list on the left. Mark
             your answers:
             A. if none of the sets in the right list are the same as those in the left list
             B. if only one of the sets in the right list is the same as those in the left
                 list
             C. if only two of the sets in the right list are the same as those in the left
                 list
             D. if all three sets in the right list are the same as those in the left list

19. 7354183476   7354983476   19.____
     4474747744   4474747774
     57914302311   57914302311

20. 7143592185   7143892185   20.____
     8344517699   8344518699
     9178531263   9178531263

21. 2572114731   257214731   21.____
     8806835476   8806835476
     8255831246   8255831246

22. 331476853821   331476858621   22.____
     6976658532996   6976655832996
     3766042113715   3766042113745

23. 8806663315   8806663315   23.____
     74477138449   74477138449
     211756663666   211756663666

24. 99000696996   99000696996   24.____
     53022219743   53022219843
     4171171117717   4171171177717

25. 24400222433004   24400222433004   25.____
     5300030055000355   5300030055500355
     20000075532002022   20000075532002022

26. 611166640660001116   61116664066001116   26.____
     7111300117001100733   7111300117001100733
     26666446664476518   26666446664476518

Questions 27-30.

DIRECTIONS: Questions 27 through 30 are to be answered by picking the answer which is in
             the correct numerical order, from the lowest number to the highest number, in
             each question.

27. A. 44533, 44518, 44516, 44547   27.____
     B. 44516, 44518, 44533, 44547
     C. 44547, 44533, 44518, 44516
     D. 44518, 44516, 44547, 44533

28. A. 95587, 95593, 95601, 95620   28.____
     B. 95601, 95620, 95587, 95593
     C. 95593, 95587, 95601, 95620
     D. 95620, 95601, 95593, 95587

29. A. 232212, 232208, 232232, 232223   29.____
     B. 232208, 232223, 232212, 232232
     C. 232208, 232212, 232223, 232232
     D. 232223, 232232, 232208, 232212

30. A. 113419, 113521, 113462, 113588   30.____
     B. 113588, 113462, 113521, 113419
     C. 113521, 113588, 113419, 113462
     D. 113419, 113462, 113521, 113588

KEY (CORRECT ANSWERS)

1.	C	11.	A	21.	C
2.	B	12.	C	22.	A
3.	D	13.	A	23.	D
4.	A	14.	A	24.	A
5.	C	15.	C	25.	C
6.	B	16.	B	26.	C
7.	D	17.	B	27.	B
8.	A	18.	B	28.	A
9.	D	19.	B	29.	C
10.	C	20.	B	30.	D

NAME AND NUMBER CHECKING

EXAMINATION SECTION
TEST 1

DIRECTIONS: Questions 1 through 17 consist of sets of names and addresses. In each question, the name and address in Column II should be an exact copy of the name and address in Column I.

If there is:
a mistake only in the name, mark your answer A;
a mistake only in the address, mark your answer B;
a mistake in both name and address, mark your answer C;
NO mistake in either name or address, mark your answer D.

SAMPLE QUESTION

Column I

Column II

Christina Magnusson
288 Greene Street
New York, N.Y. 10003

Christina Magnusson
288 Greene Street
New York, N.Y. 10013

Since there is a mistake only in the address (the zip code should be 10003 instead of 10013), the answer to the sample question is B.

COLUMN I

COLUMN II

1. Ms. Joan Kelly
   313 Franklin Ave.
   Brooklyn, N.Y. 11202

   Ms. Joan Kielly
   318 Franklin Ave.
   Brooklyn, N.Y. 11202

   1.____

2. Mrs. Eileen Engel
   47-24 86 Road
   Queens, N.Y. 11122

   Mrs. Ellen Engel
   47-24 86 Road
   Queens, N.Y. 11122

   2.____

3. Marcia Michaels
   213 E. 81 St.
   New York, N.Y. 10012

   Marcia Michaels
   213 E. 81 St.
   New York, N.Y. 10012

   3.____

4. Rev. Edward J. Smyth
   1401 Brandeis Street
   San Francisco, Calif. 96201

   Rev. Edward J. Smyth
   1401 Brandies Street
   San Francisco, Calif. 96201

   4.____

5. Alicia Rodriguez
   24-68 81 St.
   Elmhurst, N.Y. 11122

   Alicia Rodriguez
   2468 81 St.
   Elmhurst, N.Y. 11122

   5.____

6. Ernest Eisemann
   21 Columbia St.
   New York, N.Y. 10007

   Ernest Eisermann
   21 Columbia St.
   New York, N.Y. 10007

   6.____

Column I	COLUMN II	
7. Mr. & Mrs. George Petersson 87-11 91st Avenue Woodhaven, N.Y. 11421	Mr. & Mrs. George Peterson 87-11 91st Avenue Woodhaven, N.Y. 11421	7.____
8. Mr. Ivan Klebnikov 1848 Newkirk Avenue Brooklyn, N.Y. 11226	Mr. Ivan Klebikov 1848 Newkirk Avenue Brooklyn, N.Y. 11622	8.____
9. Samuel Rothfleisch 71 Pine Street New York, N.Y. 10005	Samuel Rothfleisch 71 Pine Street New York, N.Y. 10005	9.____
10. Mrs. Isabel Tonnessen 198 East 185th Street Bronx, N.Y. 10458	Mrs. Isabel Tonnessen 189 East 185th Street Bronx, N.Y. 10458	10.____
11. Esteban Perez 173 Eighth Street Staten Island, N.Y. 10306	Estaban Perez 173 Eighth Street Staten Island, N.Y. 10306	11.____
12. Esta Wong 141 West 68 St. New York, N.Y. 10023	Esta Wang 141 West 68 St. New York, N.Y. 10023	12.____
13. Dr. Alberto Grosso 3475 12th Avenue Brooklyn, N.Y. 11218	Dr. Alberto Grosso 3475 12th Avenue Brooklyn, N.Y. 11218	13.____
14. Mrs. Ruth Bortlas 482 Theresa Ct. Far Rockaway, N.Y. 11691	Ms. Ruth Bortlas 482 Theresa Ct. Far Rockaway, N.Y. 11169	14.____
15. Mr. & Mrs. Howard Fox 2301 Sedgwick Ave. Bronx, N.Y. 10468	Mr. & Mrs. Howard Fox 231 Sedgwick Ave. Bronx, N.Y. 10468	15.____
16. Miss Marjorie Black 223 East 23 Street New York, N.Y. 10010	Miss Margorie Black 223 East 23 Street New York, N.Y. 10010	16.____
17. Michelle Herman 806 Valley Rd. Old Tappan, N.J. 07675	Michelle Hermann 806 Valley Dr. Old Tappan, N.J. 07675	17.____

KEY (CORRECT ANSWERS)

1.	C		6.	A
2.	A		7.	A
3.	D		8.	C
4.	B		9.	D
5.	B		10.	B

11. A
12. A
13. D
14. C
15. B
16. A
17. C

TEST 2

DIRECTIONS: Questions 1 through 15 are to be answered SOLELY on the instructions given below. *PRINT THE LETTER OF THE CORRECT ANSWER IN THE SPACE AT THE RIGHT.*

INSTRUCTIONS:

In each of the following questions, the 3-line name and address in Column I is the master-list entry, and the 3-line entry in Column 2 is the information to be checked against the master list. If there is one line that does not match, mark your answer A; if there are two lines that do not match, mark your answer B; if all three lines do not match, mark your answer C; if the lines all match exactly, mark your answer D.

SAMPLE QUESTION

Column I
Mark L. Field
11-09 Prince Park Blvd.
Bronx, N.Y. 11402

Column II
Mark L. Field
11-99 Prince Park Way
Bronx, N.Y. 11401

The first lines in each column match exactly. The second lines do not match since 11-09 does not match 11-99; and Blvd. does not match Way. The third lines do not match either since 11402 does not match 11401. Therefore, there are two lines that do not match, and the CORRECT answer is B.

COLUMN I	COLUMN II	
1. Jerome A. Jackson 1243 14th Avenue New York, N.Y. 10023	Jerome A. Johnson 1234 14th Avenue New York, N.Y. 10023	1.____
2. Sophie Strachtheim 33-28 Connecticut Ave. Far Rockaway, N.Y. 11697	Sophie Strachtheim 33-28 Connecticut Ave. Far Rockaway, N.Y. 11697	2.____
3. Elisabeth N.T. Gorrell 256 Exchange St. New York, N.Y. 10013	Elizabeth N.T. Gorrell 256 Exchange St. New York, N.Y. 10013	3.____
4. Maria J. Gonzalez 7516 E. Sheepshead Rd. Brooklyn, N.Y. 11240	Maria J. Gonzalez 7516 N. Shepshead Rd. Brooklyn, N.Y. 11240	4.____
5. Leslie B. Brautenweiler 21 57A Seiler Terr. Flushing, N.Y. 11367	Leslie B. Brautenwieler 21-75A Seiler Terr. Flushing, N.J. 11367	5.____
6. Rigoberto J. Peredes 157 Twin Towers, #18F Tottenville, S.I., N.Y.	Rigoberto J. Peredes 157 Twin Towers, #18F Tottenville, S.I., N.Y.	6.____

COLUMN I	COLUMN II	
7. Pietro F. Albino P.O. Box 7548 Floral Park, N.Y. 11005	Pietro F. Albina P.O. Box 7458 Floral Park, N.Y. 11005	7.____
8. Joanne Zimmermann Bldg. SW, Room 314 532-4601	Joanne Zimmermann Bldg. SW, Room 314 532-4601	8.____
9. Carlyle Whetstone Payroll Div.-A, Room 212A 262-5000, ext. 471	Caryle Whetstone Payroll Div.-A, Room 212A 262-5000, ext. 417	9.____
10. Kenneth Chiang Legal Council, Room 9745 (201) 416-9100, ext. 17	Kenneth Chiang Legal Counsel, Room 9745 (201) 416-9100, ext. 17	10.____
11. Ethel Koenig Personnel Services Division, Room 433; 635-7572	Ethel Hoenig Personal Services Division, Room 433; 635-7527	11.____
12. Joyce Ehrhardt Office of the Administrator, Room W56; 387-8706	Joyce Ehrhart Office of the Administrator, Room W56; 387-7806	12.____
13. Ruth Lang EAM Bldg., Room C101 625-2000, ext. 765	Ruth Lang EAM Bldg., Room C110 625-2000, ext. 765	13.____
14. Anne Marie Ionozzi Investigations, Room 827 576-4000, ext. 832	Anna Marie Ionozzi Investigation, Room 827 566-4000, ext. 832	14.____
15. Willard Jameson Fm C Bldg., Room 687 454-3010	Willard Jamieson Fm C Bldg., Room 687 454-3010	15.____

KEY (CORRECT ANSWERS)

1.	B		6.	D
2.	D		7.	B
3.	A		8.	D
4.	A		9.	B
5.	C		10.	A

11.	C
12.	B
13.	A
14.	C
15.	A

———

TEST 3

DIRECTIONS: Questions 1 through 10 are to be answered on the basis of the following instructions. *PRINT THE LETTER OF THE CORRECT ANSWER IN THE SPACE AT THE RIGHT.*

INSTRUCTIONS:

For each such set of names, addresses, and numbers listed in Columns I and II, select your answer from the following options:
A. The names in Columns I and II are different.
B. The addresses in Columns I and II are different.
C. The numbers in Columns I and II are different.
D. The names, addresses, and numbers in Columns I and II are identical.

COLUMN I	COLUMN II	
1. Francis Jones 62 Stately Avenue 96-12446	Francis Jones 62 Stately Avenue 96-21446	1.____
2. Julio Montez 19 Ponderosa Road 56-73161	Julio Montez 19 Ponderosa Road 56-71361	2.____
3. Mary Mitchell 2314 Melbourne Drive 68-92172	Mary Mitchell 2314 Melbourne Drive 68-92172	3.____
4. Harry Patterson 25 Dunne Street 14-33430	Harry Patterson 25 Dunne Street 14-34330	4.____
5. Patrick Murphy 171 West Hosmer Street 93-81214	Patrick Murphy 171 West Hosmer Street 93-18214	5.____
6. August Schultz 816 St. Clair Avenue 53-40149	August Schultz 816 St. Claire Avenue 53-40149	6.____
7. George Taft 72 Runnymede Street 47-04033	George Taft 72 Runnymede Street 47-04023	7.____
8. Angus Henderson 1418 Madison Street 81-76375	Angus Henderson 1418 Madison Street 81-76375	8.____
9. Carolyn Mazur 12 Riverview Road 38-99615	Carolyn Mazur 12 Rivervane ftoad 38-99615	9.____

COLUMN I	COLUMN II	
10. Adele Russell 1725 Lansing Lane 72-91962	Adela Russell 1725 Lansing Lane 72-91962	10.____

KEY (CORRECT ANSWERS)

1.	C	6.	B
2.	C	7.	C
3.	D	8.	D
4.	C	9.	B
5.	C	10.	A

TEST 4

DIRECTIONS: Questions 1 through 20 test how good you are at catching mistakes in typing or printing. In each question, the name and address in Column II should be an exact copy of the name and address in Column I. Mark your answer

    A. if there is no mistake in either name or address;
    B. if there is a mistake in both name and address;
    C. if there is a mistake only in the name;
    D. if there is a mistake only in the address.

PRINT THE LETTER OF THE CORRECT ANSWER IN THE SPACE AT THE RIGHT.

COLUMN I   COLUMN II

1. Milos Yanocek   Milos Yanocek   1.____
    33-60 14 Street   33-60 14 Street
    Long Island City, N.Y. 11011   Long Island City, N.Y. 11001

2. Alphonse Sabattelo   Alphonse Sabbattelo   2.____
    24 Minnetta Lane   24 Minetta Lane
    New York, N.Y. 10006   New York, N.Y. 10006

3. Helen Steam   Helene Stearn   3.____
    5 Metropolitan Oval   5 Metropolitan Oval
    Bronx, N.Y. 10462   Bronx, N.Y. 10462

4. Jacob Weisman   Jacob Weisman   4.____
    231 Francis Lewis Boulevard   231 Francis Lewis Boulevard
    Forest Hills, N.Y. 11325   Forest Hills, N.Y. 11325

5. Riccardo Fuente   Riccardo Fuentes   5.____
    134 West 83 Street   134 West 88 Street
    New York, N.Y. 10024   New York, N.Y. 10024

6. Dennis Lauber   Dennis Lauder   6.____
    52 Avenue D   52 Avenue D
    Brooklyn, N.Y. 11216   Brooklyn, N.Y. 11216

7. Paul Cutter   Paul Cutter   7.____
    195 Galloway Avenue   175 Galloway Avenue
    Staten Island, N.Y. 10356   Staten Island, N.Y. 10365

8. Sean Donnelly   Sean Donnelly   8.____
    45-58 41 Avenue   45-58 41 Avenue
    Woodside, N.Y. 11168   Woodside, N.Y. 11168

9. Clyde Willot   Clyde Willat   9.____
    1483 Rockaway Avenue   1483 Rockway Avenue
    Brooklyn, N.Y. 11238   Brooklyn, N.Y. 11238

COLUMN I	COLUMN II	
10. Michael Stanakis 419 Sheriden Avenue Staten Island, N.Y. 10363	Michael Stanakis 419 Sheraden Avenue Staten Island, N.Y. 10363	10.____
11. Joseph DiSilva 63-84 Saunders Road Rego Park, N.Y. 11431	Joseph Disilva 64-83 Saunders Road Rego Park, N.Y. 11431	11.____
12. Linda Polansky 2225 Fenton Avenue Bronx, N.Y. 10464	Linda Polansky 2255 Fenton Avenue Bronx, N.Y. 10464	12.____
13. Alfred Klein 260 Hillside Terrace Staten Island, N.Y. 15545	Alfred Klein 260 Hillside Terrace Staten Island, N.Y. 15545	13.____
14. William McDonnell 504 E. 55 Street New York, N.Y. 10103	William McConnell 504 E. 55 Street New York, N.Y. 10108	14.____
15. Angela Cipolla 41-11 Parson Avenue Flushing, N.Y. 11446	Angela Cipola 41-11 Parsons Avenue Flushing, N.Y. 11446	15.____
16. Julie Sheridan 1212 Ocean Avenue Brooklyn, N.Y. 11237	Julia Sheridan 1212 Ocean Avenue Brooklyn, N.Y. 11237	16.____
17. Arturo Rodriguez 2156 Cruger Avenue Bronx, N.Y. 10446	Arturo Rodrigues 2156 Cruger Avenue Bronx, N.Y. 10446	17.____
18. Helen McCabe 2044 East 19 Street Brooklyn, N.Y. 11204	Helen McCabe 2040 East 19 Street Brooklyn,. N.Y. 11204	18.____
19. Charles Martin 526 West 160 Street New York, N.Y. 10022	Charles Martin 526 West 160 Street New York, N.Y. 10022	19.____
20. Morris Rabinowitz 31 Avenue M Brooklyn, N.Y. 11216	Morris Rabinowitz 31 Avenue N Brooklyn, N.Y. 11216	20.____

KEY (CORRECT ANSWERS)

1.	D	11.	B
2.	B	12.	D
3.	C	13.	A
4.	A	14.	B
5.	B	15.	B
6.	C	16.	C
7.	D	17.	C
8.	A	18.	D
9.	B	19.	A
10.	D	20.	D

TEST 5

DIRECTIONS: In copying the addresses below from Column A to the same line in Column B, an Agent-in-Training made some errors. For Questions 1 through 5, if you find that the Agent made an error in

only one line, mark your answer A;
only two lines, mark your answer B;
only three lines, mark your answer C;
all four lines, mark your answer D.

EXAMPLE

Column A

24 Third Avenue
5 Lincoln Road
50 Central Park West
37-21 Queens Boulevard

Column B

24 Third Avenue
5 Lincoln Street
6 Central Park West
21-37 Queens Boulevard

Since errors were made on only three lines, namely the second, third, and fourth, the COR-RECT answer is C.
PRINT THE LETTER OF THE CORRECT ANSWER IN THE SPACE AT THE RIGHT.

Column A

Column B

1. 57-22 Springfield Boulevard
   94 Gun Hill Road
   8 New Dorp Lane
   36 Bedford Avenue

   75-22 Springfield Boulevard
   94 Gun Hill Avenue
   8 New Drop Lane
   36 Bedford Avenue

   1._____

2. 538 Castle Hill Avenue
   54-15 Beach Channel Drive
   21 Ralph Avenue
   162 Madison Avenue

   538 Castle Hill Avenue
   54-15 Beach Channel Drive
   21 Ralph Avenue
   162 Morrison Avenue

   2._____

3. 49 Thomas Street
   27-21 Northern Blvd.
   86 125th Street
   872 Atlantic Ave.

   49 Thomas Street
   21-27 Northern Blvd.
   86 125th Street
   872 Baltic Ave.

   3._____

4. 261-17 Horace Harding Expwy.
   191 Fordham Road
   6 Victory Blvd.
   552 Oceanic Ave.

   261-17 Horace Harding Pkwy.
   191 Fordham Road
   6 Victoria Blvd.
   552 Ocean Ave.

   4._____

5. 90-05 38th Avenue
   19 Central Park West
   9281 Avenue X
   22 West Farms Square

   90-05 36th Avenue
   19 Central Park East
   9281 Avenue X
   22 West Farms Square

   5._____

KEY (CORRECT ANSWERS)

1. C
2. A
3. B
4. C
5. B

_____

TEST 6

Questions 1-10.

DIRECTIONS: For Questions 1 through 10, choose the letter in Column II next to the number which EXACTLY matches the number in Column I. *PRINT THE LETTER OF THE CORRECT ANSWER IN THE SPACE AT THE RIGHT.*

COLUMN I

COLUMN II

1. 14235
   A. 13254
   B. 12435
   C. 13245
   D. 14235
   1._____

2. 70698
   A. 90768
   B. 60978
   C. 70698
   D. 70968
   2._____

3. 11698
   A. 11689
   B. 11986
   C. 11968
   D. 11698
   3._____

4. 50497
   A. 50947
   B. 50497
   C. 50749
   D. 54097
   4._____

5. 69635
   A. 60653
   B. 69630
   C. 69365
   D. 69635
   5._____

6. 1201022011
   A. 1201022011
   B. 1201020211
   C. 1202012011
   D. 1021202011
   6._____

7. 3893981389
   A. 3893891389
   B. 3983981389
   C. 3983891389
   D. 3893981389
   7._____

8. 4765476589
   A. 4765476598
   B. 4765476588
   C. 4765476589
   D. 4765746589
   8._____

<u>COLUMN I</u>   <u>COLUMN II</u>

9. 8679678938   A. 8679687938   9._____
                                                        B. 8679678938
                                                        C. 8697678938
                                                        D. 8678678938

10. 6834836932   A. 6834386932   10._____
                                                        B. 6834836923
                                                        C. 6843836932
                                                        D. 6834836932

Questions 11-15.

DIRECTIONS: For Questions 11 through 15, determine how many of the symbols in Column
               Z are exactly the same as the symbol in Column Y.
               If none is exactly the same, answer A;
               if only one symbol is exactly the same, answer B;
               if two symbols are exactly the same, answer C;
               if three symbols are exactly the same, answer D.

<u>COLUMN Y</u>   <u>COLUMN Z</u>

11. A123B1266   A123B1366   11._____
                                            A123B1266
                                            A133B1366
                                            A123B1266

12. CC28D3377   CD22D3377   12._____
                                            CC38D3377
                                            CC28C3377
                                            CC28D2277

13. M21AB201X   M12AB201X   13._____
                                            M21AB201X
                                            M21AB201Y
                                            M21BA201X

14. PA383Y744   AP383Y744   14._____
                                            PA338Y744
                                            PA388Y744
                                            PA383Y774

15. PB2Y8893   PB2Y8893   15._____
                                            PB2Y8893
                                            PB3Y8898
                                            PB2Y8893

KEY (CORRECT ANSWERS)

1.	D	6.	A
2.	C	7.	D
3.	D	8.	C
4.	B	9.	B
5.	D	10.	D

11.	C
12.	A
13.	B
14.	A
15.	D

COURTROOM TERMS

A/K/A: Acronym that stands for "also known as" and introduces any alternative or assumed names or aliases of an individual. A term to indicate another name by which a person is known.

Arraignment: The bringing of a defendant before the court to answer the matters charged against him in an indictment or information. The defendant is read the charges and must respond with his plea.

Arrest: Deprivation of one's liberty by legal authority.

Bail: An amount of money set by the court to procure the release of a person from legal custody; this money is to be forfeited if the defendant fails to appear for trial.

Beyond a Reasonable Doubt: The standard of proof required for a finding of guilty in a criminal matter. Satisfied to a moral certainty. This is a higher standard of proof than that required in a civil matter (preponderance of the evidence).

Co-Defendant: Any additional defendant or respondent in the same case.

Confession: A voluntary statement made by a person charged with a crime wherein said person acknowledges his/her guilt of the offense charged and discloses participation in the act.

Controlled Dangerous Substance: That group of legally designated drugs, which, by statute, it is illegal to possess or distribute.

Criminal complaint: The initial written notice to a defendant that he/she is being charged with a public offense.

Due Process of Law: The exercise of the powers of the government with the safeguards for the protection of individual rights as set forth in the constitution, statutes, and common case law.

Felony: A crime of a more serious nature than a misdemeanor, the exact nature of which is defined by state statute and which is punishable by a term of imprisonment exceeding one year or by death.

Grand Jury: A jury of inquiry whose duty is to receive complaints and accusations in criminal cases, hear the evidence presented on the part of the state, and determine whether to indict (see "indictment" below).

Impeach: As used in the Law of Evidence, to call into question the truthfulness of a witness, by means of introducing evidence to discredit him or her.

Indictment: A written accusation presented by a grand jury after having been presented with evidence, charging that a person named therein has done some act, or has been guilty of some omission that by law is a public offense.

Miranda Warnings: The compulsory advisement of a person's rights prior to any custodial interrogation; these include: a) the right to remain silent; b) that any statement made may be used against him/her; c) the right to an attorney; d) the appointment of counsel if the accused cannot afford his or her own attorney. Unless these rights are given, any evidence obtained in an interrogation cannot be used in the individual's trial against him/her.

Misdemeanor: Offense lower than felony and generally punishable by a fine or imprisonment other than in a penitentiary.

Motion to Quash: Application to the court to set aside the complaint, indictment or subpoena due to a lack of probable cause to arrest the defendant, or in matters heard by a grand jury, due to evidence not properly presented to the grand jury.

Motion to Sever: Application to the court made when there are two defendants charged with the same crimes or who acted jointly in the commission of a crime, when their attorneys feel it would be in their best interest if they had separate trials.

Motion to Suppress Evidence: Application to the court to prevent evidence from being presented at trial when said evidence has been obtained by illegal means. It applies to physical evidence, statements made by defendant when not advised by counsel or through wiretapping, prior convictions, etc..

Parole: A conditional release from custody at the discretion of the paroling authority prior to his or her completing the prison sentence imposed. During said release the offender is required to observe conditions of this status under the supervision of a parole agency.

Plea: A defendant's formal answer in court to the charges contained in a charging document.

Guilty: A plea by the defendant in which he acknowledges guilt either of the offense charged or of a less serious offense pursuant to an agreement with the prosecuting attorney. It should be understood, however, that the court may not be obliged to recognize this.

Nolo Contendere: A plea that is admissible in some jurisdictions, in which the defendant states that he does not contest the charges against him. Also called "no contest", this plea has the same effect as a guilty plea, except that it cannot be used against the defendant in civil actions arising out of the same incident which gave rise to the criminal charges.

Not Guilty: A plea of innocence by the defendant.

Not Guilty by Reason of Insanity: A plea that is sometimes entered in conjunction with the "not guilty" plea.

Double Jeopardy: A plea entered by a defendant who has been tried for an offense wherein he asserts that he cannot be tried a second time for said offense, unless he successfully secured a new trial after an appeal, or after a motion for a new trial was granted by the trial court.

Police Report: The official report made by any police officer involved with the incident or appearing after the incident, setting forth the officer's observations and statements of parties and witnesses. It can be used as evidence in a trial.

Pre-Trial Intervention: Utilized in some states when a defendant is accused of a first offense, to divert the defendant from the criminal justice system.

Probation: To allow a person convicted of a minor offense to go at large, under a suspension of sentence, during good behavior, and generally under the supervision of a probation officer.

Prosecutor: The attorney who prosecutes defendants for crimes, in the name of the government.

Search Warrant: A written order, issued by the court, directing the police to search a specified location for particular personal property (stolen or illegally possessed).

Speedy Trial: Mandate by the government that all criminal trials must take place within a specified time after arrest.

Writ of Habeas Corpus: A mandate issued from a court requiring that an individual be brought before the court.

GLOSSARY OF LEGAL TERMS

TABLE OF CONTENTS

GLOSSARY OF LEGAL TERMS

A

ACTION - "Action" includes a civil action and a criminal action.

A FORTIORI - A term meaning you can reason one thing from the existence of certain facts.

A POSTERIORI - From what goes after; from effect to cause.

A PRIORI - From what goes before; from cause to effect.

AB INITIO - From the beginning.

ABATE - To diminish or put an end to.

ABET - To encourage the commission of a crime.

ABEYANCE - Suspension, temporary suppression.

ABIDE - To accept the consequences of.

ABJURE - To renounce; give up.

ABRIDGE - To reduce; contract; diminish.

ABROGATE - To annul, repeal, or destroy.

ABSCOND - To hide or absent oneself to avoid legal action.

ABSTRACT - A summary.

ABUT - To border on, to touch.

ACCESS - Approach; in real property law it means the right of the owner of property to the use of the highway or road next to his land, without obstruction by intervening property owners.

ACCESSORY - In criminal law, it means the person who contributes or aids in the commission of a crime.

ACCOMMODATED PARTY - One to whom credit is extended on the strength of another person signing a commercial paper.

ACCOMMODATION PAPER - A commercial paper to which the accommodating party has put his name.

ACCOMPLICE - In criminal law, it means a person who together with the principal offender commits a crime.

ACCORD - An agreement to accept something different or less than that to which one is entitled, which extinguishes the entire obligation.

ACCOUNT - A statement of mutual demands in the nature of debt and credit between parties.

ACCRETION - The act of adding to a thing; in real property law, it means gradual accumulation of land by natural causes.

ACCRUE - To grow to; to be added to.

ACKNOWLEDGMENT - The act of going before an official authorized to take acknowledgments, and acknowledging an act as one's own.

ACQUIESCENCE - A silent appearance of consent.

ACQUIT - To legally determine the innocence of one charged with a crime.

AD INFINITUM - Indefinitely.

AD LITEM - For the suit.

AD VALOREM - According to value.

ADJECTIVE LAW - Rules of procedure.

ADJUDICATION - The judgment given in a case.

ADMIRALTY - Court having jurisdiction over maritime cases.

ADULT - Sixteen years old or over (in criminal law).

ADVANCE - In commercial law, it means to pay money or render other value before it is due.

ADVERSE - Opposed; contrary.

ADVOCATE - (v.) To speak in favor of;
              (n.) One who assists, defends, or pleads for another.

AFFIANT - A person who makes and signs an affidavit.

AFFIDAVIT - A written and sworn to declaration of facts, voluntarily made.

AFFINITY- The relationship between persons through marriage with the kindred of each other; distinguished from consanguinity, which is the relationship by blood.

AFFIRM - To ratify; also when an appellate court affirms a judgment, decree, or order, it means that it is valid and right and must stand as rendered in the lower court.

AFOREMENTIONED; AFORESAID - Before or already said.

AGENT - One who represents and acts for another.

AID AND COMFORT - To help; encourage.

ALIAS - A name not one's true name.

ALIBI - A claim of not being present at a certain place at a certain time.

ALLEGE - To assert.

ALLOTMENT - A share or portion.

AMBIGUITY - Uncertainty; capable of being understood in more than one way.

AMENDMENT - Any language made or proposed as a change in some principal writing.

AMICUS CURIAE - A friend of the court; one who has an interest in a case, although not a party in the case, who volunteers advice upon matters of law to the judge. For example, a brief amicus curiae.

AMORTIZATION - To provide for a gradual extinction of (a future obligation) in advance of maturity, especially, by periodical contributions to a sinking fund which will be adequate to discharge a debt or make a replacement when it becomes necessary.

ANCILLARY - Aiding, auxiliary.

ANNOTATION - A note added by way of comment or explanation.

ANSWER - A written statement made by a defendant setting forth the grounds of his defense.

ANTE - Before.

ANTE MORTEM - Before death.

APPEAL - The removal of a case from a lower court to one of superior jurisdiction for the purpose of obtaining a review.

APPEARANCE - Coming into court as a party to a suit.

APPELLANT - The party who takes an appeal from one court or jurisdiction to another (appellate) court for review.

APPELLEE - The party against whom an appeal is taken.

APPROPRIATE - To make a thing one's own.

APPROPRIATION - Prescribing the destination of a thing; the act of the legislature designating a particular fund, to be applied to some object of government expenditure.

APPURTENANT - Belonging to; accessory or incident to.

ARBITER - One who decides a dispute; a referee.

ARBITRARY - Unreasoned; not governed by any fixed rules or standard.

ARGUENDO - By way of argument.

ARRAIGN - To call the prisoner before the court to answer to a charge.

ASSENT - A declaration of willingness to do something in compliance with a request.

ASSERT - Declare.

ASSESS - To fix the rate or amount.

ASSIGN - To transfer; to appoint; to select for a particular purpose.

ASSIGNEE - One who receives an assignment.

ASSIGNOR - One who makes an assignment.

AT BAR - Before the court.

AT ISSUE - When parties in an action come to a point where one asserts something and the other denies it.

ATTACH - Seize property by court order and sometimes arrest a person.

ATTEST - To witness a will, etc.; act of attestation.

AVERMENT - A positive statement of facts.

B

BAIL - To obtain the release of a person from legal custody by giving security and promising that he shall appear in court; to deliver (goods, etc.) in trust to a person for a special purpose.

BAILEE - One to whom personal property is delivered under a contract of bailment.

BAILMENT - Delivery of personal property to another to be held for a certain purpose and to be returned when the purpose is accomplished.

BAILOR - The party who delivers goods to another, under a contract of bailment.

BANC (OR BANK) - Bench; the place where a court sits permanently or regularly; also the assembly of all the judges of a court.

BANKRUPT - An insolvent person, technically, one declared to be bankrupt after a bankruptcy proceeding.

BAR - The legal profession.

BARRATRY - Exciting groundless judicial proceedings.

BARTER - A contract by which parties exchange goods for other goods.

BATTERY - Illegal interfering with another's person.

BEARER - In commercial law, it means the person in possession of a commercial paper which is payable to the bearer.

BENCH - The court itself or the judge.

BENEFICIARY - A person benefiting under a will, trust, or agreement.

BEST EVIDENCE RULE,THE - Except as otherwise provided by statute, no evidence other than the writing itself is admissible to prove the content of a writing. This section shall be known and may be cited as the best evidence rule.

BEQUEST - A gift of personal property under a will.

BILL - A formal written statement of complaint to a court of justice; also, a draft of an act of the legislature before it becomes a law; also, accounts for goods sold, services rendered, or work done.

BONA FIDE - In or with good faith; honestly.

BOND - An instrument by which the maker promises to pay a sum of money to another, usually providing that upon performances of a certain condition the obligation shall be void.

BOYCOTT - A plan to prevent the carrying on of a business by wrongful means.

BREACH - The breaking or violating of a law, or the failure to carry out a duty.

BRIEF - A written document, prepared by a lawyer to serve as the basis of an argument upon a case in court, usually an appellate court.

BURDEN OF PRODUCING EVIDENCE - The obligation of a party to introduce evidence sufficient to avoid a ruling against him on the issue.

BURDEN OF PROOF - The obligation of a party to establish by evidence a requisite degree of belief concerning a fact in the mind of the trier of fact or the court. The burden of proof may require a party to raise a reasonable doubt concerning the existence of nonexistence of a fact or that he establish the existence or nonexistence of a fact by a preponderance of the evidence, by clear and convincing proof, or by proof beyond a reasonable doubt.

Except as otherwise provided by law, the burden of proof requires proof by a preponderance of the evidence.

BUSINESS, A - Shall include every kind of business, profession, occupation, calling or operation of institutions, whether carried on for profit or not.

BY-LAWS - Regulations, ordinances, or rules enacted by a corporation, association, etc., for its own government.

C

CANON - A doctrine; also, a law or rule, of a church or association in particular.

CAPIAS - An order to arrest.

CAPTION - In a pleading, deposition or other paper connected with a case in court, it is the heading or introductory clause which shows the names of the parties, name of the court, number of the case on the docket or calendar, etc.

CARRIER - A person or corporation undertaking to transport persons or property.

CASE - A general term for an action, cause, suit, or controversy before a judicial body.

CAUSE - A suit, litigation or action before a court.

CAVEAT EMPTOR - Let the buyer beware. This term expresses the rule that the purchaser of an article must examine, judge, and test it for himself, being bound to discover any obvious defects or imperfections.

CERTIFICATE - A written representation that some legal formality has been complied with.

CERTIORARI - To be informed of; the name of a writ issued by a superior court directing the lower court to send up to the former the record and proceedings of a case.

CHANGE OF VENUE - To remove place of trial from one place to another.

CHARGE - An obligation or duty; a formal complaint; an instruction of the court to the jury upon a case.

CHARTER - (n.) The authority by virtue of which an organized body acts;

 (v.) in mercantile law, it means to hire or lease a vehicle or vessel for transportation.

CHATTEL - An article of personal property.

CHATTEL MORTGAGE - A mortgage on personal property.

CIRCUIT - A division of the country, for the administration of justice; a geographical area served by a court.

CITATION - The act of the court by which a person is summoned or cited; also, a reference to legal authority.

CIVIL (ACTIONS)- It indicates the private rights and remedies of individuals in contrast to the word "criminal" (actions) which relates to prosecution for violation of laws.

CLAIM (n.) - Any demand held or asserted as of right.

CODICIL - An addition to a will.

CODIFY - To arrange the laws of a country into a code.

COGNIZANCE - Notice or knowledge.

COLLATERAL - By the side; accompanying; an article or thing given to secure performance of a promise.

COMITY - Courtesy; the practice by which one court follows the decision of another court on the same question.

COMMIT - To perform, as an act; to perpetrate, as a crime; to send a person to prison.

COMMON LAW - As distinguished from law created by the enactment of the legislature (called statutory law), it relates to those principles and rules of action which derive their authority solely from usages and customs of immemorial antiquity, particularly with reference to the ancient unwritten law of England. The written pronouncements of the common law are found in court decisions.

COMMUTE - Change punishment to one less severe.

COMPLAINANT - One who applies to the court for legal redress.

COMPLAINT - The pleading of a plaintiff in a civil action; or a charge that a person has committed a specified offense.

COMPROMISE - An arrangement for settling a dispute by agreement.

CONCUR - To agree, consent.

CONCURRENT - Running together, at the same time.

CONDEMNATION - Taking private property for public use on payment therefor.

CONDITION - Mode or state of being; a qualification or restriction.

CONDUCT - Active and passive behavior; both verbal and nonverbal.

CONFESSION - Voluntary statement of guilt of crime.

CONFIDENTIAL COMMUNICATION BETWEEN CLIENT AND LAWYER - Information transmitted between a client and his lawyer in the course of that relationship and in confidence by a means which, so far as the client is aware, discloses the information to no third persons other than those who are present to further the interest of the client in the consultation or those to whom disclosure is reasonably necessary for the transmission of the information or the accomplishment of the purpose for which the lawyer is consulted, and includes a legal opinion formed and the advice given by the lawyer in the course of that relationship.

CONFRONTATION - Witness testifying in presence of defendant.

CONSANGUINITY - Blood relationship.

CONSIGN - To give in charge; commit; entrust; to send or transmit goods to a merchant, factor, or agent for sale.

CONSIGNEE - One to whom a consignment is made.

CONSIGNOR - One who sends or makes a consignment.

CONSPIRACY - In criminal law, it means an agreement between two or more persons to commit an unlawful act.

CONSPIRATORS - Persons involved in a conspiracy.

CONSTITUTION - The fundamental law of a nation or state.

CONSTRUCTION OF GENDERS - The masculine gender includes the feminine and neuter.

CONSTRUCTION OF SINGULAR AND PLURAL - The singular number includes the plural; and the plural, the singular.

CONSTRUCTION OF TENSES - The present tense includes the past and future tenses; and the future, the present.

CONSTRUCTIVE - An act or condition assumed from other parts or conditions.

CONSTRUE - To ascertain the meaning of language.

CONSUMMATE - To complete.

CONTIGUOUS - Adjoining; touching; bounded by.

CONTINGENT - Possible, but not assured; dependent upon some condition.

CONTINUANCE - The adjournment or postponement of an action pending in a court.

CONTRA - Against, opposed to; contrary.

CONTRACT - An agreement between two or more persons to do or not to do a particular thing.

CONTROVERT - To dispute, deny.

CONVERSION - Dealing with the personal property of another as if it were one's own, without right.

CONVEYANCE - An instrument transferring title to land.

CONVICTION - Generally, the result of a criminal trial which ends in a judgment or sentence that the defendant is guilty as charged.

COOPERATIVE - A cooperative is a voluntary organization of persons with a common interest, formed and operated along democratic lines for the purpose of supplying services at cost to its members and other patrons, who contribute both capital and business.

CORPUS DELICTI - The body of a crime; the crime itself.

CORROBORATE - To strengthen; to add weight by additional evidence.

COUNTERCLAIM - A claim presented by a defendant in opposition to or deduction from the claim of the plaintiff.

COUNTY - Political subdivision of a state.

COVENANT - Agreement.

CREDIBLE - Worthy of belief.

CREDITOR - A person to whom a debt is owing by another person, called the "debtor."

CRIMINAL ACTION - Includes criminal proceedings.

CRIMINAL INFORMATION - Same as complaint.

CRITERION (sing.)

CRITERIA (plural) - A means or tests for judging; a standard or standards.

CROSS-EXAMINATION - Examination of a witness by a party other than the direct examiner upon a matter that is within the scope of the direct examination of the witness.

CULPABLE - Blamable.

CY-PRES - As near as (possible). The rule of *cy-pres* is a rule for the construction of instruments in equity by which the intention of the party is carried out *as near as may be*, when it would be impossible or illegal to give it literal effect.

D

DAMAGES - A monetary compensation, which may be recovered in the courts by any person who has suffered loss, or injury, whether to his person, property or rights through the unlawful act or omission or negligence of another.

DECLARANT - A person who makes a statement.

DE FACTO - In fact; actually but without legal authority.

DE JURE - Of right; legitimate; lawful.

DE MINIMIS - Very small or trifling.

DE NOVO - Anew; afresh; a second time.

DEBT - A specified sum of money owing to one person from another, including not only the obligation of the debtor to pay, but the right of the creditor to receive and enforce payment.

DECEDENT - A dead person.

DECISION - A judgment or decree pronounced by a court in determination of a case.

DECREE - An order of the court, determining the rights of all parties to a suit.

DEED - A writing containing a contract sealed and delivered; particularly to convey real property.

DEFALCATION - Misappropriation of funds.

DEFAMATION - Injuring one's reputation by false statements.

DEFAULT - The failure to fulfill a duty, observe a promise, discharge an obligation, or perform an agreement.

DEFENDANT - The person defending or denying; the party against whom relief or recovery is sought in an action or suit.

DEFRAUD - To practice fraud; to cheat or trick.

DELEGATE (v.)- To entrust to the care or management of another.

DELICTUS - A crime.

DEMUR (v.) - To dispute the sufficiency in law of the pleading of the other side.

DEMURRAGE - In maritime law, it means, the sum fixed or allowed as remuneration to the owners of a ship for the detention of their vessel beyond the number of days allowed for loading and unloading or for sailing; also used in railroad terminology.

DENIAL - A form of pleading; refusing to admit the truth of a statement, charge, etc.

DEPONENT - One who gives testimony under oath reduced to writing.

DEPOSITION - Testimony given under oath outside of court for use in court or for the purpose of obtaining information in preparation for trial of a case.

DETERIORATION - A degeneration such as from decay, corrosion or disintegration.

DETRIMENT - Any loss or harm to person or property.

DEVIATION - A turning aside.

DEVISE - A gift of real property by the last will and testament of the donor.

DICTUM (sing.)

DICTA (plural) - Any statements made by the court in an opinion concerning some rule of law not necessarily involved nor essential to the determination of the case.

DIRECT EVIDENCE - Evidence that directly proves a fact, without an inference or presumption, and which in itself if true, conclusively establishes that fact.

DIRECT EXAMINATION - The first examination of a witness upon a matter that is not within the scope of a previous examination of the witness.

DISAFFIRM - To repudiate.

DISMISS - In an action or suit, it means to dispose of the case without any further consideration or hearing.

DISSENT - To denote disagreement of one or more judges of a court with the decision passed by the majority upon a case before them.

DOCKET (n.) - A formal record, entered in brief, of the proceedings in a court.

DOCTRINE - A rule, principle, theory of law.

DOMICILE - That place where a man has his true, fixed and permanent home to which whenever he is absent he has the intention of returning.

DRAFT (n.) - A commercial paper ordering payment of money drawn by one person on another.

DRAWEE - The person who is requested to pay the money.

DRAWER - The person who draws the commercial paper and addresses it to the drawee.

DUPLICATE - A counterpart produced by the same impression as the original enlargements and miniatures, or by mechanical or electronic re-recording, or by chemical reproduction, or by other equivalent technique which accurately reproduces the original.

DURESS - Use of force to compel performance or non-performance of an act.

E

EASEMENT - A liberty, privilege, or advantage without profit, in the lands of another.

EGRESS - Act or right of going out or leaving; emergence.

EIUSDEM GENERIS - Of the same kind, class or nature. A rule used in the construction of language in a legal document.

EMBEZZLEMENT - To steal; to appropriate fraudulently to one's own use property entrusted to one's care.

EMBRACERY - Unlawful attempt to influence jurors, etc., but not by offering value.

EMINENT DOMAIN - The right of a state to take private property for public use.

ENACT - To make into a law.

ENDORSEMENT - Act of writing one's name on the back of a note, bill or similar written instrument.

ENJOIN - To require a person, by writ of injunction from a court of equity, to perform or to abstain or desist from some act.

ENTIRETY - The whole; that which the law considers as one whole, and not capable of being divided into parts.

ENTRAPMENT - Inducing one to commit a crime so as to arrest him.

ENUMERATED - Mentioned specifically; designated.

ENURE - To operate or take effect.

EQUITY - In its broadest sense, this term denotes the spirit and the habit of fairness, justness, and right dealing which regulate the conduct of men.

ERROR - A mistake of law, or the false or irregular application of law as will nullify the judicial proceedings.

ESCROW - A deed, bond or other written engagement, delivered to a third person, to be delivered by him only upon the performance or fulfillment of some condition.

ESTATE - The interest which any one has in lands, or in any other subject of property.

ESTOP - To stop, bar, or impede.

ESTOPPEL - A rule of law which prevents a man from alleging or denying a fact, because of his own previous act.

ET AL. (alii) - And others.

ET SEQ. (sequential) - And the following.

ET UX. (uxor) - And wife.

EVIDENCE - Testimony, writings, material objects, or other things presented to the senses that are offered to prove the existence or non-existence of a fact.

Means from which inferences may be drawn as a basis of proof in duly constituted judicial or fact finding tribunals, and includes testimony in the form of opinion and hearsay.

EX CONTRACTU

EX DELICTO - In law, rights and causes of action are divided into two classes, those arising *ex contractu* (from a contract) and those arising *ex delicto* (from a delict or tort).

EX OFFICIO - From office; by virtue of the office.

EX PARTE - On one side only; by or for one.

EX POST FACTO - After the fact.

EX POST FACTO LAW - A law passed after an act was done which retroactively makes such act a crime.

EX REL. (relations) - Upon relation or information.

EXCEPTION - An objection upon a matter of law to a decision made, either before or after judgment by a court.

EXECUTOR (male)

EXECUTRIX (female) - A person who has been appointed by will to execute the will.

EXECUTORY - That which is yet to be executed or performed.

EXEMPT - To release from some liability to which others are subject.

EXONERATION - The removal of a burden, charge or duty.

EXTRADITION - Surrender of a fugitive from one nation to another.

F

F.A.S.- "Free alongside ship"; delivery at dock for ship named.

F.O.B.- "Free on board"; seller will deliver to car, truck, vessel, or other conveyance by which goods are to be transported, without expense or risk of loss to the buyer or consignee.

FABRICATE - To construct; to invent a false story.

FACSIMILE - An exact or accurate copy of an original instrument.

FACTOR - A commercial agent.

FEASANCE - The doing of an act.

FELONIOUS - Criminal, malicious.

FELONY - Generally, a criminal offense that may be punished by death or imprisonment for more than one year as differentiated from a misdemeanor.

FEME SOLE - A single woman.

FIDUCIARY - A person who is invested with rights and powers to be exercised for the benefit of another person.

FIERI FACIAS - A writ of execution commanding the sheriff to levy and collect the amount of a judgment from the goods and chattels of the judgment debtor.

FINDING OF FACT - Determination from proof or judicial notice of the existence of a fact. A ruling implies a supporting finding of fact; no separate or formal finding is required unless required by a statute of this state.

FISCAL - Relating to accounts or the management of revenue.

FORECLOSURE (sale) - A sale of mortgaged property to obtain satisfaction of the mortgage out of the sale proceeds.

FORFEITURE - A penalty, a fine.

FORGERY - Fabricating or producing falsely, counterfeited.

FORTUITOUS - Accidental.

FORUM - A court of justice; a place of jurisdiction.

FRAUD - Deception; trickery.

FREEHOLDER - One who owns real property.

FUNGIBLE - Of such kind or nature that one specimen or part may be used in the place of another.

G

GARNISHEE - Person garnished.

GARNISHMENT - A legal process to reach the money or effects of a defendant, in the possession or control of a third person.

GRAND JURY - Not less than 16, not more than 23 citizens of a county sworn to inquire into crimes committed or triable in the county.

GRANT - To agree to; convey, especially real property.

GRANTEE - The person to whom a grant is made.

GRANTOR - The person by whom a grant is made.

GRATUITOUS - Given without a return, compensation or consideration.

GRAVAMEN - The grievance complained of or the substantial cause of a criminal action.

GUARANTY (n.) - A promise to answer for the payment of some debt, or the performance of some duty, in case of the failure of another person, who, in the first instance, is liable for such payment or performance.

GUARDIAN - The person, committee, or other representative authorized by law to protect the person or estate or both of an incompetent (or of a *sui juris* person having a guardian) and to act for him in matters affecting his person or property or both. An incompetent is a person under disability imposed by law.

GUILTY - Establishment of the fact that one has committed a breach of conduct; especially, a violation of law.

H

HABEAS CORPUS - You have the body; the name given to a variety of writs, having for their object to bring a party before a court or judge for decision as to whether such person is being lawfully held prisoner.

HABENDUM - In conveyancing; it is the clause in a deed conveying land which defines the extent of ownership to be held by the grantee.

HEARING - A proceeding whereby the arguments of the interested parties are heared.

HEARSAY - A type of testimony given by a witness who relates, not what he knows personally, but what others have told hi, or what he has heard said by others.

HEARSAY RULE, THE - (a) "Hearsay evidence" is evidence of a statement that was made other than by a witness while testifying at the hearing and that is offered to prove the truth of the matter stated; (b) Except as provided by law, hearsay evidence is inadmissible; (c) This section shall be known and may be cited as the hearsay rule.

HEIR - Generally, one who inherits property, real or personal.

HOLDER OF THE PRIVILEGE - (a) The client when he has no guardian or conservator; (b) A guardian or conservator of the client when the client has a guardian or conservator; (c) The personal representative of the client if the client is dead; (d) A successor, assign, trustee in dissolution, or any similar representative of a firm, association, organization, partnership, business trust, corporation, or public entity that is no longer in existence.

HUNG JURY - One so divided that they can't agree on a verdict.

HUSBAND-WIFE PRIVILEGE - An accused in a criminal proceeding has a privilege to prevent his spouse from testifying against him.

HYPOTHECATE - To pledge a thing without delivering it to the pledgee.

HYPOTHESIS - A supposition, assumption, or toehry.

I

I.E. (id est) - That is.

IB., OR IBID.(ibidem) - In the same place; used to refer to a legal reference previously cited to avoid repeating the entire citation.

ILLICIT - Prohibited; unlawful.

ILLUSORY - Deceiving by false appearance.

IMMUNITY - Exemption.

IMPEACH - To accuse, to dispute.

IMPEDIMENTS - Disabilities, or hindrances.

IMPLEAD - To sue or prosecute by due course of law.

IMPUTED - Attributed or charged to.

IN LOCO PARENTIS - In place of parent, a guardian.

IN TOTO - In the whole; completely.

INCHOATE - Imperfect; unfinished.

INCOMMUNICADO - Denial of the right of a prisoner to communicate with friends or relatives.

INCOMPETENT - One who is incapable of caring for his own affairs because he is mentally deficient or undeveloped.

INCRIMINATION - A matter will incriminate a person if it constitutes, or forms an essential part of, or, taken in connection with other matters disclosed, is a basis for a reasonable inference of such a violation of the laws of this State as to subject him to liability to punishment therefor, unless he has become for any reason permanently immune from punishment for such violation.

INCUMBRANCE - Generally a claim, lien, charge or liability attached to and binding real property.

INDEMNIFY - To secure against loss or damage; also, to make reimbursement to one for a loss already incurred by him.

INDEMNITY - An agreement to reimburse another person in case of an anticipated loss falling upon him.

INDICIA - Signs; indications.

INDICTMENT - An accusation in writing found and presented by a grand jury charging that a person has committed a crime.

INDORSE - To write a name on the back of a legal paper or document, generally, a negotiable instrument

INDUCEMENT - Cause or reason why a thing is done or that which incites the person to do the act or commit a crime; the motive for the criminal act.

INFANT - In civil cases one under 21 years of age.

INFORMATION - A formal accusation of crime made by a prosecuting attorney.

INFRA - Below, under; this word occurring by itself in a publication refers the reader to a future part of the publication.

INGRESS - The act of going into.

INJUNCTION - A writ or order by the court requiring a person, generally, to do or to refrain from doing an act.

INSOLVENT - The condition of a person who is unable to pay his debts.

INSTRUCTION - A direction given by the judge to the jury concerning the law of the case.

INTERIM - In the meantime; time intervening.

INTERLOCUTORY - Temporary, not final; something intervening between the commencement and the end of a suit which decides some point or matter, but is not a final decision of the whole controversy.

INTERROGATORIES - A series of formal written questions used in the examination of a party or a witness usually prior to a trial.

INTESTATE - A person who dies without a will.

INURE - To result, to take effect.

IPSO FACTO - By the fact iself; by the mere fact.

ISSUE (n.) The disputed point or question in a case,

J

JEOPARDY - Danger, hazard, peril.

JOINDER - Joining; uniting with another person in some legal steps or proceeding.

JOINT - United; combined.

JUDGE - Member or members or representative or representatives of a court conducting a trial or hearing at which evidence is introduced.

JUDGMENT - The official decision of a court of justice.

JUDICIAL OR JUDICIARY - Relating to or connected with the administration of justice.

JURAT - The clause written at the foot of an affidavit, stating when, where and before whom such affidavit was sworn.

JURISDICTION - The authority to hear and determine controversies between parties.

JURISPRUDENCE - The philosophy of law.

JURY - A body of persons legally selected to inquire into any matter of fact, and to render their verdict according to the evidence.

L

LACHES - The failure to diligently assert a right, which results in a refusal to allow relief.

LANDLORD AND TENANT - A phrase used to denote the legal relation existing between the owner and occupant of real estate.

LARCENY - Stealing personal property belonging to another.

LATENT - Hidden; that which does not appear on the face of a thing.

LAW - Includes constitutional, statutory, and decisional law.

LAWYER-CLIENT PRIVILEGE - (1) A "client" is a person, public officer, or corporation, association, or other organization or entity, either public or private, who is rendered professional legal services by a lawyer, or who consults a lawyer with a view to obtaining professional legal services from him; (2) A "lawyer" is a person authorized, or reasonably believed by the client to be authorized, to practice law in any state or nation; (3) A "representative of the lawyer" is one employed to assist the lawyer in the rendition of professional legal services; (4) A communication is "confidential" if not intended to be disclosed to third persons other than those to whom disclosure is in furtherance of the rendition of professional legal services to the client or those reasonably necessary for the transmission of the communication.

General rule of privilege - A client has a privilege to refuse to disclose and to prevent any other person from disclosing confidential communications made for the purpose of facilitating the rendition of professional legal services to the client, (1) between himself or his representative and his lawyer or his lawyer's representative, or (2) between his lawyer and the lawyer's representative, or (3) by him or his lawyer to a lawyer representing another in a matter of common interest, or (4) between representatives of the client or between the client and a representative of the client, or (5) between lawyers representing the client.

LEADING QUESTION - Question that suggests to the witness the answer that the examining party desires.

LEASE - A contract by which one conveys real estate for a limited time usually for a specified rent; personal property also may be leased.

LEGISLATION - The act of enacting laws.

LEGITIMATE - Lawful.

LESSEE - One to whom a lease is given.

LESSOR - One who grants a lease

LEVY - A collecting or exacting by authority.

LIABLE - Responsible; bound or obligated in law or equity.

LIBEL (v.) - To defame or injure a person's reputation by a published writing.

(n.) - The initial pleading on the part of the plaintiff in an admiralty proceeding.

LIEN - A hold or claim which one person has upon the property of another as a security for some debt or charge.

LIQUIDATED - Fixed; settled.

LIS PENDENS - A pending civil or criminal action.

LITERAL - According to the language.

LITIGANT - A party to a lawsuit.

LITATION - A judicial controversy.

LOCUS - A place.

LOCUS DELICTI - Place of the crime.

LOCUS POENITENTIAE - The abandoning or giving up of one's intention to commit some crime before it is fully completed or abandoning a conspiracy before its purpose is accomplished.

M

MALFEASANCE - To do a wrongful act.

MALICE - The doing of a wrongful act Intentionally without just cause or excuse.

MANDAMUS - The name of a writ issued by a court to enforce the performance of some public duty.

MANDATORY (adj.) Containing a command.

MARITIME - Pertaining to the sea or to commerce thereon.

MARSHALING - Arranging or disposing of in order.

MAXIM - An established principle or proposition.

MINISTERIAL - That which involves obedience to instruction, but demands no special discretion, judgment or skill.

MISAPPROPRIATE - Dealing fraudulently with property entrusted to one.

MISDEMEANOR - A crime less than a felony and punishable by a fine or imprisonment for less than one year.

MISFEASANCE - Improper performance of a lawful act.

MISREPRESENTATION - An untrue representation of facts.

MITIGATE - To make or become less severe, harsh.

MITTIMUS - A warrant of commitment to prison.

MOOT (adj.) Unsettled, undecided, not necessary to be decided.

MORTGAGE - A conveyance of property upon condition, as security for the payment of a debt or the performance of a duty, and to become void upon payment or performance according to the stipulated terms.

MORTGAGEE - A person to whom property is mortgaged.

MORTGAGOR - One who gives a mortgage.

MOTION - In legal proceedings, a "motion" is an application, either written or oral, addressed to the court by a party to an action or a suit requesting the ruling of the court on a matter of law.

MUTUALITY - Reciprocation.

N

NEGLIGENCE - The failure to exercise that degree of care which an ordinarily prudent person would exercise under like circumstances.

NEGOTIABLE (instrument) - Any instrument obligating the payment of money which is transferable from one person to another by endorsement and delivery or by delivery only.

NEGOTIATE - To transact business; to transfer a negotiable instrument; to seek agreement for the amicable disposition of a controversy or case.

NOLLE PROSEQUI - A formal entry upon the record, by the plaintiff in a civil suit or the prosecuting officer in a criminal action, by which he declares that he "will no further prosecute" the case.

NOLO CONTENDERE - The name of a plea in a criminal action, having the same effect as a plea of guilty; but not constituting a direct admission of guilt.

NOMINAL - Not real or substantial.

NOMINAL DAMAGES - Award of a trifling sum where no substantial injury is proved to have been sustained.

NONFEASANCE - Neglect of duty.

NOVATION - The substitution of a new debt or obligation for an existing one.

NUNC PRO TUNC - A phrase applied to acts allowed to be done after the time when they should be done, with a retroactive effect.("Now for then.")

O

OATH - Oath includes affirmation or declaration under penalty of perjury.

OBITER DICTUM - Opinion expressed by a court on a matter not essentially involved in a case and hence not a decision; also called dicta, if plural.

OBJECT (v.) - To oppose as improper or illegal and referring the question of its propriety or legality to the court.

OBLIGATION - A legal duty, by which a person is bound to do or not to do a certain thing.

OBLIGEE - The person to whom an obligation is owed.

OBLIGOR - The person who is to perform the obligation.

OFFER (v.) - To present for acceptance or rejection.

(n.) - A proposal to do a thing, usually a proposal to make a contract.

OFFICIAL INFORMATION - Information within the custody or control of a department or agency of the government the disclosure of which is shown to be contrary to the public interest.

OFFSET - A deduction.

ONUS PROBANDI - Burden of proof.

OPINION - The statement by a judge of the decision reached in a case, giving the law as applied to the case and giving reasons for the judgment; also a belief or view.

OPTION - The exercise of the power of choice; also a privilege existing in one person, for which he has paid money, which gives him the right to buy or sell real or personal property at a given price within a specified time.

ORDER - A rule or regulation; every direction of a court or judge made or entered in writing but not including a judgment.

ORDINANCE - Generally, a rule established by authority; also commonly used to designate the legislative acts of a municipal corporation.

ORIGINAL - Writing or recording itself or any counterpart intended to have the same effect by a person executing or issuing it. An "original" of a photograph includes the negative or any print therefrom. If data are stored in a computer or similar device, any printout or other output readable by sight, shown to reflect the data accurately, is an "original."

OVERT - Open, manifest.

P

PANEL - A group of jurors selected to serve during a term of the court.

PARENS PATRIAE - Sovereign power of a state to protect or be a guardian over children and incompetents.

PAROL - Oral or verbal.

PAROLE - To release one in prison before the expiration of his sentence, conditionally.

PARITY - Equality in purchasing power between the farmer and other segments of the economy.

PARTITION - A legal division of real or personal property between one or more owners.

PARTNERSHIP - An association of two or more persons to carry on as co-owners a business for profit.

PATENT (adj.) - Evident.

(n.) - A grant of some privilege, property, or authority, made by the government or sovereign of a country to one or more individuals.

PECULATION - Stealing.

PECUNIARY - Monetary.

PENULTIMATE - Next to the last.

PER CURIAM - A phrase used in the report of a decision to distinguish an opinion of the whole court from an opinion written by any one judge.

PER SE - In itself; taken alone.

PERCEIVE - To acquire knowledge through one's senses.

PEREMPTORY - Imperative; absolute.

PERJURY - To lie or state falsely under oath.

PERPETUITY - Perpetual existence; also the quality or condition of an estate limited so that it will not take effect or vest within the period fixed by law.

PERSON - Includes a natural person, firm, association, organization, partnership, business trust, corporation, or public entity.

PERSONAL PROPERTY - Includes money, goods, chattels, things in action, and evidences of debt.

PERSONALTY - Short term for personal property.

PETITION - An application in writing for an order of the court, stating the circumstances upon which it is founded and requesting any order or other relief from a court.

PLAINTIFF - A person who brings a court action.

PLEA - A pleading in a suit or action.

PLEADINGS - Formal allegations made by the parties of their respective claims and defenses, for the judgment of the court.

PLEDGE - A deposit of personal property as a security for the performance of an act.

PLEDGEE - The party to whom goods are delivered in pledge.

PLEDGOR - The party delivering goods in pledge.

PLENARY - Full; complete.

POLICE POWER - Inherent power of the state or its political subdivisions to enact laws within constitutional limits to promote the general welfare of society or the community.

POLLING THE JURY - Call the names of persons on a jury and requiring each juror to declare what his verdict is before it is legally recorded.

POST MORTEM - After death.

POWER OF ATTORNEY - A writing authorizing one to act for another.

PRECEPT - An order, warrant, or writ issued to an officer or body of officers, commanding him or them to do some act within the scope of his or their powers.

PRELIMINARY FACT - Fact upon the existence or nonexistence of which depends the admissibility or inadmissibility of evidence. The phrase "the admissibility or inadmissibility of evidence" includes the qualification or disqualification of a person to be a witness and the existence or nonexistence of a privilege.

PREPONDERANCE - Outweighing.

PRESENTMENT - A report by a grand jury on something they have investigated on their own knowledge.

PRESUMPTION - An assumption of fact resulting from a rule of law which requires such fact to be assumed from another fact or group of facts found or otherwise established in the action.

PRIMA FACUE - At first sight.

PRIMA FACIE CASE - A case where the evidence is very patent against the defendant.

PRINCIPAL - The source of authority or rights; a person primarily liable as differentiated from "principle" as a primary or basic doctrine.

PRO AND CON - For and against.

PRO RATA - Proportionally.

PROBATE - Relating to proof, especially to the proof of wills.

PROBATIVE - Tending to prove.

PROCEDURE - In law, this term generally denotes rules which are established by the Federal, State, or local Governments regarding the types of pleading and courtroom practice which must be followed by the parties involved in a criminal or civil case.

PROCLAMATION - A public notice by an official of some order, intended action, or state of facts.

PROFFERED EVIDENCE - The admissibility or inadmissibility of which is dependent upon the existence or nonexistence of a preliminary fact.

PROMISSORY (NOTE) - A promise in writing to pay a specified sum at an expressed time, or on demand, or at sight, to a named person, or to his order, or bearer.

PROOF - The establishment by evidence of a requisite degree of belief concerning a fact in the mind of the trier of fact or the court.

PROPERTY - Includes both real and personal property.

PROPRIETARY (adj.) - Relating or pertaining to ownership; usually a single owner.

PROSECUTE - To carry on an action or other judicial proceeding; to proceed against a person criminally.

PROVISO - A limitation or condition in a legal instrument.

PROXIMATE - Immediate; nearest

PUBLIC EMPLOYEE - An officer, agent, or employee of a public entity.

PUBLIC ENTITY - Includes a national, state, county, city and county, city, district, public authority, public agency, or any other political subdivision or public corporation, whether foreign or domestic.

PUBLIC OFFICIAL - Includes an official of a political dubdivision of such state or territory and of a municipality.

PUNITIVE - Relating to punishment.

Q

QUASH - To make void.

QUASI - As if; as it were.

QUID PRO QUO - Something for something; the giving of one valuable thing for another.

QUITCLAIM (v.) - To release or relinquish claim or title to, especially in deeds to realty.

QUO WARRANTO - A legal procedure to test an official's right to a public office or the right to hold a franchise, or to hold an office in a domestic corporation.

R

RATIFY - To approve and sanction.

REAL PROPERTY - Includes lands, tenements, and hereditaments.

REALTY - A brief term for real property.

REBUT - To contradict; to refute, especially by evidence and arguments.

RECEIVER - A person who is appointed by the court to receive, and hold in trust property in litigation.

RECIDIVIST - Habitual criminal.

RECIPROCAL - Mutual.

RECOUPMENT - To keep back or get something which is due; also, it is the right of a defendant to have a deduction from the amount of the plaintiff's damages because the plaintiff has not fulfilled his part of the same contract.

RECROSS EXAMINATION - Examination of a witness by a cross-examiner subsequent to a redirect examination of the witness.

REDEEM - To release an estate or article from mortgage or pledge by paying the debt for which it stood as security.

REDIRECT EXAMINATION - Examination of a witness by the direct examiner subsequent to the cross-examination of the witness.

REFEREE - A person to whom a cause pending in a court is referred by the court, to take testimony, hear the parties, and report thereon to the court.

REFERENDUM - A method of submitting an important legislative or administrative matter to a direct vote of the people.

RELEVANT EVIDENCE - Evidence including evidence relevant to the credulity of a witness or hearsay declarant, having any tendency in reason to prove or disprove any disputed fact that is of consequence to the determination of the action.

REMAND - To send a case back to the lower court from which it came, for further proceedings.

REPLEVIN - An action to recover goods or chattels wrongfully taken or detained.

REPLY (REPLICATION) - Generally, a reply is what the plaintiff or other person who has instituted proceedings says in answer to the defendant's case.

RE JUDICATA - A thing judicially acted upon or decided.

RES ADJUDICATA - Doctrine that an issue or dispute litigated and determined in a case between the opposing parties is deemed permanently decided between these parties.

RESCIND (RECISSION) - To avoid or cancel a contract.

RESPONDENT - A defendant in a proceeding in chancery or admiralty; also, the person who contends against the appeal in a case.

RESTITUTION - In equity, it is the restoration of both parties to their original condition (when practicable), upon the rescission of a contract for fraud or similar cause.

RETROACTIVE (RETROSPECTIVE) - Looking back; effective as of a prior time.

REVERSED - A term used by appellate courts to indicate that the decision of the lower court in the case before it has been set aside.

REVOKE - To recall or cancel.

RIPARIAN (RIGHTS) - The rights of a person owning land containing or bordering on a water course or other body of water, such as lakes and rivers.

S

SALE - A contract whereby the ownership of property is transferred from one person to another for a sum of money or for any consideration.

SANCTION - A penalty or punishment provided as a means of enforcing obedience to a law; also, an authorization.

SATISFACTION - The discharge of an obligation by paying a party what is due to him; or what is awarded to him by the judgment of a court or otherwise.

SCIENTER - Knowingly; also, it is used in pleading to denote the defendant 's guilty knowledge.

SCINTILLA - A spark; also the least particle.

SECRET OF STATE - Governmental secret relating to the national defense or the international relations of the United States.

SECURITY - Indemnification; the term is applied to an obligation, such as a mortgage or deed of trust, given by a debtor to insure the payment or performance of his debt, by furnishing the creditor with a resource to be used in case of the debtor's failure to fulfill the principal obligation.

SENTENCE - The judgment formally pronounced by the court or judge upon the defendant after his conviction in a criminal prosecution.

SET-OFF - A claim or demand which one party in an action credits against the claim of the opposing party.

SHALL and MAY - "Shall" is mandatory and "may" is permissive.

SITUS - Location.

SOVEREIGN - A person, body or state in which independent and supreme authority is vested.

STARE DECISIS - To follow decided cases.

STATE - "State" means this State, unless applied to the different parts of the United States. In the latter case, it includes any state, district, commonwealth, territory or insular possession of the United States, including the District of Columbia.

STATEMENT - (a) Oral or written verbal expression or (b) nonverbal conduct of a person intended by him as a substitute for oral or written verbal expression.

STATUTE - An act of the legislature. Includes a treaty.

STATUTE OF LIMITATION - A statute limiting the time to bring an action after the right of action has arisen.

STAY - To hold in abeyance an order of a court.

STIPULATION - Any agreement made by opposing attorneys regulating any matter incidental to the proceedings or trial.

SUBORDINATION (AGREEMENT) - An agreement making one's rights inferior to or of a lower rank than another's.

SUBORNATION - The crime of procuring a person to lie or to make false statements to a court.

SUBPOENA - A writ or order directed to a person, and requiring his attendance at a particular time and place to testify as a witness.

SUBPOENA DUCES TECUM - A subpoena used, not only for the purpose of compelling witnesses to attend in court, but also requiring them to bring with them books or documents which may be in their possession, and which may tend to elucidate the subject matter of the trial.

SUBROGATION - The substituting of one for another as a creditor, the new creditor succeeding to the former's rights.

SUBSIDY - A government grant to assist a private enterprise deemed advantageous to the public.

SUI GENERIS - Of the same kind.

SUIT - Any civil proceeding by a person or persons against another or others in a court of justice by which the plaintiff pursues the remedies afforded him by law.

SUMMONS - A notice to a defendant that an action against him has been commenced and requiring him to appear in court and answer the complaint.

SUPRA - Above; this word occurring by itself in a book refers the reader to a previous part of the book.

SURETY - A person who binds himself for the payment of a sum of money, or for the performance of something else, for another.

SURPLUSAGE - Extraneous or unnecessary matter.

SURVIVORSHIP - A term used when a person becomes entitled to property by reason of his having survived another person who had an interest in the property.

SUSPEND SENTENCE - Hold back a sentence pending good behavior of prisoner.

SYLLABUS - A note prefixed to a report, especially a case, giving a brief statement of the court's ruling on different issues of the case.

T

TALESMAN - Person summoned to fill a panel of jurors.

TENANT - One who holds or possesses lands by any kind of right or title; also, one who has the temporary use and occupation of real property owned by another person (landlord), the duration and terms of his tenancy being usually fixed by an instrument called "a lease."

TENDER - An offer of money; an expression of willingness to perform a contract according to its terms.

TERM - When used with reference to a court, it signifies the period of time during which the court holds a session, usually of several weeks or months duration.

TESTAMENTARY - Pertaining to a will or the administration of a will.

TESTATOR (male)

TESTATRIX (female) - One who makes or has made a testament or will.

TESTIFY (TESTIMONY) - To give evidence under oath as a witness.

TO WIT - That is to say; namely.

TORT - Wrong; injury to the person.

TRANSITORY - Passing from place to place.

TRESPASS - Entry into another's ground, illegally.

TRIAL - The examination of a cause, civil or criminal, before a judge who has jurisdiction over it, according to the laws of the land.

TRIER OF FACT - Includes (a) the jury and (b) the court when the court is trying an issue of fact other than one relating to the admissibility of evidence.

TRUST - A right of property, real or personal, held by one party for the benefit of another.

TRUSTEE - One who lawfully holds property in custody for the benefit of another.

U

UNAVAILABLE AS A WITNESS - The declarant is (1) Exempted or precluded on the ground of privilege from testifying concerning the matter to which his statement is relevant; (2) Disqualified from testifying to the matter; (3) Dead or unable to attend or to testify at the hearing because of then existing physical or mental illness or infirmity; (4) Absent from the hearing and the court is unable to compel his attendance by its process; or (5) Absent from the hearing and the proponent of his statement has exercised reasonable diligence but has been unable to procure his attendance by the court's process.

ULTRA VIRES - Acts beyond the scope and power of a corporation, association, etc.

UNILATERAL - One-sided; obligation upon, or act of one party.

USURY - Unlawful interest on a loan.

V

VACATE - To set aside; to move out.

VARIANCE - A discrepancy or disagreement between two instruments or two aspects of the same case, which by law should be consistent.

VENDEE - A purchaser or buyer.

VENDOR - The person who transfers property by sale, particularly real estate; the term "seller" is used more commonly for one who sells personal property.

VENIREMEN - Persons ordered to appear to serve on a jury or composing a panel of jurors.

VENUE - The place at which an action is tried, generally based on locality or judicial district in which an injury occurred or a material fact happened.

VERDICT - The formal decision or finding of a jury.

VERIFY - To confirm or substantiate by oath.

VEST - To accrue to.

VOID - Having no legal force or binding effect.

VOIR DIRE - Preliminary examination of a witness or a juror to test competence, interest, prejudice, etc.

W

WAIVE - To give up a right.

WAIVER - The intentional or voluntary relinquishment of a known right.

WARRANT (WARRANTY) (v.) - To promise that a certain fact or state of facts, in relation to the subject matter, is, or shall be, as it is represented to be.

WARRANT (n.) - A writ issued by a judge, or other competent authority, addressed to a sheriff, or other officer, requiring him to arrest the person therein named, and bring him before the judge or court to answer or be examined regarding the offense with which he is charged.

WRIT - An order or process issued in the name of the sovereign or in the name of a court or judicial officer, commanding the performance or nonperformance of some act.

WRITING - Handwriting, typewriting, printing, photostating, photographing and every other means of recording upon any tangible thing any form of communication or representation, including letters, words, pictures, sounds, or symbols, or combinations thereof.

WRITINGS AND RECORDINGS - Consists of letters, words, or numbers, or their equivalent, set down by handwriting, typewriting, printing, photostating, photographing, magnetic impulse, mechanical or electronic recording, or other form of data compilation.

Y

YEA AND NAY - Yes and no.

YELLOW DOG CONTRACT - A contract by which employer requires employee to sign an instrument promising as condition that he will not join a union during its continuance, and will be discharged if he does join.

Z

ZONING - The division of a city by legislative regulation into districts and the prescription and application in each district of regulations having to do with structural and architectural designs of buildings and of regulations prescribing use to which buildings within designated districts may be put.

Made in the USA
Middletown, DE
05 October 2023